T0311454

China's Economic Reform and Development during the 13th Five-Year Plan Period

"Five-Year Plans" have been a cornerstone of Chinese social and economic development initiatives since 1953. During the thirteenth of these periods between 2016 and 2020, the global economy has experienced instability after the financial crisis, as well as political and economic reconfiguration. Drawing on modern economic theory, this book comprehensively discusses China's economic development in this crucial phase.

The book analyzes the international economic environment and asks how China's continued reform and opening-up can fit with the new era of economic globalization. It also presents the difficulties China faces in such fields as urbanization, the coordination of regional development and urban–rural integration, economic reform, and the reform of factor markets and state-owned enterprises.

The book outlines many medium-term development rules along with key characteristics of China's economy, helping international readers fully understand likely future trajectories for the Chinese economy.

Lin Gang is the dean, professor, and doctoral supervisor at the Institute of China's Economic Reform and Development, Renmin University of China. His research areas include ownership theory, economic growth theory, economic system reform, and economic methodology.

Wang Yiming is the executive director of the China Society of Macroeconomics and vice chairman of the Chinese Association for Regional Economics. He has been engaged in macroeconomic research for a long time, mainly in the fields of macroeconomic policy, economic and social development planning, scientific and technological progress and policy, industrial development and policy, and regional economy and policy.

Ma Xiaohe is the executive vice president of the Institute of China's Economic Reform and Development, Renmin University of China, and the associate dean and researcher at the Academy of Macroeconomic Research, National Development and Reform Commission. His research focus is regional economy.

Gao Debu is professor and doctoral supervisor at the School of Economics, Renmin University of China, vice president of the China Economic Reform and Development Research Institute, and researcher at the Collaborative Innovation Center for Socialism with Chinese Characteristics. He has been engaged in research on political economics and economic history for a long time.

China Perspectives

The *China Perspectives* series focuses on translating and publishing works by leading Chinese scholars writing about both global topics and China-related themes. It covers humanities and social sciences, education, media and psychology, as well as many interdisciplinary themes.

This is the first time any of these books have been published in English for international readers. The series aims to put forward a Chinese perspective, give insights into cutting-edge academic thinking in China, and inspire researchers globally.

Titles in economics include:

Trade Openness and China's Economic Development
Miaojie Yu

Perceiving Truth and Ceasing Doubts
What Can We Learn from 40 Years of China's Reform and Opening-Up?
Cai Fang

Demographic Perspective of China's Economic Development
Cai Fang

Inflation in China
Microfoundations, Macroeconomic Dynamics and Monetary Policy
Chengsi Zhang

China's Economic Reform and Development during the 13th Five-Year Plan Period
Edited by Lin Gang, Wang Yiming, Ma Xiaohe, Gao Debu

Cultural Economics
Li Yining

For more information, please visit https://www.routledge.com/series/CPH

China's Economic Reform and Development during the 13th Five-Year Plan Period

Edited by
Lin Gang, Wang Yiming,
Ma Xiaohe, and Gao Debu

 Routledge
Taylor & Francis Group

LONDON AND NEW YORK

This book is published with financial support from the fund for building world-class universities (disciplines) of Renmin University of China.

First published in English 2021
by Routledge
2 Park Square, Milton Park, Abingdon, Oxon OX14 4RN

and by Routledge
52 Vanderbilt Avenue, New York, NY 10017

Routledge is an imprint of the Taylor & Francis Group, an informa business

British Library Cataloguing-in-Publication Data
A catalogue record for this book is available from the British Library

Library of Congress Cataloging-in-Publication Data
A catalog record has been requested for this book

ISBN: 978-1-138-09005-7 (hbk)
ISBN: 978-1-315-10879-7 (ebk)

Typeset in Times New Roman
by codeMantra

Contents

Figures

Tables

Contributors

Gao Debu, the professor and doctoral supervisor of the School of Economics, Renmin University of China, vice president of China Economic Reform and Development Research Institute, researcher of Collaborative Innovation Center for Socialism with Chinese Characteristics. He has been engaged in political economics and economic history research for a long time.

Lin Gang, the dean, professor, and doctoral supervisor in the Institute of China's Economic Reform and Development, Renmin University of China. His research areas are ownership theory, economic growth theory, economic system reform, economic methodology, and so forth.

Wu Huifang, working at Beijing Miyun District Finance Bureau, Master of Economics.

Yang Jing, a researcher and Doctor of Economics of Research Institute of Marxism, Chinese Academy of Social Sciences (CASS).

Bi Jiyao, the director and researcher of Institute of Foreign Economic Research, NDRC, part-time professor and doctoral supervisor of World Economics in the Institute of China's Economic Reform and Development, Renmin University of China.

Song Li, the deputy director and researcher of Economic Research Institute, NDRC, professor and postgraduate supervisor in Graduate School at Chinese Academy of Social Sciences (CASS), and professor and doctoral supervisor of Political Economics in the Institute of China's Economic Reform & Development, Renmin University of China.

Chen Liang, an associate professor and Doctor of Economics of Institute of China's Economic Reform and Development, Renmin University of China.

Zhang Peili, an associate professor at Renmin University of China, PhD in Economics, specializing in the study on China's economic reform and development.

Wang Qingyun, deputy director and researcher of Training Center, NDRC, part-time professor and doctoral supervisor of Political Economics in the Institute of China's Economic Reform & Development, Renmin University of China.

Liu Shujie, director and researcher of Economic Research Institute, NDRC, part-time professor and doctoral supervisor of political economics in the Institute of China's Economic Reform & Development, Renmin University of China. He has twice been granted the "Science and Technology Progress Award of the State Development Planning Commission".

Yang Tianyu, professor in the School of Economics, Renmin University of China. His research focuses on income distribution and structural transformation. His papers were published in *Developing Economies and Economic Research.*

Jiang Wei, doctoral student in the Institute of China's Economic Reform and Development at Renmin University of China, PhD in economics, specializing in the study on China's economic reform and development.

Ma Xiaohe, executive vice president in the Institute of China's Economic Reform and Development, Renmin University of China, and the associate dean and researcher at the Academy of Macroeconomic Research, National Development and Reform Commission (NDRC). His research focus is regional economy.

Xia Xiaohua, an associate professor of economics in the School of Economics at Renmin University of China. He has published over 40 peer-reviewed articles in international journals such as *Energy Policy, Communications in Nonlinear Science and Numerical Simulation, Ecological Modelling, and Journal of Environmental Informatics.*

ChenYanbin, professor and associate dean of School of Economics, Renmin University of China. His research interest is macroeconomics. He put forward the concept of "Big Macroeconomics".

Zhang Yansheng, secretary-general of academic committee, NDRC, part-time professor and doctoral supervisor of World Economics in the Institute of China's Economic Reform and Development, Renmin University of China. He served as the director and researcher of Institute of Foreign Economics, NDRC, and was granted the Sun Yefang Economic Science Award.

Wang Yiming, executive director of China Society of Macroeconomics, CSM, and vice chairman of Chinese Association for Regional Economics (CARE). He has been engaged in macroeconomic research for a long time, mainly in the fields of macroeconomic policy, economic and social development planning, scientific and technological progress and policy, industrial development and policy, and regional economy and policy.

Chen Yongjun, distinguished professor and doctoral supervisor in the School of Business, Renmin University of China, a leading scholar of industrial economics of the national key disciplines, a member of School Administration Committee at Renmin University of China, and vice president of the Institute of China's Economic Reform and Development. He was granted the special allowance from the government by the State Council.

Sun Yongmei, an associate professor in the Institute of China's Economic Reform and Development at Renmin University of China. Sun's research is mainly concerned with the problem of economic growth and urbanization of China.

1 Strategic Choice in Adjustment and Transition

Train of Thought on Social and Economic Development in "13th Five-Year Plan" Period

The "13th Five-Year Plan" is the period of building a well-off society, the decisive moment of realizing the first centennial goal, and the critical point of paving the foundation for the second centennial goal aiming for decisive achievements by comprehensively deepening reform and governing, subject to laws. The uniqueness of the "13th Five-Year Plan" period requires us to fully grasp the new role of China in the global pattern adjustment, to adapt to the new requirement of transit in development stages, and to plan for scientific development to a higher level, with a wider vision.

I Global Economic Adjustment and the New Role of China

In the "13th Five-Year Plan" period, as the global economy is still trying to come to terms with adjustment periods after the financial crisis, the economic globalization and international economy show a new momentum. With the new opportunities brought by a new technical revolution and industrial reform, Chinese economy's share of global economy continues to rise. However, as new developments take place with China's emergence in the global economy and its relation with the world, the external environment for China will be more complicated.

A Global Economy Still in Adjustment and Transition Period

1 World Economy Recovering Slowly in Adjustment and Differentiation

For a short period in the forthcoming days, the world economy will experience moderate and low growth, with new changes in growth pattern as follows. First would be the "two wheel drive" of China's economy and the US economy". The US economy will gradually step out of the shadow of the crisis and enter a new growth, with an enhanced role of driving the global economy. On the other hand, China's economy will continue to grow at both medium and high speed and will be an important driving force for global economy as structural reforms accelerate. Second is the "double speed growth" in developed countries. The economic recovery of the eurozone is difficult and slow while that of Japan remains depressed, which is in sharp contrast with the economic recovery of the United States. Third is the "two-way differentiation" of emerging economies. The economic growth of China and India is expected to be at a relatively rapid speed, while that of Russia, Brazil, and other countries that have a high dependency on energy resource will significantly slow down. Thus, low and medium growth in world economy will become the new normal. According to the International Monetary Fund's forecast, the average annual growth rate of world economy from 2016 to 2020 will be about 3.9% – the growth rate of developed countries and developing countries, respectively, will be 2.3% and 5.4%. Compared with the average level of growth rate before the financial crisis, from 2003 to 2007, the three aspects were, respectively, decreased by 0.9, 0.5, and 2.3 percentage points. Economic growth in developing countries is still significantly higher than that in developed countries. Their proportion of global economy will be on a continuous rise, but with a slowdown in momentum for catching-up. The slow recovery and growth of world economy, on the whole, is conducive to China's expansion of foreign trade export. However, the low and medium growth in the global economic environment is likely to weaken the external demand for China's exports.

2 *International Economic and Trade Rules Confronted with Major Adjustments*

Influenced by the slowdown in global economy, multilateral trading system, and expansion of global supply chain, international trade is entering a low-growth phase. The US-led Trans-Pacific Partnership Agreement (TPP) and Trans-Atlantic Trade and Investment Partnership Agreement (TTIP) agreements aimed to build high standard of large-scale free trade across the two continents, with the focus on competition and neutrality, labor rights, and environmental standards, for the purpose of reshaping global economic and trade rules. This will either significantly raise the threshold for China in order to participate in economic globalization or may cause loss due to transfer of trade and investment. Developed countries actively promoted the negotiation of Trade-in Service Agreement (TISA) and the expansion of Information Technology Agreement (ITA) and strengthened technical trade measures to create competitive advantages. Many aspects of the adjustment of global economic imbalances and trade rules are in line with the objectives of China's intensification of reform and expansion of opening-up, which will further advance its reform and opening-up and also bring new challenges.

3 *New Changes in World's Energy Resource Layout*

With the shift in energy production and consumption, the pattern of world energy resource continues to change profoundly. World energy production shifted from the East to the West, and North America has now become the new global energy production center. The United States has made a major breakthrough in the technology of exploration and development of shale gas and shale oil, thus significantly increasing production of oil and gas. In 2020, the overall US energy self-sufficiency rate will reach 93.5%, which will make change it from being the largest energy consumption country to an energy production country. Canada's deep-sea oil mining has made significant progress, which will make it a new energy supply country. Meanwhile, energy demand in Asia is expanding rapidly, thus shifting world energy demand from the West to the East. According to the International Energy Agency, it is predicted that by 2020, Asia's oil imports will account for 65% of international crude oil trade and 27% of global oil production. Oil-producing areas in the Middle East, Russia and Central Asia, vigorously promoted the eastward strategy in search for new alternative markets. The disputes on natural gas in Russia and European countries triggered the restructuring of energy layout in Europe and Asia. Europe proposed to establish a unified energy market, increase import of shale gas from the United States, implement diversification of energy supply, vigorously develop new energy, and reduce dependence on the oil and gas resource from Russia. The changes in world energy and resources layout will make the supply of international energy resources in China more diversified, which will increase the risks.

4 International Monetary System Tends to New Changes

With the ongoing recovery of the US economy, the US dollar is becoming stronger. Since 2012, the exchange rate of US dollar has continuing to increase, exerting great impact on global prices of assets and bulk commodity. The decline in the prices of bulk commodity in the international market led to a decrease in the income of resource-exporting countries and a sharp decline in import, which resulted in a rebound of China's export growth. Some European countries, emerging economies, and Japan sought growth through currency devaluation, which resulted in great fluctuation of exchange rates of major international currencies. This, in turn, seriously affected global economic recovery, with the international community appealing for reform of international monetary system. Although in the long run there would be no fundamental change in the USD-centered international monetary system, the world economic pattern and strength comparison will change significantly as a result of the rapid rise of emerging powers. To set up a more diversified and balanced international monetary system is an irresistible trend. The new changes in international monetary system are conducive to promoting internationalization of renminbi (RMB), but it will increase the exchange rate risk of China's foreign economy and the uncertainty of inflow and outflow of international capital.

4   *Strategic Choice in Adjustment and Transition*

5   *Global Governance Structure Reform Facing New Challenges*

After the international financial crisis, the status of emerging markets and developing countries was remarkably improved. It is hard for developed countries to dominate global governance alone. AIIB (Asian Infrastructure Investment Bank) and NDB (BRICS New Development Bank) have become key projects for emerging economies to reshape international economic order. The game between developed and developing countries becomes more complicated and fierce. The general trend indicates that in the process of promoting global economic rebalance, mutually expanding market opening up, reforming international monetary and financial system, responding to climate changes, and ensuring energy and resource security and food safety, the opinion of developing countries needs to be given importance and fair and efficient system of global governance needs to be established. Change will be accompanied by readjustment of interests, inevitably with contradictions and conflicts. In this process, China, as world's largest goods trade country and the second largest economy, ought to play a greater role. However, the developed countries led by the United States are not willing to give up for their dominance in rule-making. The reform of global governance structure will be difficult and will have profound impact on the relation between China and global economy.

B Accelerated Breeding of New Scientific and Technical Revolution and Industrial Change

1 New Scientific and Technical Revolution to Promote New Industrial Change

At present, the development of information technology is leading to a path of a major breakthrough and reform. The development of new technology such as Internet of Things, big data, cloud computing, mobile Internet, and 3D printing promoted the upgrade and update of information technology; triggered technical reform in industry, energy, agriculture, and medical treatment; advanced the diversification of the industrial reform with affluent connotation; led to high performance computing, broadband network, new materials, smart production, genetic engineering medicine, biomedical engineering, solar battery, electric vehicles and so forth; and profoundly changed traditional production mode and lifestyle of people. Scientific and technical revolution and industrial reform are historically integrated with the transformation of China's economic development mode, which not only created opportunities for China to be at par with the developed countries, but also posed the risk of the widening gap. As the new technical revolution and industrial reform are still in embryonic stage in in the race for a breakthrough, China and the developed countries are standing at the same starting line. It provides China with a "once-in-a-century" opportunity to speed up industrialization to achieve leapfrog development. Meanwhile, a new industrial revolution resulted in the decline of the assembling cost in manufacturing process. In this regard, the comparative advantage of low labor cost in China will be significantly weakened, while it will become more pressing for it to establish new advantage in core technology to catch-up with new technical revolution and industrial reform.

2 New Manufacturing Paradigm and Business Mode to Take Shape

A new industrial revolution promoted the change of production mode. Different from the traditional production mode pursuing "scale, centralization and standardization" on the basis of mature mainstream technology, the new production mode adheres to "flexibility, diversification and decentralization" upon support of innovative technology, provides a "final solution" to the customers, and shifts the value-added center of value chain from production sector to service sector. To adapt to the new production mode, the new business mode of cross-border e-commerce, mobile Internet, free search offerings, and energy management contracting emerged in a short period. In addition, the crossover development between Internet financing, new media service, O2O and other new types of operation and industries greatly changed the market structure and competition pattern. China's new manufacturing paradigm and business mode are proactive, but the transformation of traditional large-scale manufacturing paradigm and business mode is also confronted with many challenges.

3 In-depth Adjustment of Global Pattern of Industrial Division of Labor

After the international financial crisis, major developed countries implemented the "reindustrialization" strategy to actively attract the reflux of medium and high-end manufacturing industries, trying to revive the real economy. Emerging economies relied on lower cost advantage to attract labor-intensive industries, thereby crowding out and replacing China's market share. For a time in the forthcoming days, major developed countries will continue their dominance over the global manufacturing industry, strengthen the monopoly, and control over industrial core technology, thus further consolidating their position in the high-end industrial chain; on the other hand, emerging economies will continue to display their comprehensive cost advantages and enhance their competitiveness in labor-intensive industry, especially in low-end manufacturing. China's cost factors like labor and land are on a collective rise, which weakened the traditional competitive advantage of manufacturing. In this regard, some labor-intensive industries, especially those in the low-end product market, will be replaced by the developing countries, with lower costs. Meanwhile, China accelerated industrial restructuring and upgrading, developed strategic emerging industries, and fostered new competitive advantages aided by technology, brand, quality, and service. With the growing competition between China and the developed countries in high-end manufacturing, including new energy, new materials, energy-saving, and environmental protection, China's industrial development has been squeezed by both the developed countries and the emerging economies and confronted with the situation of "being contained in the front and chased behind".

4 New Industrial Change to Advance Institutional Reform in Relevant Countries

After the financial crisis, in order to enhance economic vitality and transfer technology innovation to industrial production, Western developed countries systematically arranged for industrial adjustments including adjusting government policy, strengthening construction of information infrastructure, and creating new policy environment for industrial reform in macro policies; undertook innovation of enterprise organization system and governance structure by creating new institutional environment for industrial reform on micro basis; and strengthened market functions by breaking departmental monopoly and creating new market environment for industrial reform in market structure. International efforts to speed up institutional innovation around new industrial revolution not only provided China with experience to expedite industrial system innovation but also put forward higher requirements for deepening reform.

C New Change in Relation between China and the World

1 China Remaining Important Power Source for World Economic Growth

In 2014, China's GDP totaled USD10.4 trillion, accounting for 13.3% of the global GDP, as shown in Figure 1.1, with 9.1 percentage points lower than the United States, but with, respectively, 7.4 and 10.6 percentage points higher than that of Japan and India. In the past few years, the rate of contribution of China's total GDP to world economic growth has been steady between 20% and 30%. In 2009, it was more than 60%, as shown in Figure 1.2. Although China's economic growth rate decreased year-over-year since 2010, the expansion of middle-income group resulted in huge consumption potential, further promoting new urbanization will create a huge demand for investment and consumption and comprehensively deepening reform will stimulate new impetus for economic growth. China still maintains its economic growth at medium and high speed in the "13th Five-Year Plan" period. With the continuous stable economic growth, China's total economic output in 2020 is expected to be close to the United States; also, it is believed that it will form interactive relation with world economy and thus continue to be important power source of world economic growth through trade, investment, and financial channels.

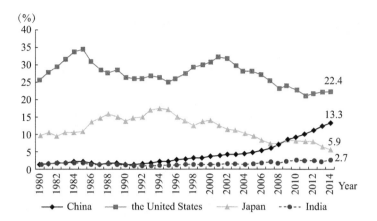

Figure 1.1 Proportion of total economic output of China, the United States, Japan, and India in world economic output from 1980 to 2014.

Source: calculated on the basis of WDI.

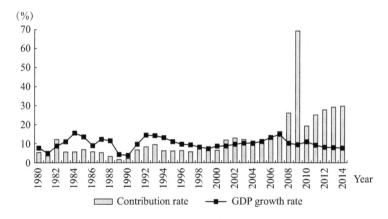

Figure 1.2 Curve of China's contribution rate to global economic growth and China's economic growth.

Source: calculated on the basis of WDI.

2 China's Oversea Investment Scale in Continuous Expansion

In 2014, China became world's largest trading country, world's largest foreign capital recipient, and world's third largest oversea investor. With low growth in world economy as the new normal, China's dependence on exports to promote economic growth was weakened. China's export growth will be a percentage point of single digit. In the coming years, China's export growth will be slower than its economic growth. Additionally, China's import will also

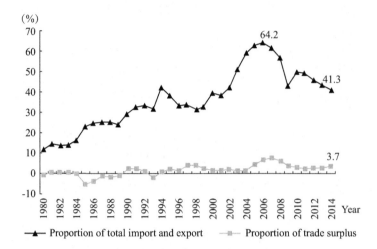

Figure 1.3 Share of China's total import and export and trade surplus in China's GDP from 1980 to 2014.
Source: National Bureau of Statistics.

slow down, with a remarkable decrease in the proportion of total amount of import and export goods and trade surplus in GDP, as shown in Figure 1.3. In addition, China's import will continue to expand, and it is expected to exceed USD10 trillion in the "13th Five-Year Plan" period. Besides, China will constantly lift restrictions on investment admission, explore the management mode of national treatment and negative list before admission, and actively expand the opening up in finance, education, culture, health care, and other services; additionally,, it will speed up the implementation of the "going out" strategy, especially in energy and resource, infrastructure, and advantageous manufacturing. It is estimated that China's overseas investment will exceed USD500 billion in the "13th Five-Year Plan" period, which will provide strong support for globalization layout and interaction between China and world economy.

3   Rise of Status of RMB in International Monetary System

China's economy grows at a high rate, with its foreign trade and investment constantly expanding and its foreign exchange reserves ranking top in the world. Its banks and other financial institutions quickened their pace of "going out", which enhanced China's status in global financial system. In the "13th Five-Year Plan" period, China will expedite the internationalization and upgrade the status of RMB in international monetary system: it will expand the application range of RMB in cross-border trade and investment, promote convertibility of capital account and reform of RMB exchange rate formation mechanism, and accelerate the development of RMB offshore business.. The speedup in the process of international-ization of RMB will be conducive to change the international financial system dominated by the Western countries, thus increasing the impact of fluctuation in international financial market on domestic financial system and the pressure of financial stability maintenance and financial risks prevention.

4 Continuous Rise of China's Influence and Say

With the substantial increase of economic strength and comprehensive national strength, China actively participated in global governance and promoted international order to a more fair and reasonable direction. Moreover, China will play a greater role in multilateral affairs through the multilateral platforms of G20, Shanghai Cooperation Organization, and BRICS cooperation mechanism. Meanwhile, China's influence in global po-litical, economic, and military security has significantly increased. Relevant parties relied more on China in terms of major international and regional issues, gave more importance to their cooperation with China, and put for-ward demands for China's role in global economy rebalance, response to climate change, protection of intellectual property rights, and opening up of markets. Developed countries required China to assume more international responsibilities and obligations, while developing countries expected China to find a solution to international poverty alleviation and foreign aid. This role is conducive to enhancing the influence and say of China, which will be further lay the stage for its role in the international affairs.

II New Normal and New Challenges in China's Economic Development

In the "13th Five-Year Plan" period, Chinese will represent in a broader sense at a deeper level the characteristics of its entry into a new stage of de-velopment. The correct understanding of the transition of the economic and social development phase in the "13th Five-Year Plan" period and the new requirements for transition is vital for the choice of development strategy during the period.

A Economic Development into New Normal

The transformation from the old normal to the new normal, through eco-nomic slowdown and gear-shifting, is in essence the process of structural adjustment and impetus conversion. In this sense, the new normal for China is the shift from rapid growth stage to efficient growth stage, as well as the historic change from big to the strong.

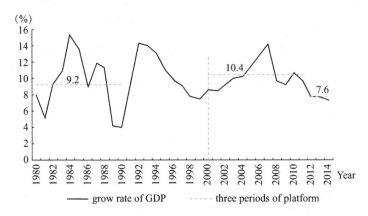

Figure 1.4 Curve of growth rate of China's GDP since 1980 in three periods of platform.

Note: The three periods of platform are from 1980 to 1990, from 2000 to 2011, and from 2012 to 2014.

1 Slowdown and Gear-shifting of Economy Growth

To shift from high-speed growth to medium and high-speed growth is the basic characteristic of the new normal. China's annual economic growth was 7.7% from 2012 to 2013, 7.3% in 2014, and expected to be 7% in 2015, all of which were in the bracket of medium- and high-speed growth from 7% to 8%. Compared with the two periods from 1980 to 1990 and from 2000 to 2011, China's economic growth slowed down, as shown in Figure 1.4. In the "13th Five-Year Plan" period, the economic growth will decline with the decrease in the potential growth rate, with corresponding adjustment in growth rate. Different from the past 30 years, with the advent of the new normal stage, the working-age population began to decrease, the dependency ratio of population gradually increased, and the savings rate and investment rate tended to decline. In addition, the transfer of labor and other production factors from agricultural sector to non-agricultural sector slowed down, thus contributing less to the rise of total factor productivity (TFP); in contrast, technical progress and human capital were not enough to replace the contribution of cross-sectoral transfer of production factors to the rise of TFP. Under the combined effect of these factors, the potential growth rate tended to decline. Economic slowdown and gear-shifting were difficult to avoid, but, at the same time, the quality and efficiency of economic growth significantly improved, and therefore the whole society's labor productivity and TFP will continue to go upward.

2 Structural Adjustment, Optimization, and Upgrade

Different from the rapid expansion of manufacturing capacity in the past catch-up stage, upon the entry into the new normal, the manufacturing

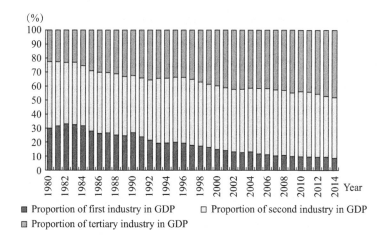

Figure 1.5 Proportion of China's added value in three industries in China's GDP from 1980 to 2014.

Source: National Bureau of Statistics.

sector is faced with enormous pressure to absorb excess capacity, thus narrowing the expansion of industrial scale. Meanwhile, the development in education, culture, medical, tourism, pension, and other services was expedited. In 2013, the proportion of China's service sector's added value in China's GDP surpassed the secondary industry for the first time. In 2014, the proportion of service in GDP was raised to 48.20%, a rise of 1.3 percentage points over the previous year, with 5.6 percentage points higher than that of the secondary industry, as shown in Figure 1.5. Meanwhile, the proportion of high-tech industries in the value added of industries above designated size was raised up to 10.6% in 2014. With the rapid development of the Internet and e-commerce-related new business activities, in 2014, national online retail volume experienced a year-on-year rise by 49.70%, with courier business growth up 51.9%. A new generation of information technology, biomedicine, high-end equipment manufacturing, new energy, and other emerging industries was on a rapid rise, with a growing share in the total economic output. In the "13th Five-Year Plan" period, structural reform will be quickened, which will create more favorable conditions and environment for structural adjustment and upgrade.

3 Continuous Change of Growth Momentum

After entering the new normal, China was confronted with relative excess capacity, with the representation as follows: its labor costs was on a rise; bearing capacity of resource environment was close to the ceiling; the room for expansion by relying on high-intensity input grew smaller and smaller;

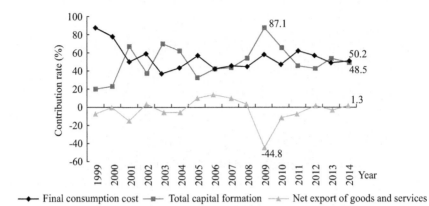

Figure 1.6 Contribution rate of consumption, investment, and exports to China's economic growth.
Source: National Bureau of Statistics.

the main source of economic development changed from large-scale expansion of production capacity to increase of production efficiency; and the enhancement of efficiency and effectiveness became the main focus. With the acceleration in the income of urban and rural residents, the middle-income group expanded, consumption gradually became the main driving force of economic growth, and the role of investment and export in promoting economic growth was weakened. In 2014, the contribution rate of final consumption expenditure to economic growth was 50. 2%, 0.7 percentage points higher than that of total capital formation to economic growth, as shown in Figure 1.6. In addition, the driving role of scientific and technical progress in economic growth was enhanced. In recent years, the number of patent applications was significantly increased, and its growth rate was remarkably accelerated. In the "13th Five-Year Plan" period, the new growth momentum will continue to increase and will gradually replace the traditional impetus. The continuous advancement of impetus transformation will create the conditions for formation of new dynamic mechanism.

B Forthcoming Challenges and Risks

In the new normal of economic development, the traditional comparative advantages that supported China's rapid economic growth were weakened; the restriction of various constraints and structural contradictions were enhanced; some deep-seated contradictions in social transition were highlighted; and the maintenance of sustained and healthy economic development were faced with many difficulties and challenges.

1 Inclination of Rise in Labor Costs

With the change of population structure in China, the working-age population showed a negative growth. In 2012, China's working-age population, aged from 16 to 59, declined for the first time, with a net reduction of 2.05 million people. In 2013 and 2014, the reduction was, respectively, 2.44 million and 3.71 million people. The dependency ratio of population increased year-on-year. Meanwhile, China's labor participation rate also showed a downward trend. In the "13th Five-Year Plan" period, the total labor supply will fall, as transferable young labor force from rural areas is limited. Thus, the comparative advantage of low labor cost will be significantly weakened. The changing trend in labor supply and demand will accelerate labor costs at a more rapid space, resulting in the increased dependency on labor productivity and technical innovation for maintenance of sustained and rapid economic growth.

2 Declining Tendency of Rate of Savings and Investment

Over the past 30 years, China's savings rate continued to increase, which was mostly ascribed to the constant decline of dependency ratio in population. However, this situation will change as the population structure changes. The empirical analysis shows that the savings rate is inversely related to the dependency ratio in population – the rise of one percentage point will lead to the fall of savings rate by 0.8 percentage point. As the dependency ratio in population increases, the savings rate at the higher level will be adjusted downward and will directly cause decrease in the investment rate. From Figure 1.7, we can find that the investment rate decreased from

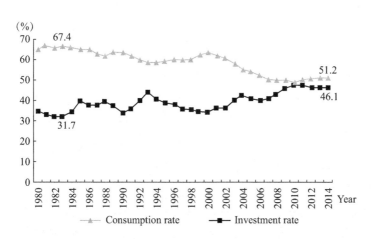

Figure 1.7 Changes in China's consumption rate and investment rate from 1980 to 2014.

Source: National Bureau of Statistics.

47.2% in 2010 to 46.1% in 2014. In addition, as the marginal return of investment diminishes, the situation of high-speed economic growth depending on high-speed investment growth will change. The investment efficiency must be increased in the meantime by displaying the key role of investment in economic growth.

3   Lack of R&D Innovation Capability in Enterprises

In the face of the global new momentum of industrial revolution centered on manufacturing industry, digitalization, and intellectualization, the problems of Chinese enterprises in research and development field were gradually exposed. Most large-scale industrial enterprises had little R&D activities, or the R&D activities were at low level. In 2013, only 14.80% of the industrial enterprises above designated size had R&D activities. R&D expenditures accounted for only 0.8% of main business income of enterprises. However, R&D expenditures of foreign enterprises accounted for more than 3% of main business income of enterprises in 1980s, while that of multinational companies above 5%. It can be seen that the innovation capability of Chinese enterprises is still insufficient, and the enterprises with independent intellectual property rights account for only a small proportion, with low quality in terms of intellectual property rights. China's traditional industrial system, with high dependence on low-end processing and assembly, low technical innovation, and poor brand recognition, found it increasingly difficult to adapt to the change resulting from a competitive environment. If China does not speed up upgrading R&D capacity to promote industrial and technical progress, the existing technical route and productivity will face the risk of elimination. Therefore, it is crucial for China to promote market-oriented technical innovation led by enterprises.

4   Stage of Large-scale Expansion of Manufacturing Basically Came to an End

The expansion of manufacturing sector is an important drive for China's rapid economic growth. However, after the rapid expansion of manufacturing capacity, major manufacturing sectors are faced with severe overcapacity in recent years. In 2014, China's steel output reached 1.12 billion tons, with supply exceeding demand. The installed power-generating capacity reached 1.36 billion kilowatts, and the output of automobiles was 23.725 million units, close to the upper limit of productivity. The demand for bulk products such as steel and cement and durable goods like automobiles ranked top in the world. Due to the impact of adjustment of economic structure and constraints of resource and environment, the future demand for many products will get gradually close to the historical peak and then enter a stage of stable growth or fall after hitting the peak. For a time in the near future, the scale of China's manufacturing expansion will be gradually narrowed. Some industries are confronted with tremendous pressure to absorb excess productivity. Generally speaking, the stage of "project launching" for development of manufacturing industry is basically over, and the main source of power for industrial development is shifted from large-scale expansion of productivity to increase of production efficiency.

5 Obvious Increase in Social Contradictions

Although the Gini coefficient in China dropped from 0.491 in 2008 to 0.469 in 2014, it is still at a high level and the income gap is still large. In some monopolized industries, there is a stark contrast between the high salary, high welfare, and high guarantee of an enterprise's senior managers and the low salary, low welfare, and low guarantee of the low-income group, including migrant workers, flexible employees, and other staff who are in a dire state, which made the actual income gap greater than the nominal one. The miniaturization of family in urban and rural areas, the ownership of housing asset, and the marketization of employment highlighted the diversity, independence, and selectivity of social subjects, and the social interest pattern become more complicated and diversified. The interests of different groups expanded but the mechanism of coordinating their interests was absent, which resulted in occurrence of conflict of interest and disputes. Meanwhile, with the improvement of material life, people's awareness of their democratic rights increased; hence, their need to exercise their rights and interests grew constantly and they put forward new demands for innovation in social management. If these demands are not handled properly, they will manifest into potential contradictions.

6 Continuous Intensification of Hard Constraints in Ecological Environment

We can say that in the past rapid growth period, the leeway for resource environment was relatively large. However, after the new normal, with the continuous expansion of economic scale and increase in consumption of energy and resources, the hard constraints and rigid pressure of resource environment gradually increased. The amounts of pollutants discharged in China reached at a high level, highlighting the characteristics of diversified sources, complex types, enlarged areas, and persistent effects of pollution. As the scale of industry continues to expand and the consumption of energy resource increases, the rigid pressure on ecological environment will further increase. The disorderly transfer of industries will also exacerbate ecological damage in some ecologically fragile areas. China has promised to the international community that by 2020, the emission of carbon dioxide per unit of GDP will be reduced by 40% to 45% compared with that in 2005, which will act as a significant constraint to the excessive growth of energy consumption. With the increasing demand for ecological environment from all walks of life, the hard constraints of resource environment facing the economic development will be gradually strengthened.

7 Rise of Dominant Pressure of Potential Risks

In the growth mode in pursuit of speed and efficiency, when economic growth slows down, the amplification of fiscal revenue and corporate profits will also fall sharply. Meanwhile, the scale of debt and credit was expanded for a time in the past, which increased potential risks in promoting economic growth. Local government financing platforms for large-scale loans led to potential debt risks, while the real estate and financial system gradually accumulated risks. Upon the slowdown of economic growth, various potential risks will be revealed, and contradictions and challenges will be significantly increased.

C Development Potential and Advantage

Reform and opening up in the last 30 years has resulted in China's material and technical foundation becoming stronger, human capital exhibiting scale and cumulative effects, and development potential and comprehensive advantages showing great promise.

1 Substantial Improvement of Scientific and Technical Innovation Capability

In recent years, China's investment in science and technology has increased on a remarkable rise, with great advancement in scientific and technical innovation. In 2014, China's R&D expenditure reached RMB1.34 trillion, accounting for 2.09% of China's GDP, 0.35 percentage points higher than that in 2010. In the "13th Five-Year Plan" period, along with the continuous growth in investment of research and development, science and technology innovation ability, especially enterprise technology innovation capability, will be greatly improved. On the basis of effective breakthrough of a number of core technologies, China can further improve the TFP contribution to its economic growth, weaken the influence of reduction of savings rates and slowdown of capital investment growth, and inject new impetus for economic growth.

2 Accelerated Formation of New Demographic Dividend

With the decrease in working-age population, the aged tendency of population accelerated and the savings rate decreased. The original demographic dividend will gradually disappear. Meanwhile, with the reduction in the proportion of children population among human population, the human capital investment per capita of both the country and the family will improve. The improvement in the labor force quality made it possible for China to create and cultivate the new demographic dividend after the demographic dividend of working-age population disappeared. Every year, there are more than seven million college graduates in China, of which more than six million have received secondary occupation education and skills training; in addition, more than three lakh students have returned from foreign countries. Among the urban population aged 25 to 34, 34% received higher education, close to the average level of Organisation for Economic Co-operation and Development (OECD) countries, which promoted the traditional quantity dividend of medium and low-end population to shift to the quality dividend of medium and high-end talents and created conditions for advancement of economic growth to medium and high-end level.

3 Accelerated Development of Urbanization

In 2014, China's urban resident population reached 749 million – an increase of 18.05 million over the previous year – and the urbanization rate was 54.8%. Though the latter was slightly higher than the average level of the world, it was significantly lower than that of Japan and South Korea, as shown in Figure 1.8. Compared with the countries and regions with similar GDP per capita, it was obviously lower, which indicated China's huge potential for urbanization in the future. In the "13th Five-Year Plan" period, China's urbanization rate will exceed 60%, which will create huge demand for investment in urban infrastructure and residential construction, great need

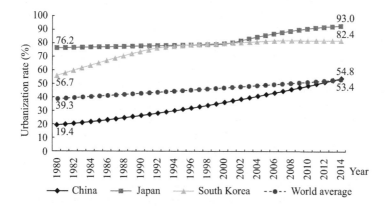

Figure 1.8 Comparison of urbanization rate between China, Japan, and South Korea.

Source: National Bureau of Statistics, World Bank.

for consumption because of citizenization of the population transferred from rural areas, and the strong pull on economic growth.

4 Expedite Expansion of Domestic Market

Recently, although domestic consumption growth had decreased, it still exceeded the growth rate of GDP. In the "13th Five-Year Plan" period, with the rapid increase in labor salary and continuous improvement of social security, residents' consumption will significantly increase, China's domestic market will accelerate the growth of expansion of its overall size, and China's domestic consumption rate might go on a gradual rise. In particular, with the rapid growth of the middle-income group, the proportion of high-end service-type and development-centric consumption, especially in medical care, transportation, communication, education, culture, and entertainment, will gradually grow; meanwhile, consumption in network, information, and other industries will continue to emerge. The constant occurrence of new forms of consumption will become a strong drive for sustained economic development.

5 Great Room to Maneuver for Regional Development

Great regional differences objectively led to the complementarity of China's factor development and industrial development and increased the leeway for China's economic growth. For example, the industries in the coastal areas that lost comparative advantage can be shifted to China's inland, which will extend their life cycle. Such unique space to maneuver, that is, transfer of domestic industries, enables maintaining the comparative advantage of low-cost labor force so that each region can use its dynamic comparative advantages at different industrial levels.

6 Enormous Potential for Deepening Reform

Deepening reforms will effectively improve efficiency of resource allocation, increase overall factor productivity, and help maintain the momentum of economic growth. Although the reform will be more difficult to push forward under the restriction of the "more complicated and diversified pattern of interests" as compared with the previous period, the space for reform remains substantial. Since the Third Plenary Session of the 18th CPC Central Committee, the CPC Central Committee made a series of strategic deployment, significantly accelerated the pace of reform, intensified decentralization, and promoted the reform of state-owned enterprises, investing and financing system, and financial and taxation system that affect the overall situation. It will release a huge institutional bonus and provide an inexhaustible motive force for economic growth.

III Overall Thinking and Development Prospect in "13th Five-Year Plan" Period

A General Thinking

Exalt the Chinese characteristic socialism theory banner; adhere to Deng Xiaoping Theory and the important thought of "Three Represents" and Scientific Outlook on Development as guidance; thoroughly implement the spirit of Comrade Xi Jinping series of important speech, fully completed in accordance with the strategic layout of well-off society, deepening the reform, according to the law of ruling the country, comprehensive strictly, adhere to the development is the first priority, to lead the new the normal demands of economic development, accelerate the transformation of economic development, and comprehensively improve the quality and efficiency of economic development, and strive to achieve the number of expansion to improve the quality, the factor driven to innovation driven, high growth to high growth of the conversion, to ensure timely build the well-off society and lay a more solid foundation for the realization of the great rejuvenation of the Chinese nation Chinese dream.

1 To Ensure Build-up of Well-off Society on Schedule

To build a well-off society in an all-round manner by 2020 is an important component of China's dream of realizing the great rejuvenation of the Chinese nation. The "13th Five-Year Plan" period is a decisive stage for building a moderately prosperous society. Compared with the overall well-off society that has been realized in 2000, a comprehensive well-off society is built with a wider coverage and at a higher level. With efforts in the past ten years or so, the construction of a comprehensive well-off society made great headway. However, as the overall plan for promoting economic, political, cultural, social, and ecological progress was proposed at the 18th National Congress of the Communist Party of China, there are still "short boards" in the comprehensive well-off society, which include poverty population which is still large; issues concerning agriculture, farmer, and rural areas are still prominent; development is still lagging behind in former revolutionary base areas, areas inhabited by minority, remote and border areas, and poverty-stricken areas; resource and environmental situation is still severe; and social civilization still needs to be improved. In the "13th Five-Year Plan" period, it is important for the Chinese government to focus on the purpose of providing people with better education, more stable jobs, more satisfactory income, more reliable social security, higher-level health care service, more comfortable living conditions, and more beautiful environment; these can be achieved by overcoming the difficulties by making breakthrough in the "short boards" and thus ensuring the timely realization of the goal for a comprehensive well-off society.

2 *To Accelerate Transformation of Economic Development Mode*

China's economic development entered into the new normal, with profound change in the conditions and environment for factor-driven development. The original development method is difficult to continue. As such, if there is no transformation, there will be no way out. The transformation of economic development mode lies in the transition from extensive scale and speed growth to intensive quality growth, and from reliance on factor-driven mode to reliance on efficiency-driven and innovation-driven way, which will bring about the transition from high-speed growth to high-efficiency growth. In the case of slowdown in economy growth and increase of factor costs, it is only by increasing factor productivity that the rise of labor costs be effectively offset, the investment marginal output maintain stable growth, enterprises maintain or get close to the profitability over the past period of rapid growth, the accumulated foam and risks be gradually released, and the pressure on resource and environment be gradually mitigated. Therefore, the main theme of economic development in the "13th Five-Year Plan" period should be to promote the transformation from factor-driven to efficiency- and innovation-driven and to push forward the leap of economic growth from high-speed growth to high-efficiency growth.

3 *To Focus on All-round Improvement in Quality and Efficiency of*
   Economic Development

From the macro perspective, improving the quality of economic development should be based on the increase of national economic input-output rate, labor productivity, rate of return on investment, total factor productivity, and sustainability of economic development. The increase in the efficiency of economic development is mainly reflected in the rise of labor remuneration and income of residents, as well as in the increase of enterprise profits and financial revenues. To enhance quality and efficiency of economic development, there is a need to improve the labor productivity and the contribution rate of technical progress to economic growth. The focus should be to increase the input of science and technology and human capital and display the critical role of technical growth in increasing production efficiency so as to make economic development rely more on technical progress, increase in worker quality, and innovation drive of management. Centered by the goal of comprehensively improving quality and efficiency of economic development, it is important to achieve the unified upgrade in quantity, speed, and quality. In other words, it is necessary to achieve sustainable rapid growth with high quality and efficiency, which are on a constant rise.

B Outlook on Economic Growth in "13th Five-Year Plan" Period

In the "13th Five-Year Plan" period, the impact of international financial crisis will continue, the US dollar will remain in appreciation mode, international capital flow will intensify, market fluctuation will increase, bulk commodities will generally remain in the transformation from recession to recovery, and the world will stay in low inflation period. China's economic development has entered the critical phase of further structural adjustment and transit from the old impetus to the new one. Some major periodic and turning changes will successively appear. Active or passive structural adjustment and asset restructuring will be accelerated, the impact of release of local risks will be enhanced, and the declination of potential growth rate caused by the transformation in the growth stage is difficult to reverse in a short term. In this process, if you can avoid systemic risks, the periodic platform at the time of medium and high-speed growth is expected to come into being, and economic growth will pick up slightly after its stabilization, with limited range.

In the case of demand, export remains low speed growth in fluctuation. As the price of bulk commodities stabilizes, export growth is expected to go up after 2017. Influenced by income growth and consumption mode change, the overall growth rate of consumption will exhibit steady trend. The investment will be the vital variable, leading to changes in demand; real estate investment will gradually bottom out and infrastructure investment growth will remain higher than the growth of fiscal income. Led by real estate and export, manufacturing investment and other investment are expected to rebound.

From the supply side, the effective labor supply, which is determined by the working-age population and the labor participation rate, will begin to decline in 2016. Due to the decline in investment growth, the pace of capital formation will continue to slow down. With accumulation of innovation factors and structural reform, the growth of TFP ceased to decline and showed a small pick-up, which became a positive factor in supply.

Considering the change of demand and supply as well as of the long-term trend, in the context of the orderly advancement of reform with controllable risks, a momentum of rapid growth will continue in the "13th Five-Year Plan" period. With primary expectation, the annual average economic growth rate will be slightly higher than 6.5%. From the perspective of growth momentum, the contribution of consumption and TFP to economic growth will increase. The contribution rate of consumption to economic growth will increase by more than 1 percentage point every year, and the contribution rate of TFP will gradually increase. In terms of industrial structure, the proportion of service industry will steadily increase, while that of the secondary industry will continuously decline.

To maintain medium and high-speed growth in the "13th Five-Year Plan" period is an important condition to achieve the goal of doubling the

GDP and urban and rural residents' income in 2020 compared to 2010, which is the basis to keep sustainable and healthy economic development and create conditions for structural adjustment and impetus shift. Given the huge economic volume of China, if there is a decrease in inertia in the process of economic growth and gear-shifting, the downward trend will tend to be out of control. When the growth rate is too low, it will be easy for economic foam to crack with intensive release of risks. In addition, it will be hard for enterprises to increase input in R&D and innovation, along with the change of market and social expectation. Therefore, in order to keep the economy developing at a reasonable rate, it is necessary to achieve medium and high-speed growth on the basis of structural adjustment and impetus transition.

C   Conditions to Maintain High Growth in "13th Five-Year Plan" Period

1   Economic Growth Remaining Great Potential

In the recent 30 or so years since the reform and opening up, China has become the second largest economy in the world due to its rapid growth of economy. However, in 2014, China's total GDP was only 59.5% of the US total GDP, with greater gap in terms of GDP per capita. The per capita GDP of China was only 13.9% of that of the US, as shown in Figure 1.9, and still lower than the world average GDP, suggesting that China is still in the period of growth by catch-up. As there is still room for industrialization and urbanization, China can learn and absorb the world advanced technology to improve the TFP and maintain medium and high-speed growth of economy.

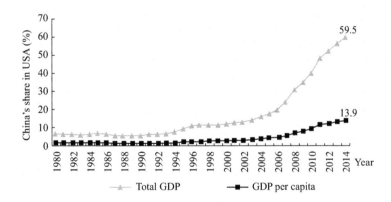

Figure 1.9 Share of China's total GDP and GDP per capita in the USA from 1980 to 2014.

Source: calculated on the basis of WDI.

2 Breeding of New Focus on Demand

Currently, China has not completed its industrialization and urbanization due to a huge gap in development between regions. There is great responsibility and pressure on China to transform 260 million migrant workers into urban labor market, and to rid 70 million poor people of poverty, to move 100 million residents in squatter settlements into new houses. Besides, there is a great need for investment in people's livelihood, environmental protection, water conservancy, and city transformation. In the case of fixed capital stock per capita, China is only about one-fifth of the United States, as shown in Figure 1.10, but has huge potential for investment. In the "13th Five-Year Plan" period, consumption will play a more important role; new hot spots of consumption in information, health, health care, pension, culture, entertainment, and tourism will emerge in an endless stream; traditional consumption will exhibit personalized features, and in combination with electronic commerce, it will fuel more diversified demands.

3 Still Room for Higher Productivity

There is still a considerable gap between China's total factor productivity and that of developed countries. Let us assume that the total factor productivity of the United States is 1, then that of Japan and South Korea will be, respectively, equivalent to 71% and 69% of that of the US, while that of China will be only 41%, as shown in Figure 1.11. By improving allocation of factors within and between departments through innovative technologies, management, and business modes, China will have its TFP remain stable and promote effective accumulation of capital. In the past years, the

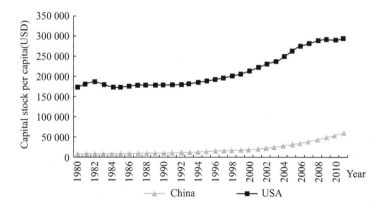

Figure 1.10 Comparison of capital stock per capita under current PPP between China and USA from 1980 to 2010.
Data source: calculated on the basis of PWT.

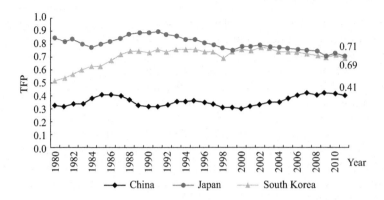

Figure 1.11 Comparison of TFP between China, Japan, and South Korea from 1980 to 2010.

Data source: calculated on the basis of PWT. Suppose the TFP of the US is 1.

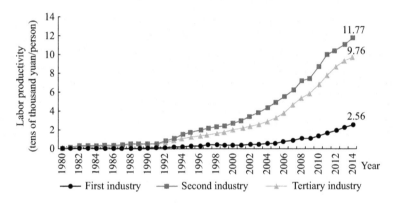

Figure 1.12 Differences in labor productivity between China's three industries from 1980 to 2014.

Source: National Bureau of Statistics.

transfer of labor and other factors of production from agricultural sectors to non-agricultural sectors and from state-owned sectors to private sectors was the main way to enhance factor productivity. As Figure 1.12 shows, the labor productivity of China's secondary and tertiary industries is significantly higher than that of its primary industry. After entering the new stage, the space of the reallocation of resources between departments was reduced. However, there was still great room to improve the efficiency through inter-departmental transfer of factors and through merger and acquisition among enterprises. The variation coefficient can reflect capital output efficiency of different sectors within the manufacturing industry. It is estimated that China's variation coefficient is 1.3, while that of the US is only 0.3, which indicates that that China has greater room to enhance efficiency through factor transfer between industries. By breaking monopoly and introducing competition, more resource was transferred from low-efficiency industries to high-efficiency industries and from low-output enterprises to high-output enterprises. To make up for the "short boards" in industry and enterprise efficiency, China can greatly improve the total factor productivity and transfuse new impetus for economic development.

4 Broad Space for Industry Transformation and Upgrade

In recent years, the Internet, cloud computing, new materials, robotics, energy conservation, environmental protection, and other emerging industries have developed rapidly, with increasingly prominent trend of integration with traditional industries. China has become world's largest Internet and mobile Internet economy. The effect of the Internet on the transformation of the consumer has already appeared, and the transformation of the supply chain and production has just begun. Led by the new information technology and the Internet, China's economy will form new competitive advantages in the process of transformation of traditional industries. In addition, through the advancement of "The Belt and Road" construction and the acceleration of international cooperation in equipment manufacturing capacity, China will be further integrated into global division of labor; foreign investment and trade growth will be further released; and factor flow of capital, technology, talent, and information will be more comprehensive; all of these are conducive to further enhance China's competitiveness of products and services.

5 Great Room for Catch-up between Internal Regions

With the rapid development of high-speed train and highways as well as the quick upgrade of information infrastructure network, factor flow between different areas will be more convenient. The comparative advantage of each region will be further displayed, which provides strong support for the central and western regions to release growth potential. It is impossible to maintain a high rate of growth for a long time in the future. In the eastern coastal areas, a number of high-level growth poles dependent on city belts or city clusters are successively formed. At present, many innovative and green cities have emerged. The flow of various factors within regions and between regions has become more effective, with more obvious spillover effect of knowledge. Besides, the promoting effect of intensification of distribution of labor on productivity has become increasingly prominent.

IV Strategies and Decisions for Major Issues in "13th Five-Year Plan" Period

In the "13th Five-Year Plan" period, we should ensure the establishment of a comprehensive well-off society, accelerate the transformation of economic development mode, improve the overall quality and efficiency of economic development, and deal with various challenges in the middle-income population so as to resolve the risks in the process from high-speed growth to medium and high-speed growth. It also means that the task to be fulfilled will be more difficult than ever. Compared with the countries that have surpassed the "middle income trap", China is still in the initial stage of modernization. The industrialization process is greatly compressed in time with more highlighted structural problems, which requires us to aim at the overall relations and situations and the long-term critical areas, as well as to implement major strategies and take strategic countermeasures against prominent contradictions and problems.

A Implementation of Innovation-Driven Development Strategy

At present, a new technical revolution and industrial revolution intersect with the new normal of China, which provides critical moments for the enhancement of the drive of innovation to economic growth. It requires great efforts in implementing innovation-driven strategies and promoting economic growth from factor-driven to innovation-driven modes.

1 Enhancing Enterprises' Dominant Position in Innovation

At present, less than 15% of China's industrial enterprises above the designated size are engaged in R&D. Enterprises have little aspiration and little impetus for innovation. Innovation requires enterprises to fully compete in the market, which requires the market to play a decisive role in resource allocation, mainly by discovering and fostering new growth points in the market. It is necessary for China to guide the optimization of capital, talent, technology, and other innovative factors according to market orientation; lead innovative resource to focus on enterprises; improve the mechanism for transfer of technical results from scientific research institutes and universities to enterprises; enhance the support for innovation of small and medium enterprises; help enterprises get rid of their excess reliance on the processing and manufacturing sectors that consume much energy resource; rely more on research and development, design, market development, brand building, and intangible capital investment; meet diversified and personalized demands; as well as advance the transition from traditional manufacturing to new manufacturing based on R&D.

2   Integration of Scientific Innovation and Industrial Transition and Upgrade

Innovation is the industrialization process of scientific and technical achievements, and it must be carried out to create new growth points and be implemented in the industrial transformation and upgrading. The development of new industries and technology innovation makes breakthroughs in key aspects of research and development, design, standards, brand, and supply chain management; strives to master the core technology; improve the proportion of high value-added sectors; increase product knowledge, technology, and human capital content; strengthen R&D capability; support the development of high-tech industry technology, knowledge-intensive, high value-added operations, and equipment manufacturing industry to promote high-tech industries, from the main assembly point, to the manufacturing shift, and to independent research and development.

3   Mobilization of Initiative of Innovation and Entrepreneurship in the Whole Society

China should create a favorable policy environment for mass entrepreneurship and innovation. More effective measures should be implemented to speed up the transformation of government functions to promote fair competition in the market. The innovation incentive mechanism should be strengthened, especially for researchers, to encourage grassroots entrepreneurship and micro innovation, so that they become the life goal of young people. More importance should be attached to display the entrepreneurship, to encourage enterprises to make efforts into the R&D, and for application of new technologies, new products, and new technique. The innovation of industrial organization, management, and business mode of enterprises should be encouraged to make thousands and thousands of enterprises to become the subject of innovation.

4   Expedite Formation of Institutional Mechanism with Innovation-Driven Development

To achieve innovation-driven development, the most fundamental thing is to get rid of institutional obstacles and set up an institutional environment conducive to efficient allocation of innovative resource and full release of innovation potential. It is important to drive stock reform with increments, such as to construct a group of new R&D institutions in the emerging fields of the Internet of Things, big data, cloud computing, and electric automobiles, so as to produce a number of original achievements of scientific research and promote the further reform of the existing research institutes. It is necessary to deepen the reform of property right system for scientific and technical achievements; improve the market mechanism for transformation of achievements; change revenue distribution for technical achievements; and encourage all types of enterprises to mobilize the enthusiasm of innovation of researchers through equity, options, bonuses, and other incentives. More emphasis should be placed on the protection of intellectual property rights and the strengthening of law enforcement. It is also important to strengthen financial support for innovation; establish venture capital guiding fund; make good use of private equity, equity-based crowd-funding, and other financing tools; and support the development of venture capital and angel investment, so as to mobilize the whole society to put in more enthusiasm in innovation investment.

B Increase of Investment in Human Capital

In the context of the decline of working-age population and the speedup of aged tendency of population, fundamental factors, such as increasing investment in human capital, strengthening high-end skill training and higher education system construction, and releasing population quality dividend, are adapted to the changes in the supply and demand of labor force to accelerate the cultivation of new competitive advantages.

1 Establishment of Modern Educational System

It is important for China to make innovation in the content and methods of teaching by structuring the whole teaching process in a way that addresses scientific spirit, creative thinking, and creative ability for vigorous cultivation of innovative talents. China should promote connotative development of higher education with a focus on talent fostering, improving quality of education, strengthening the innovation ability construction of universities and colleges, and supporting the participation of universities and colleges in the construction of national innovation system. In addition, China should accelerate the construction of modern occupational education, enhance the practicability of occupational education, cultivate a large number of technical talents, and strengthen the occupational skill training and job skill training for migrant workers. Furthermore, China should strengthen the inclusiveness and fairness of basic education, continuously increase financial investment in basic education, consolidate and improve compulsory education, expedite the popularization of preschool education and high school education, improve the quality of basic education, and narrow the gap between urban and rural education.

2 Speeding Up Reform of Educational System

It is advisable to provide universities and colleges with more autonomy in running schools, encourage the establishment of private-owned, small-size, high-level research institutions, and lift the limitation for the cooperative operation of schools between foreign first-class universities and colleges and domestic ones. In addition, it is necessary to promote a number of local universities and colleges to be transformed into those focusing on applied technology or occupational education. Besides, it is important to advance the reform of enrollment and examination system for higher education. It is also of significance to implement the evaluation system combined with academic achievements examination and comprehensive quality in high school, so as to reverse the trend of exam-oriented education and establish and improve multiple admission mechanisms.

3 Reform of Talent Flow Mechanism

It is necessary to improve the position management of the staff to eradicate barriers to the flow of talent system and promote the rational flow of researchers in scientific research institutions and enterprises. It is important to eliminate the obstacles that flow inside and outside of the system, establish the "revolving door" mechanism with Chinese characteristics, and encourage the flow of professional talents in academic institutions, government departments, enterprises, and non-profit organizations. Besides, it is advisable to perfect the incentive mechanism for talents to go to the basic and arduous positions for startup of business. It is also important to promote classified reform of talent evaluation mechanism and titling system.

4 Stimulating Potential of Human Capital

It is important for China to create a culture that encourages innovation and tolerates failures in order to encourage innovative talents to develop innovation and startup business. In addition, it is necessary for China to reconstruct the incentive mechanism for entrepreneurial activities, with a view to respect and protect entrepreneurs' personal property rights and stabilize the expectation and confidence of property owners. Besides, it is also vital to expedite the urbanization of migrant workers, especially the second generation of migrant workers, to make them at par with the urban people and to stimulate their enthusiasm for economic development and entrepreneurial activities.

C Advancing Rise of Quality and Efficiency and Upgrade in Industries

After entering the new stage of development, the fundamental way to tap the growth potential of China's economy lies in the revitalization of real economy, which, in turn, depends on upgrading the quality and efficiency of industries for improving industrial value chain and raising added value of products.

1 Accelerating Cultivation of New Economic Growth Points

It is important to adapt to the new changes of international industry competition; accelerate the cultivation of emerging industries in the field of industrial robots, information network, integrated circuits, new energy, new materials, and biological medicine; promote the development of intelligent manufacturing, distributed energy, online shopping, Internet banking, and other new manufacturing and service formats; and encourage enterprises to make progress in R&D, design, standards, branding, and supply chain management. Besides, China needs to promote the plan of "Made in China 2025", encourage qualified enterprises to upgrade according to "Industry 4.0", carry out the "Internet plus", and make optimum use of the latest achievements and advanced intelligent manufacturing technology by means of information technology revolution, advance upgrade of manufacturing quality, and efficiency. By 2025, China should make its overall manufacturing reach world level, with the establishment of world's leading technology system and industrial system.

2 Speeding Up Transition and Upgrade of Traditional Industries

As traditional industry is still the main battlefield for economic development, China should promote structural tax-cut and implement inclusive taxation policy in an effort to reduce the burden of enterprises. Besides, China should further promote the integration of manufacturing industry and the Internet, accelerate the pace of technical innovation, establish a stable high-skilled staff team, and enhance the value creativity and market competitiveness of enterprises. It is advisable for China to make comprehensive use of economic, legal, and administrative means; accelerate the elimination of traditional heavy chemical industries which are prone to have high energy consumption, high emission, and low added value; improve access standards in terms of environmental protection, energy consumption, and technology; speed up technical progress, management innovation, industrial restructuring, and layout optimization; and encourage the transnational management of heavy chemical industry. It is also of significance to improve the quality of labor, enhance human capital accumulation, and encourage traditional labor-intensive industries to transform its operations into manufacturing and service integrated with labor, knowledge, and skills; these factors will help advance the transition and upgrade of traditional labor-intensive industries and processing trade.

3 Establishment of Market Clearing Mechanism for
  Excess Capacity

China should formulate enforcement regulations related to of bankruptcy and implement it as soon as possible, so as to stop transfusion of fiscal funds and bank capital into "Zombie Enterprises" (unprofitable and debt-laden enterprises backed by investors or government) and release the idle resource. Regarding the institutional obstacles against the exit of enterprises, China should accelerate the promulgation of instruction, specific policies and measures on personnel placement, corporate debt cancellation after verification, asset disposal, bankruptcy reorganization, and corporate restructuring. Besides, China should release financial support policies conducive to clearing excess capacity and raise special funds used for solving problems of personnel placement and debt disposal in clearing excess capacity. It is also advisable for China to actively explore the market-oriented means of clearing excess capacity, such as establishing national market for overcapacity transaction, allowing cross-regional transaction of productivity index on the basis of rational distribution of overcapacity exit index.

4 Quickening Development of Producer Services

Productive service industry has become a key link to improve the added value in the manufacturing industry and production efficiency in the service industry. It is important to focus on encouraging the development of financial insurance, business service, technology service, information service, and creative production services; expedite the development of productive service sectors of R&D, design, standards, logistics, marketing, branding, and supply chain management; increase the added value, knowledge, technology and human capital content in the manufacturing industry; keep up with the new trend of service industry transfer and accelerated development of service outsourcing worldwide; and actively and steadily expand the range of opening up of service industries, as well as undertake international service transfer and service outsourcing in software, telecommunications service, financial service, and management consultation.

D Actively Promoting Urbanization Centered by Human

Urbanization is China's biggest potential domestic demand. Promotion of urbanization, especially to accelerate the citizenization of the migrant of rural people, will create a huge demand for investment and consumption in order to absorb excess production capacity and will continue to create demands for investment in infrastructure and housing. This economic growth will not be from too much reliance on external demands as it was in the past, but from dependence on the coordinated drives of domestic and external demands.

1 Promoting New Urbanization Centered by Human

To orderly advance the citizenization of rural migrant workers is the core of new urbanization. In 2013, the gap between China's urbanization rate

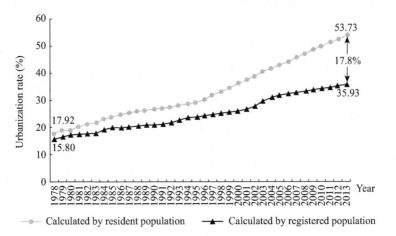

Figure 1.13 Gap between China's urbanization rate calculated by resident population and that by registered population.

Note: The data for China's urbanization rate calculated by resident population were from China Statistical Yearbook in 2014; the data for China's urbanization rate calculated by registered population weer from China Population Statistical Yearbook from 1949 to 1985, China Population Statistical Yearbook from 1988 to 2006; and China Population and Employment Statistics Yearbook from 2007 to 2014.

calculated by resident population and that by registered population was 17.8 percentage points, as shown in Figure 1.13. It is necessary to accelerate the breakthrough in the dualistic separation system for urban and rural areas, reform the household registration system with different standards for urban and rural areas, fully implement system of residential pass for rural migrant workers, as well as establish and improve the basic public service supply mechanism on the basis of living years and other conditions in order to realize the full coverage of basic public services for urban residential population. It is also important to promote the implementation of the system of linking up the augmentation of financial transfer payment and urban construction land with the number of households absorbing rural migrant workers and phase out the difference between urban-registered permanent residence and rural ones, thus disconnecting the registered permanent residence with public service. In addition, it is advisable to create urban investment and financing system, establish transparent issuing system for local government bonds, and publicize the cooperative mode between the government and social capital in public infrastructure and public utility.

2 Advancing Reform of Rural Land Management System

It is important for China to gradually narrow the scope of land requisition, improve the land requisition compensation standard, develop a reasonable standardized, diversified security mechanism for landless farmers, and include all the qualified farmers whose lands were expropriated, into pension, medicare, and other means of urban social security. In accordance with the planning and purpose, rural collective operational construction land should be allowed for divestment, lease, share-holding, and entrance into the market as state-owned land, with the same rights and same prices. It is necessary to protect usufruct of rural residence base, carefully and steadily push forward the system of mortgage, guarantee and transfer of farmers' housing property on a pilot basis, and explore the mechanism for voluntarily exit from rural homestead. In addition, farmers should be given the rights of possession, use, revenue-earning and transfer on contracted land, as well as the mortgage and guarantee of contract and management rights; these actions will lower the inhibitions of rural farmers to transfer contract and management rights to professional households, family farms, farmers' cooperatives, and agricultural enterprises in the open markets for development of various forms of scale management.

3 Actively and Steadily Developing Urban Agglomerations and Metropolitan Areas

It is of significance to further optimize the development of the three-city clusters of the Yangtze River Delta, Pearl River Delta, and Beijing-Tianjin-Hebei Region; promote the construction of the internationalized urban system centered by the cosmopolises of Shanghai, Beijing, and Guangzhou; speed up the development of the city clusters of Liaodong Peninsula, Shandong Peninsula, and the west coast of the Taiwan Strait; actively cultivate the emerging city clusters with good basic conditions and great potential for development like the Beibu Gulf, the Middle Reaches of the Yangtze River, the Chengdu-Chongqing Region, Central China, and Guanzhong region. The enhancement of these regions will help in the absorption of rural migrant workers so that more and more qualified capable migrant people settle down there, gradually integrate themselves into the immigrant location, and turn into urban people.

4 Speeding Up Development of Small and Medium Cities and Small Towns

It is important to enhance the overall carrying capacity of small and medium-sized cities and small towns; expedite the promulgation of supporting policies of finance-taxation, investment, and financing for development of small towns and industries; strengthen the functions of developing industries so that they provide public services, attract employment, and gather population of small towns; and promote the employment nearby and citizenization nearby of rural migrant workers. Besides, it is necessary to rapidly implement the relaxation of those policies with limitation against the settlement of rural migrant workers into small and medium-sized cities and small towns, especially counties and hub towns, promote their settlement in small and medium-sized cities and small towns, and endow them with equal basic public service as the local urban residents.

5 Strengthening Sustainable Development Capacity of Cities and Towns

It is important to make reasonable planning of the size of urban population; strictly control the occupation of cultivated land; establish the institutional mechanism for economical use of land, water, and energy resource; and develop resource-saving and environment-friendly cities and towns. The size and layout of cities should be adapted to local soil and water resource, environmental capacity, and geological structure. The situation of prioritizing management over planning in city development should be changed into both strengthening urban planning supervision and improving urban comprehensive management.

E Promoting Regional Coordinated Development

For a time in the nearer future, China's regional development pattern will undergo new adjustment, which will make it difficult to advance regional coordinated development. In the context of the concentration of production factors to advantageous regions, it is necessary to optimize the allocation of resource and factors between regions, promote regional coordinated development, accelerate the equalization of basic public services, increase the support to underdeveloped areas, and form the new regional development pattern with complementary advantages, positive interaction, and coordinated development.

1 Adhering to Overall Strategy of Regional Development

It is important for China to improve the development of western regions, rejuvenate the rusty belt of Northeast China and other old industrial bases, rapidly develop central regions, and prioritize the development of eastern regions. In this regard, the overall framework of regional development with "three vertical and three horizontal axes" should be established, with the horizontal axes including the Yangtze River Economic Belt, Longhai-Lanxin Economic Belt, and Pearl River-Xijiang River Economic Belt, and the vertical axes including the Coastal Economic Belt, Jingguang-Jingha Economic Belt, and Bao-Kun Economic Belt. On the basis of the optimized and focused development along these axes, the pattern of regional development across the east and west and linking the north and south will take shape.

2 *Greater Efforts to Build Key Economic Zones*

It is vital for China to actively plan the new layout for regional development linked with main lines of transportation with great rivers and land routes, which is detailed as follows: to implement the synergetic development strategy of Beijing, Tianjin, and Hebei so as to promote the development of the Bohai Sea region and lead the development of northern hinterland; to carry out the development strategy of the Yangtze River Economic Belt, on the basis of the Yangtze golden waterway, supported by the Yangtze River Delta, the Middle Reaches of the Yangtze River, and Chengdu-Chongqing City Cluster, with a view to accelerate the construction of the Yangtze River Economic Belt; to build bay area economy with international influence and competitiveness, on the basis of the Greater Pearl River Delta City Cluster, driving the development of the Pearl River-Xijiang River Economic Belt and enhancing the cooperation of the places in the Pan-Pearl River Delta.

3 *Improvement in Policy System in Innovation Regions*

It is important to establish the new regional development mechanism with solid market norms, free factor flow, sustainable resource and environment, complete transfer payment mechanism, effectively bonded main functional areas, and equal access to basic public service. For such purpose, China should increase the transfer payment capacity to old revolutionary base areas, ethnic minority areas, border areas, and poor areas, especially to raise support to these areas in the fields of compulsory education and human resource development, so as to enhance self-development of underdeveloped areas. China should also increase efforts in assistance and targeted aid to the areas with particular difficulties and further improve the long-term assistance mechanism.

4 *Enhancing Network Support Function for Infrastructure*

The modern infrastructure network plays an important role in promoting the coordinated development of urban and rural areas. In this regard, it is vital to accelerate the improvement of national railway network and to build fast passenger transport system that are safe, low-cost, and have high efficiency. Besides, it is important to strengthen the fast and efficient connection within and between city clusters pivoted by integrated transport hubs with fast railways and highways at the core. In addition, it is vital to strengthen the construction of logistics infrastructure network; create a convenient and reliable, high-quality, and professional freight system; optimize the passenger terminals' functions of collecting and distributing; improve convenience and compatibility in cargo integrated reloading, promote the smooth convergence and efficient transit of various transportation means, raise logistics efficiency; and reduce logistics costs between regions.

F Implementation of Green Low-Carbon Development Strategy

It is the overall guiding policy of China to integrate the construction of eco-logical civilization into its whole process of economic and social develop-ment, which requires the reduction of consumption and emission of energy resource, effective reversal of increasing deterioration of ecological environ-ment, as well as the transformation from the process of pressure release in resource environment to that of technical progress and industrial upgrade.

1 Developing Clean and Renewable Energy Source

The unreasonable energy consumption structure and the high proportion of fossil energy, especially coal, in production and consumption of primary energy source are the main causes for the growing greenhouse gas emis-sion and increasingly critical air pollution. China must speed up the devel-opment of clean energy and renewable energy, and gradually increase the proportion of non-fossil energy in production and consumption of primary energy source, which can be specified as follows: to develop the technology of clean and efficient use of coal and raise the energy efficiency in the whole development and utilization of coal and pollutant emission standards; to accelerate the development of natural gas and other clean fossil energy to promote the development of shale gas and other unconventional oil and gas resource; to expand hydroelectric scale to advance the construction of large hydropower stations; to actively develop nuclear power on the basis of ensuring safety; to expand the scale of grid-tied wind power generation by speeding up the construction of the eight major wind power generation bases at tens of millions of kilowatts in the "three northern areas of China" (Northeast China, North China, and West China) and coastal areas, speed-ing up the construction of small and medium-sized wind power stations in the inland areas, developing nautical wind power generation technology, and strengthening the construction of grid-tied supporting projects; to promote the diversified utilization of solar energy by building large-scale photovoltaic power plants, encouraging the development of distributed pho-tovoltaic power generation, and supporting demonstration of distributed energy system projects; to develop biomass energy according to local condi-tions and encourage the development of technologies of methane electricity generation and power generation with waste incineration and landfill gas; to accelerate the exploration of geothermal energy, ocean energy, and other renewable energy resource; and to improve the development and utilization of the aforementioned energy resources.

2 Building Low-Carbon-Based Systems for Industry, Architecture, and Transportation

It is vital for China to advance the R&D and application of low-carbon technology in key industries; gradually set up industrial emission standards;

strengthen technical transformation for energy saving in the industries of power, steel, building materials, nonferrous metals, and chemical industry; implement mandatory energy-efficiency labeling, expand the scope of energy-saving product certification, and push forward contract energy management and energy auditing. Besides, it is important for China to strengthen the construction and management of low-carbon in the cities, develop low-carbon architecture, and renovate the existing urban buildings into the new ones in accordance with energy-efficiency standards. Furthermore, it is necessary for China to accelerate rail transportation and other low-carbon transportation means, encourage public transportation, improve transportation efficiency, and improve low-carbon-oriented traffic restriction regulations and standards.

3 Strengthening Environmental Governance and Ecological Restoration

China should create the coordinated governance mode between basins, between regions, and between urban and rural areas to advance the overall prevention and treatment of air pollution, water pollution, soil pollution, and so on, by means of the following measures: to focus on areas with critical mixed atmospheric pollution like Beijing, Tianjin, and Hebei and further improve the mechanism of regional coordinated governance and management mode and enhance prevention against air pollution; to continuously strengthen the protection of source of drinking water, actively prevent and treat groundwater pollution, and enhance comprehensive treatment of major drainage areas and sensitive areas; to control soil pollution by strengthening the management of soil pollution in main areas and adjusting the usage of seriously polluted land; to speed up the construction of urban sewage, garbage treatment facilities, and other pollution treatment infrastructure and improve the charging operation mechanism that can effectively cover costs; and to focus on the environmental risk analysis and investigation on main areas, carry out environmental security assessment on soil, groundwater, and drinking water source, and resolutely prevent large-scale environmental events.

4 Active Response to Climate Change

It is vital for China to establish a system for "double control" over total carbon emission and intensity, and strengthen objective assessment responsibility system in the governments at all levels to control greenhouse gas emission. It is necessary for China to gradually establish a unified national carbon emission trading market and to study and formulate the proposal for setting up of national carbon emission trading volume and quota allocation. Besides, it is important to strengthen the R&D and industrialized input in energy conservation; increase of energy efficiency, clean coal, advanced nuclear power, carbon capture and storage, and other low-carbon and zero-carbon technology; promote the industrial development of low-carbon and zero-carbon technology; implement low-carbon technical demonstration projects; and strengthen the popularization and application of low-carbon technology. Furthermore, it is also of significance to establish and improve the statistics, monitoring, and evaluation system adapted to the requirements of the goal of control over greenhouse gas emission, as well as to establish and improve the monitoring system for whole greenhouse gas emission to strengthen the assessment on all subjects of liability.

5 Innovating Environmental Protection System

It is advisable for China to improve the pollutant emission permit system, promote the compensated use for pollutant-discharge right and trading pilot, and advance the measure for the third party to control environmental pollution. Besides, it is important to explore the establishment of diversified compensation mechanism, gradually increase the transfer payment in key ecological function areas, and improve the incentive and restraint mechanism of linking funds allocation with ecological protection effectiveness. In addition, it is of significance to promote the establishment of horizontal ecological compensation between regions and formulate measures of horizontal ecological compensation. Furthermore, it is vital to strictly enforce the system of compensation for ecological damage to the environment, as well as to set up and improve environmental monitoring and alerting system.

G Implementation of Opening Development Strategy

In the "13th Five-Year Plan" period, the relationship between China and world economy will be more close, which will intensify China's interaction with international economy. Instead of adhering to the policy of "bringing in", China is more actively "going out". China should optimize the overall layout of opening up, accelerate the construction of The Belt and Road, and better balance the bilateral interests between "bringing in" and "going out", so as to achieve common development for mutual benefit in a win-win manner in the process of opening up.

1 Optimization of Overall Layout of Opening Up

It is of significance to create a new height for opening up in coastal areas, display the role of the Yangtze River Delta, the Pearl River Delta, and the Bohai Rim as the portal for opening up to the outside world, and build up economic areas with greater international influence. It is important to support the development of high-end industry in coastal areas, intensify R&D, and speed up the transportation from the global base of processing and assembly to the base of R&D and advanced manufacturing. Relying on the golden waterway of the Yangtze River, China should promote the development of the Yangtze River Economic Belt and develop the new corridor for the opening up both in land and in sea. On the basis of inland central cities and city clusters as well as development areas and industry cluster districts, China should accelerate the opening up of inland by actively exploring the new path to undertake industrial transfer and supporting the establishment of advanced manufacturing center in inland central cities. Besides, China should also support addition of international transport routes for passengers and freight, develop river-ocean combined transportation as well as multiple transportation like railway-water and land-aviation, and form the economic corridor to the world across the east and west and connecting the north and south. Furthermore, it is important to cultivate new pivotal points for opening up in border areas and to develop border key pilot areas of development and opening-up and border economic cooperation zones into an important platform for China to cooperate with neighboring countries, so as to steadily develop cross-border economic cooperation zone, develop energy resource importing and processing base, and make industrial cooperation oriented to surrounding markets.

2 Accelerating Construction of "The Belt and Road"

In adherence to the principle of achieving shared growth through discussion and collaboration, China should focus on the communication in policy, facilities, trading, capital, and people, as well as promote all-round cooperation with relevant countries to build a community of interest, fate, and responsibility. It is important to deepen multilevel economic and trade cooperation with relevant countries, construct global value chain with common interest, and lead the development of border and inland areas. For the purpose of rapidly forming the international channel and constructing comprehensive transportation network with safe and smooth communication at home and abroad, China should promote the linkage of infrastructures, optimize the construction of backbone channels, and connect the missing or bottleneck sections of highways or railways. It is advisable for China to deepen economic and trade cooperation with relevant countries, mutually expand the opening-up of markets, actively cultivate new trade growth points, further create trading ways, constantly improve trade facilitation, and advance the cooperation between China and countries along the Belt and Road in large-size complete sets of equipment, technology, and standards. Besides, China should increase the import of non-resource products and promote trade balance. It is important for China to strengthen the cooperation with countries alongside in industrial investment for joint establishment of a number of economic and trade cooperation zones, so as to lead the relevant countries to increase employment and people's livelihood. It is also vital for China to intensify cooperation with them in energy and resource, raise its capacity of deep processing of energy resource, and expand the scope and room for cooperation. Furthermore, China should broaden financial cooperation, actively participate in the construction of AIIB, display the role of Silk Road Funds, expand the scale and scope of bilateral currency swap, carry out more settlement on the basis of domestic currency of cross-border trade, and reduce the exchange rate risk and settlement cost of trade and investment within the regions.

3 Innovating Foreign Investment Management System

The management system of pre-establishment national treatment and negative list should be fully implemented to promote fair competition between domestic and foreign enterprises. On the basis of exploration and pilot in the four free-trade zones in Shanghai, Guangdong, Tianjin, and Fujian, China should popularize, replicate, and fully implement the management system of pre-establishment national treatment and negative list in a broader range. Meanwhile, China should also establish the foreign investment security review system adapted to such management system.

4 Orderly Expansion of Opening-Up in Service Sector

To orderly expand the opening-up of service industry is conducive not only to enhancing the competitiveness of service industry but also to promoting the integrated development of service and manufacturing in the opening-up, so as to enhance the position of China's manufacturing industry in global value chains. It is necessary to make focal opening-up at different levels in the limitation on foreign capital access to China's service industries; promote the orderly opening-up in finance, education, culture, medical treatment, and other service industries; and relax foreign access restriction on children-fostering and old-people supporting, architectural design, accounting, auditing, commerce, trade, logistics, e-commerce, and other service industries. As for the service industries with more mature conditions, intensive experiments are recommended to advance progress in opening-up.

5 Building Open and Secure Financial System

It is an important measure to develop the new system of opening-up by strengthening the two-way opening-up within and outside financial industry. On the basis of the improvement of prudential supervision and effective control of risks, China can orderly achieve the convertibility of RMB capital accounts and steadily promote the internationalization of RMB. It is vital for China to encourage the loan and investment of RMB overseas, so as to speed up the development of RMB offshore markets.

H Promotion of Inclusiveness for Shared Development

In adherence to people-orientation, China should continuously improve people's livelihood to achieve development benefit for all Chinese people in a more equal way. It is important to construct the inclusive development mechanism with equal opportunities, broad participation, and result sharing; enhance people's sense of happiness; and form a situation of economic growth with fair distribution in a harmonious society with benign interaction.

1 Improvement of Population Quality and National Health

For this purpose, China should establish the population development outlook centered by quality; adjust and optimize family planning policy; and ensure that the total population is moderate, the structure is optimized, the distribution is rational, the flow is orderly, and the quality is raised – it is the population that advances the economic development, coordinates with social construction, and fits in the resource environment. China should also make overall consideration about the aging population and the momentum of health consumption, promote the reform of medical treatment system and medical insurance system, and put forward the ideas for research on the design of the main healthcare system, development of service system, and medical industrial service. It is necessary to increase the investment in medical treatment and public health and establish fair and inclusive basic medical treatment service system. Besides, it is also important to intensify the construction of public welfare pension service facilities and promote the rise of social service supply at all levels for community-based and at-home elderly care as well as the support for the elderly by institutions. Furthermore, it is vital to encourage social cooperation and actively display the role of various social organizations and communities in supporting, respecting, and helping old people.

2 Tough Work for Poverty Alleviation and Development

It is vital for China to substantially increase the investment in poverty alleviation and release more policies and measures to benefit destitute areas and poor people, focusing on concentrated contiguous destitute areas. Besides, it is necessary for China to strengthen infrastructure construction, ecological environment protection, and basic public service supply; carry out poverty alleviation projects with the advancement of whole villages, migrant relocation, and special industrial development; and expand input in poverty alleviation to vigorously solve outstanding problems. It is necessary to take targeted measures in poverty alleviation by filing and recording the information on poor villages and poor households for accurate identification, targeted support, dynamic management, and high efficiency of poverty alleviation. It is advisable to publicize the role of the social security system to assure them with the basic living guarantee and to help the poor people who lack the ability to work or who are unable to rely on their own ability to lift themselves out of poverty above the bottom-line of living standards, thus ensuring their rights of basic living standards and livelihood. China should resolutely eliminate absolute poverty through supporting production and employment, relocation and resettlement of migrant people, ecological protection, and minimum living security policies, with a view to totally lift more than 70 million poverty-stricken people out of poverty in the "13th Five-Year Plan" period.

3 Expanding Employment by All Means

It is vital to give priority to employment and enhance the drive of economic development through employment, so as to make more workers obtain income through participation in economic activities. Besides, labor market segmentation should be broken to eliminate discrimination and restrictions and promote fair employment. It is important to improve employment and public service system, strengthen the capacity building of public employment service, and enhance the inclusiveness, pertinence, and effectiveness of employment service. In addition, it is advisable to accelerate life-long occupation training system for workers and promote their capacity of employment and entrepreneurship. Besides, it is important to improve entrepreneurship support policies and actively advance construction of business incubation base, so as to encourage small and medium-sized enterprises, small and micro enterprises, and individual businesses to promote employment driven by entrepreneurship.

4 Effectively Controlling Income Distribution Gap

In adherence to the distribution system dominated by the principle of distribution on the basis of labor and combination of various modes of distribution, China should improve the initial distribution and redistribution regulation system; optimize the initial distribution mechanism of distributing according to the share of contribution of labor, capital, knowledge, technology, management, and other factors; speed up the establishment of the redistribution adjustment mechanism by means of taxation, social security, and transfer payment; and form the long-term income growth mechanism with the synchronization of residents' income growth and economic development, labor compensation growth, and labor productivity increase. Efforts should be made to improve the income and consumption capacity of low-income residents, continuously expand middle-income groups, and enhance income adjustment in high-income groups. In addition, it is important to establish the comprehensive and classified personal income taxation system, rationally determine the scope of pre-tax deductions, adjust progressive tax rates, and reduce the tax burden of middle- and low-income groups. It is also necessary for China to further highlight the importance of creative work in the initial distribution and redistribution sectors, get rid of all distribution systems that are not conducive to innovation and creation, and make the distribution of innovation fruits occupy greater share to professional talents, scientific researchers, and management innovators.

5 Improving Social Security System

China should integrate basic endowment insurance for urban and town workers, urban residents, social old-age insurance, new rural social pension insurance and endowment insurance for farm workers, promote the realization of the overall planning nationwide, provincial seamless connection, and smooth transfer of the basic pension accounts. It is necessary for China to accelerate the coverage of basic medical insurance of the Chinese people and straighten out the convergence mechanism of urban workers' basic medical insurance, basic medical insurance for urban residents, and new rural cooperative medical insurance. Besides, it is important to raise the coverage of unemployment insurance and the relevant level for overall planning, and to further display the positive role of unemployment insurance in the basic living guarantee and employment promotion of unemployed people. In addition, it is vital to improve the social assistance system based on guaranteeing the minimum living standards and to promote the construction of special assistance systems such as medical treatment and aid against serious diseases. It is critical to push forward the overall development of welfare causes such as supporting the elderly people, helping the disabled, saving orphans, and aiding the poor; advance the transformation of social welfare from vacancy-filling type to inclusive type; build up a strong baseline for livelihood security; and develop strong basic social safety network.

6 Improving Public Security System

In order to build a safe China, China should establish the overall concept of national security, strengthen the capacity construction of all sectors of public security, coordinate professional strength with mass prevention and treatment against danger, remarkably maintain public security and guarantee social harmony, and solidly safeguard social harmony and stability. China should also strengthen food and drug safety system; form a traceable system for the whole process of production, circulation, and consumption; and build a safety chain from the production source to the consumption terminal. In addition, it is also important to strengthen Internet information security, enhance technical prevention and security management, and effectively improve anti-attack capability. Furthermore, it is vital to intensify emergency management capacity, upgrade the capabilities of non-traditional security alarming, prevention, control and rapid disposal.

I Intensifying Reform Efforts

To ensure the realization of the economic and social development goals in the "13th Five-Year Plan" period, it is critical to form an effective incentive mechanism through institutional innovation, with the aim of dealing well with the relationship between the government and markets. Under the market economy, the mechanism influences the interest distribution pattern, leads the behavior of market main body, and decides the mechanism for economic development impetus. Only when China firmly pushes forward the reform and accelerates the reform in key sectors, can it stimulate the momentum and vitality of economic and social development.

1 Deepening Reform of Administrative System

It is important for China to streamline administration and delegate more powers to lower-level governments, and to society in general, while improving regulation, as well as optimizing service reform. It is of significance for China to continuously cancel and decentralize items for administrative approval, establish and standardize administrative examination and approval management system, as well as simplify procedures, make clear time limitation, and exchange the "subtraction" of government power for the "addition" of market vitality. It is necessary to formulate a negative list of market access, clarify the list of government powers and responsibilities, and make sure that nothing should be done without the authorization of the law and the legal duties regulated by the law must be done. In addition, the focus of the government's administration should be gradually moved from the primary approval to the later service and supervision, and strictly normalize the later action in accordance with relevant regulations. It is vital for China to innovate the way of public service provided by the government and advance the diversification of the subject and the way of providing public service.

2 Pushing Forward Reform of Investment and Financing System

It is important for China to substantially shrink the scope of investment projects approved by the government and decentralize the approval authority, and to considerably simplify the pre-approval procedures for investment projects and implement the online parallel processing for project approval. It is vital to significantly ease restrictions on market access for private investment and encourage social capital to establish equity investment funds. It is advisable for Chinese government to provide investment subsidies, inject capital, and establish funds and other measures to guide society capital investment in key projects. Furthermore, it is important to actively promote the cooperative mode between the government and social capital in infrastructure, public utilities, and other fields.

3 Deepening Reform of State-Owned Enterprises and State-Owned Assets

It is vital for China to accurately define the different functions of various state-owned enterprises and make classified reforms in them. It is advisable to accelerate the pilot operation of state-owned capital investment companies, build market-oriented operation platform, and improve the management efficiency of state-owned capital. Besides, it is important to orderly implement the reform of mixed ownerships in state-owned enterprises and to encourage and normalize the equity participation by non-state-owned capital in investment projects. In addition, it is important to speed up the system reform in the fields of electric power, oil, and gas. Multiple measures should be taken to eradicate the historically formed social functions from enterprises to safeguard the legitimate rights and interests of workers. It is critical for China to improve the modern enterprise system and reform and perfect the incentive and restraint mechanism of enterprise operators.

4 Deepening Reform of Fiscal and Taxation Systems

China should improve the financial budget system; set up an open, transparent, standardized, and complete budget system; and implement interim fiscal planning management. It is advisable for China to reform the transfer payment system, reduce or combine a number of special transfer payment projects, and increase the size and proportion of general transfer payment. Besides, it is necessary to improve the definition of authority of office and right of property of the central and local governments for reasonable adjustment of income distribution in the central and local governments, and improve the mechanism of matching financial resource with authority in the central and local governments for increase of financial resource of the basic-level governments. In addition, it is important to establish and improve the coverage of state-owned capital management budget and revenue-sharing system in all state-owned enterprises and to increase the ratio of state-owned capital management budget included in the common public budget.

5 Deepening Financial System Reform

China should accelerate the interest rate marketization reform and establish and improve the market benchmark interest rate system. For this purpose, China should improve RMB exchange rate formation mechanism, give full importance to the basic role of market supply and demand in the formation of exchange rates, and enhance the flexibility of the two-way floating of RMB exchange rates. Besides, China should steadily achieve the convertibility of RMB capital accounts, expand the scope of international use of RMB, and improve RMB global clearing service system. In addition, it is important to relax financial industry access restrictions; accelerate the development of private as well as small and medium-sized financial institutions for issues of small and micro businesses and those concerning agriculture, farmer, and rural areas; and improve modern financial systems. Furthermore, it is advisable for China to strengthen the construction of multilevel capital market system, implement stock issuance registration system reform, develop regional equity market oriented to small and medium-sized enterprises, promote the securitization of credit assets, expand the issuing size of corporate bonds, and develop financial derivatives market. Last but not least, China should make innovation in financial supervision to prevent and resolve financial risks.

Bibliography

Liu Shijin. *Climbing the Height of Efficiency: Overlook for China's Economic Growth in Ten Years*, Beijing: China CITIC Press, 2015.

Wang Yiming. "Comprehensive Understanding of New Normal of China's Economy", *Qiushi*, no. 22, 2014:40–43.

Wang Yiming. "Leaping to Middle and High End in Middle and High Speed Growth", *Macroeconomic Management*, no. 10, 2014:4–6

Wang Yiming. "Advancing China's Economy from Rapid Growth to Efficient Growth", *Guangming Daily*, 2015, 5 August.

Wang Yiming. "Making Innovation Driving Force for Development", *People's Daily*, 13 April. 2015.

Wang Yiming. "Advancing ChinaWorld Bank, State Council Development Research Center, *China in 2030: Building a Modern, Harmonious and Creative Society*, Beijing: China Financial & Economics Publishing House, 2013.

2 Outlook of International Economic Environment during China's 13th Five-Year Plan Period

During the 13th Five-Year Plan period of China, as the world's multi-polarization and economic globalization intensify, the pattern of world's political and economic security is confronted with reconstruction. Great changes have taken place in growth model, industrial structure, energy territory, governance layout, monetary system, and geopolitical games, as well as in the interaction between China and world economy. The world needs to accommodate the vigorous China, and so does China to adapt to the world in continuous development. In the interaction between China and the world during the Plan period, China shall better exploit new opportunities, cope with new challenges, take initiatives to create an external environment conducive to the growth and rise of China, and safeguard and realize the interests for its own development.

I International Environmental Variation Trend in 13th Five-Year Plan Period

During the 13th Five-Year Plan period of China, as the world's multi-polarization and economic globalization intensify, the interdependence between countries will reach an unparalleled level. The developing countries and the emerging economies have been on the rise in the global politics and economy, which has been the basic trend for years. Meanwhile, new changes will take place in the growth model, industrial structure, energy territory, governance layout, monetary system, and geopolitical games.

A World Economy: In Profound Adjustment of Growth Pattern, Promising Improvement in Overall Recovery

1 Economy of USA: Still in Moderate Recovery, with Supply Side's Support to Growth Expected to Enhance

After the international financial crisis, the United States of America actively promoted structural reforms including reviving manufacturing industry, strengthening financial supervision, promoting scientific and technical innovation, and implementing large-scale stimulus for economic growth. Generally speaking, these policies and measures have achieved positive results, like the uplift of confidence of consumers and enterprises in economic growth, the gradual recovery of the two pillar industries of real estate and auto, reduction of unemployment rate and mild resurrection of economy. The economy in the United States of America went on an annual rise by 1.8%, 2.8%, and 1.9%, respectively, from 2011 to 2013.

In comparison with other developed countries, the immigration policies in the United States of America are looser and labor supply more abundant. In addition, as shale gas revolution has brought down energy prices, a large number of investment and accumulation might well lead to new scientific and technical revolution and rapid development of emerging industries. During the 13th Five-Year Plan period, the economic growth in the United States of America is likely to get support from the supply-end and therefore it will possibly maintain moderate recovery. The economic growth in the United States of America will mainly face constraints from three aspects in the future: the first is the adjustment of monetary policies, especially the rise of interest rates, which will increase the uncertainty for recovery; the second is the continuous cut of fiscal deficit, which will suppress the growth of public demand; and the third is the reduction of leverage of enterprises and residents, which will result in the uncertainty of revival of economy. In overall consideration, the annual economic growth of the United States of America during the Plan is expected to reach about 2.2%, higher than that in eurozone and Japan. The United States of America hopefully will continue to play its leading role in global industrial and technical growth, but it will find it hard to make significant contribution to stimulate demands for global growth.

2 Eurozone: Hard-to-Change Low Growth, Uncertain about Political and Institutional Factors

The eurozone has suffered from the international financial crisis and sovereign debt crisis, which make the recovery in the region slow and difficult. From 2011 to 2013, the eurozone's economy saw an annual increase by, respectively, 1.6%, −0.7%, and −0.4%. This is the external performance of the problems of rigid internal system, virtual high well-being, and loose supervision. The eurozone has been struggling to propel economic structural reforms by issuing the plan of *Europe 2020 Strategies*. However, according to the current situation, it has made slow headway, with several heavy debtor nations, under external pressure, implementing specific reforms, like deficit reduction.

Generally speaking, the sovereign debt crisis has been leveled off; technically speaking, the eurozone's economy has been rallied out of recession. Both have made consumers and enterprises rebuild their confidence in economic growth. If there is no major external crisis or unrest, the eurozone's economy is expected to maintain growth at a low rate, as that in the 12th Five-Year Plan in China. The constraints mainly stem from the aspects of policy and system. From a policy perspective, to prevent deflation, the eurozone is still strengthening quantitative easing monetary policies, which will face the problems for exit in the future. Besides, the cut in the fiscal deficit will also intensify the uncertainty for economic growth. In terms of institutional factor, the eurozone, or EU, was not always a sovereign power, and it found it hard to form a joint force in promoting structural reforms and narrowing the gap of regional development; hence, it was hard to make major breakthrough in solutions to all kinds of structural problems. At the same time, as the unemployment rate in the eurozone is more than 10%, it is a difficult to reduce unemployment and increase employment. In summary, during the 13th Five-Year Plan period, the eurozone's economy will remain, on average, at an annual growth rate of around 1%, probably with further differentiation between economies.

3 Japan: Hard to Advance Structural Reforms, Less Optimistic about Economic Growth Prospects

Japan's economy, highly dependent on external demand, was seriously impacted after the international financial crisis and sovereign debt crisis. Also because of the earthquake, tsunami, and the nuclear leakage that happened recently, the recovery of Japan's economy is undergoing a series of twists and turns. From 2011 to 2013, Japan's economy experienced an annual increase, respectively, by −0.5%, 1.4%, and 1.5%. In 2013, Japan implemented the extremely loose economic stimulus policies known as the Abenomics, including additional issuance of currency to propel depreciation of yen, increase of public financial expenditure to expand domestic demand, and promotion of structural reforms to improve market environment. According to the current situation, these policies and measures achieved certain results in boosting growth and relieving deflation.

In terms of momentum, the effect of monetary policies on wealth in Abe Economics will gradually attenuate. The Japanese government's debt accounts for over 200% of GDP, not enough to support the continuous implementation of massive stimulus policies, and whether the innate drive for Japan's economic growth goes stronger depends on the progress and result of its structural reforms. According to the current situation, Japan has raised the consumption tax and advanced[1] the reforms and measurements including the establishment of special economic zones to attract foreign technology, talents, and funds; reduced the tax burden of enterprises in capital, expenditure, and R&D investment, promoted industrial integration, restart of nuclear power station, and enterprise's participation in agriculture. In addition, Japan is also trying to join the TPP to exert reversal pressure on domestic reforms. The various structural reforms in Japan are interrelated with each other, the overall progress is difficult and the comprehensive effect is uncertain. In addition, the chronological factors, like the aging population, still exist. Once the growth and inflation go beyond synchronization, the prospect of economy will become gloom. Overall, the annual growth rate, on average, of the Japan's economy during the 13th Five-Year Plan period is about 1.5% or so.

4   Emerging Markets and Developing Countries: Entirely on a Rapid Rise, Still with Obvious Structural Problem

After the international financial crisis, emerging markets and developing countries took the lead in picking up and reviving the global economy, with their growing share in global economic output. From 2011 to 2013,[2] the economy of emerging markets and developing countries, respectively, grew by 6.3%, 5%, and 4.7%, significantly higher than the developed countries. However, owing to the factors of concepts, institutional mechanisms, and management models, structural adjustment in economy of emerging markets and developing countries lagged behind the developed countries. Additionally, due to the weak demand from foreign markets and an increasing capital outflow, the economic growth rate has significantly slowed down since 2013.

With great potential in industrialization and urbanization, abundant energy resource reserve, and abundant labor supply, emerging markets and developing countries have vigorously promoted scientific innovation and development in industries with comparative advantage in recent years, and as expected, still in a rapid growth during the 13th Five-Year Plan period. However, we also find that emerging markets and developing countries face structural problems; some heavily depend on exports and external markets, mainly on resource industry, or excessively on international capital inflow, while others are in a state of inharmonious industrialization and urbanization or a rapid rise in domestic costs. Therefore, the growth of emerging markets and developing countries will be restricted by many factors of adjustment of monetary policies, flow of international capitals, and fluctuation in bulk stock prices and capacity change of foreign demand markets. It also determines that though emerging markets and developing countries can achieve rapid growth, they find it difficult to be not dependent on the market, technology, element, and industry of developed countries. Strenuous efforts are required to decide whether to balance the economic growth and stabilize inflation stabilization, or whether to properly handle external risks and advance the structural reform of economy. Upon overall consideration, the economy of emerging markets and developing countries is expected to maintain an annual growth, on average, at the rate of about 5.5% during the 13th Five-Year Plan period, remarkably faster than developed countries, with the overall pattern of world economy still at a momentum of South Up and North Down.

5 *World Economy: Probably in Continuous Low Growth, Hopefully in Enhancing Steadiness*

There is little possibility for the momentum of world economic growth to be as it was before the crisis. On the one hand, the financial crisis has not changed the trend of economic globalization and continuous development of science and technology, with the chronological constraints for growth of world economy still existing. It is about eight years between the outbreak of international financial crisis and the advent of the 13th Five-Year Plan period. Most systemic risks have been fully released at this stage, with little possibility of crisis or turbulence. Developed countries propose re-industrialization and economic rebalancing to emphasize again the development of real economy, while emerging economies focus on expanding domestic demand and promoting the industrialization and modernization of the countries with billions of people, which is conducive to the continuous revival of world economy. On the other hand, it is impossible to succeed in one move, that is, whether to solve the problems of high unemployment, high deficits, and high debts in the developed countries, or whether to solve the structural problems in emerging markets and developing countries. Since 2014, some economies, such as Japan, European Union and Russia, have suffered slowdown in growth or even negative rise. Therefore, during the 13th Five-Year Plan period, the momentum of world economic growth will hardly go back to the level before the crisis, and will most likely be on a continuous low rise by 3%.

Global economic imbalance will be further improved. Both international financial crisis and the European sovereign debt crisis, in essence, are the mandatory adjustments on the critical imbalance of global economy. From 2004 to 2007, before the financial crisis, global economic imbalance was intensified. During this time, the current account deficit per year of the United States of America was up to 800 billion US dollars, accounting for nearly 6% of GDP and about 60% of global current account deficit. Correspondingly, the current account surplus of Japan, Germany, and Asia's emerging economies and oil-exporting countries continues to increase. After the crisis, the developed countries made active or passive adjustment on structural problems like excessive consumption, virtual high welfare, and scarcity of financial supervision, which gradually eased global economic imbalance. Such process is expected to continue during the 13th Five-Year Plan period, and the stability of global economic recovery to improve.

By and large, during the 13th Five-Year Plan period, the world economic growth mode and economic structure adjustment are estimated to maintain at a low growth before the formation of new growth model and scientific revolution. Taking into account the reduction of systemic risks, the comprehensive stability of recovery is promising to improve.

B Economic Globalization: Further Growing, Incubating Big Changes in Global Technology and Industry Development

1 Development of Economic Globalization Presents New Features and New Momentum

It is impossible to reverse the trend of economic globalization, which promotes further specialization of international industries and optimizes the distribution of elements of resources. It leads to the full play of comparative advantages of all countries, which makes countries in the world benefit to varying degrees in participating in the process of economic globalization. No country can independently develop by breaking away from the world economy. To further open up markets and push liberalization and facilitation of trade and investment remains the inevitable choice for all the countries in order to achieve economic development and prosperity. In addition, the profit-chasing nature of capital determines that the basic impetus for economic globalization still exists. Besides, further progress in technology and the blooming of markets also play an active role in continuing economic globalization further during the 13th Five-Year Plan period. Moreover, various forms of protective measures in all countries are confined to a certain extent, which limits the interference in economic globalization to a controllable range. New features and new trends will appear in economic globalization during the 13th Five-Year Plan period as follows.

First, it is difficult to experience rapid growth in international trade and transnational investment. After the international financial crisis, the developed countries adjusted the debt consumption model and slowed down the corporate and personal leverage ratio, while economic growth failed to effectively promote the growth of import demand, with a decrease in correlation between international trade and global growth. From 2003 to 2007, world economy showed an annual growth, on average, by 4.8%, and global trade volume by 8.3%. From 2010 to 2013, world economy went on a downward annual growth, on average, by 3.8%, and global trade volume by 6.2%, with a faster declination in growth rate. During the 13th Five-Year Plan period, even though world economy continues a moderate recovery, it will be still difficult for the volume of global trade to experience rapid growth. In recent years, the status of the recovery of world economy has been in overall stabilization, while foreign direct investment has plunged to the bottom. In 2012, global foreign direct investment amounted to 1.3 trillion US dollars, with a declination up to 18%, back to the level in 2009. It is estimated that it will be impossible to return to a relatively high level during the 13th Five-Year Plan period.

Second, international trade and cross-border investment are present in the layout of South Up and North Down. From the structure, the status of emerging economies and developing countries in international trade and cross-border investment continued to increase in 2012, with the utilization of foreign capital in emerging economies and developing countries accounting for 52% of the total, higher than that in the developed countries for the first time. In the future, emerging economies and developing countries will accelerate the industrialization and urbanization, continuously encourage the expansion of exports, increase importing demand, and constantly increase their share in international trade. Meanwhile, in the field of infrastructure construction and industrial development, a large amount of external investment will be attracted to continuously increase the scale of foreign direct investment. As the import demand in developed countries is weakened, in order to promote economic recovery and revitalize the manufacturing sector, they shall actively expand exports and attract capital reflux. However, because of strengthening of protectionism tendency and growth of uncertain factors, the share of the developed countries will continue to decline in international trade and transnational investment.

Third, regional economic cooperation and integration continues to infuse new momentum for economic globalization. As of July 2013, effective regional trade arrangements reported to WTO totaled 249, with 70% of them emerging in the last decade. Among them, there were 39 reported after 2012, accounting for 16% of the total. Among all these regional trade arrangements, there were 218 pertaining to the free-trade agreement, accounting for 88% of the total. All the 159 members of the WTO, except for Mongolia, are involved in one or more regional trade arrangements. It is hard to make major breakthrough in Doha Round of negotiations of the WTO. Under such context, the development of regional economic integration is accelerating and the regional trade arrangements focused on free trade agreement constantly emerging, which will continue to input new vigor for economic globalization.

2 Profound Adjustment in Global Industrial Layout, Competitive Relations

Developed countries continue to take the lead in technical innovation and industrial development, with the spreading intersection between the development of manufacturing industry and emerging economies. Boosted in science and technology innovation, the developed countries vigorously develop new industries as well as transform and upgrade traditional industries with new technology, and at the same time continue to develop finance, insurance, information, technology, accounting and legal services, and other modern service industry. As the overall competitiveness of these industries is still strong, they remain at the high-end of the international division of labor. After the crisis, the developed countries have made positive progress in revitalizing the manufacturing industry. From 2000 to 2008, the production in manufacturing industry experienced an accumulative growth of 6.2%, far lower than the GDP growth in the same period, with only 5 of the 17 subsectors maintaining growth. From 2009 to 2012, the accumulative growth was 15.2%, far higher than the GDP growth in the same period, with 14 industries maintaining upward momentum. Within the manufacturing industries, especially in terms of the labor-intensive industries of textile, wood, and furniture, as well as the capital-intensive industries of plastics, rubber, and non-metallic minerals, the sustained shrinkage before crisis was reversed. In a certain sense, the industrial development in developed countries has shown a somewhat backward trend, while in some developing countries it has shown a continuous progress by accelerating emerging industries. The increase of crossover points between both will exacerbate the trade friction in related sectors.

Emerging markets and developing countries vigorously develop industries with comparative advantages, which will strengthen the competition in between in traditional manufacturing industry. The developing countries actively utilize foreign direct investment, undertake international industrial transfer, accelerate the development of industries with comparative advantage and technology, as well as spare no efforts in developing emerging industries to narrow the gap with the developed countries. However, the developing countries will remain in the adverse in terms of technical innovation and international division of labor. In Southeast Asia, Africa, and India, labor costs are 80 to 100 US dollars per month, far lower than that in the developed countries, and even less than that in China. Relevant countries have taken measures to ease restriction on access of foreign investment and implement preferential taxation for foreign investment, which lead its manufacturing sector make positive progress in foreign investment utilization. In 2012, ASEAN utilized foreign investment, totaling 125.46 billion US dollars, up 6.7%, which made ASEAN replace China to become the world's largest destination for inflow of foreign investment. After some time, with the improvement of software and hardware, the labor-intensive industry in Southeast Asia will develop rapidly, and the competition in traditional manufacturing industry between the developing countries may be aggravated.

3 Information Technology Continues to Promote the Penetration of the Field Is Still the Main Theme of Global Industrial Transformation and Upgrading

After the international financial crisis, major developed countries and emerging economies increased investment in R&D for new energy, energy saving, and environmental protection; promoted industrialization; and continued to advance the development of information technology; meanwhile, they promoted the integration of information technology, new energy, and biotechnology, trying to seize the strategic high ground for future technical progress and industrial development. The influence of such integration on global industrial development has surfaced – new energy, 3D printing, Internet of Things, cloud computing, and other emerging industries have been flourishing; this promotes industrial organization to profoundly change and brings new impetus to global industrial transformation and upgrading. In 2012, McKinsey predicted 12 new technologies that are most likely to become the leading industry in 2020, six of them closely linked with information technology, including mobile Internet, intelligent software, Internet of Things, cloud computing, new generation of robots, and 3D printing.

The promotion and penetration of information technology will give birth to new industries and new commercial activities, and therefore constantly improve the efficiency of human production and life. In 2013, the production of global PC decreased by 10%, while that of smart phones and tablet PCs increased, respectively, by 42.3% and 50.6%. It is expected that the manufacturing industry of mobile information processing equipment in the future will continue to grow rapidly. With the popularization and application of mobile Internet, cloud computing, big data, and other new technology in traditional industries, the new commercial activities of Internet of Things, Internet finance, mobile funding, mobile healthcare, and mobile education will rapidly develop into an important supplement to traditional commercial activities. McKinsey predicts that the output of global mobile healthcare and mobile education will reach to 49 billion and 70 billion US dollars in 2020, respectively, 40 and 15 times that in 2012. The new 3D printing technology and artificial intelligence will further promote the development of personalized mode of production. More production will be completed by 3D printers and intelligent robots, while human beings will be mainly engaged in product design, which will further stimulate our potential of creativity. The integration of information technology and service industries will accelerate the development of service outsourcing in global context.

Meanwhile, emerging technology industries of renewable energy, gene diagnosis and repair, and new materials will experience rapid development; likewise, renewable energy technology, like photoelectric conversion, will be key to solve global energy problems. Once the gene technology makes a major breakthrough, fundamental changes are expected to take place in terms of intelligence and physical quality of human beings. The development of all these new technology and industries has a wide prospect. However, according to the current situation, it is still a long way for relevant technology to make a major breakthrough in industrialization. Information technology continues to permeate all aspects, which will remain the main theme for global industrial development, transformation, and upgrading during the 13th Five-Year Plan period.

4 Global Industrial Transformation and Upgrading Continuous a Long-term Gradual Process

In a certain sense, the third industrial revolution begins to take shape. Generally speaking, however, it still takes long for emerging industries to supersede traditional ones and for emerging production mode to replace traditional ones. The global industrial upgrading during the 13th Five-Year Plan period is still in a "progressive tense". Currently, the technical foundation of traditional industries has become mature, while some emerging technology remains in the early stage of growth, not enough to support emerging industries in place of traditional ones to provide a full range of goods and services. For example, considering the composition of global total energy consumption, traditional fossil energy still accounts for 80.6% consumption, whereas wind, solar, and other new energy for only 8.2% consumption. Meanwhile, in the global scope, the coexistence of uncertainty between the excess capacity of traditional industries and the development of emerging industries makes the industrial transformation and upgrading long and complicated. Of particular note, countries competing against emerging technologies and industries face increasingly fierce international competition. Signs of overcapacity occur in some sectors. Moreover, trade protectionism measures are also taken periodically in many countries. It is still early to say if the emerging industries will finally take the lead.

C Global Governance System to Restructure, Int'l Economic & Trade Rules Gradually to Approach "High Standard"

1 Global Governance System Diversified to be Fairer and More Reasonable

During the 13th Five-Year Plan period, the overall global governance is presented as South up North down. After the international financial crisis, profound changes took place in the global governance system: the position of emerging markets and developing countries significantly improved, and developed countries found it difficult to dominate the global governance alone. Competition between developed and developing countries has become more complicated and intense, especially in the maintenance of stable development of world economy, mutual expansion of markets, reshaping of international economic and trade rules, reform of international monetary and financial system, as well as issues related to climate change, safety of energy, resources, and food and other sectors. It is high time for developing countries to have some say and to establish a global governance system in consideration of both equity and efficiency.

The global governance system will be restructured in a more diversified direction. Over the years, the global governance system has formed into a pyramid-typed structure. On the top is the United Nations, responsible for coordinating the relationship between countries as well as major international affairs. In the center is an international organization and platform in charge of coordinating the safety, economy, trade, finance, and relations between powers, including the United Nations Security Council, World Trade Organization, International Monetary Fund, World Bank, G20 Summit. At the bottom are some international organizations for coordination of specific global issues, such as Intergovernmental Panel on Climate Change. In its entirety, this organization system will not fundamentally change during the 13th Five-Year Plan period, but in certain areas in emerging markets and developing countries, attempt was made to set up a mechanism in parallel with the current system. For example, on July 15, 2014, the establishment of BRICs Development Bank and its emergency reserve fund was formally announced. Since then, the financial cooperation between the BRIC countries has made substantial headway. Meanwhile, some regional organizations, like APEC Summit, have played a significant role in regional affairs, which makes them a supplement to global governance system. It can be affirmed that, along with the continuous variation of strength between developed and developing countries, the global governance system will become more diversified.

2 Emerging Economies: Upward in International Monetary and Financial System

As is well known, World Bank and International Monetary Fund are the cornerstones of international monetary and financial system. As both have long been dominated by the United States of America, Europe, and other developed countries, their decision-making and operation represent the interest of developed countries rather than that of developing ones, the reasonable appeals of which are often difficult to meet. Since the end of the international financial crisis, the international community has been calling for reforms in the international monetary system, but the developed countries still occupy the leading position. For instance, the voting rights at World Bank of the five BRIC countries accounts for only 13%, while that of the United States of America is 15%; the voting rights at the International Monetary Fund of the former is 11%, while that of the latter is 17%. Moreover, the voting right at the International Monetary Fund of either Britain or France occupies a higher percent than any one of the BRICs. The establishment of the BRICs Development Bank and its emergency reserve, in a certain sense, equivalent to that of another kind of "World Bank" and "International Monetary Fund" specifically for developing countries, has formed a new system that parallels and overlaps the current international monetary and financial system. Of particular note, the paralleling part is represented in it providing infrastructure financing for developing countries, while the overlapping one is shown in its response to global financial risks and crisis. Such situation indicates that profound and complex changes will take place in the international monetary and financial system, with the upward status of emerging markets and developing countries as the basic momentum.

On the other hand, the dominance of US dollar will continue to fall, especially in terms of its role as the main international reserve currency. Meanwhile, European sovereign debt crisis is leading the euro on the verge of collapse. According to statistics, from 2009 to 2012, the US dollar and euro denominated assets account for, respectively, from 62% and 26% to 61.2% and 24.1% of the world official foreign exchange reserve. Although US dollar remains the world's most important reserve and settlement currency, RMB is expected to play an increasingly more important role in emerging markets and developing countries.

3 High Standard FTA Streamlines Global Economic and Trade Rules

Rulemaking has become an important field in the world, especially for those major powers in the world. The United States of America has vigorously promoted the TPP and TTIP. Commonly featured with high standards, wide coverage, and comprehensive expansion of market access on the basis of national treatment and negative list management, both incorporate into negotiation the new subjects of labor standards, environmental protection, intellectual property rights, government procurement, and competitive neutrality. Both the GDP and the trade volume of the 12 members of TPP account for about 40% of all the world; while those of TTIP, namely, of European countries and the United States of America, respectively, account for 50% and 30%. Upon the execution of TPP and TTIP, an enormous free-trade area will be set up across the Pacific and the Atlantic Oceans. The terms involving labor, environmental protection, and intellectual property rights will become a new global benchmark in a sense which shall lead the reform of multilateral trading system and rise of standards of international trade rules and exert profound impact on economic globalization and global economic governance. Currently, the signing of TPP and TTIP is facing difficulties. For example, Japan meets with domestic resistance against the reduction of tariffs on agricultural products, while Europe and the United States of America have large disputes on issues about standards. However, in China's 13th Five-Year Plan, it is still a big probability event for the relevant parties to conclude both agreements. In addition, the United States of America has been advancing the negotiation of TISA, featured with high standard and wide coverage.

Also, we have to notice in the event of international financial crisis, new trends occur in the development of world science, technology, and industry: global industrial division tends to delayering; industrial and value chains continue to extend, while multinational corporations demand for cross-border allocation of resources in a broader and deeper extent as well as more and more facilitation in investment, trade, and service. TPP, TTIP, and TISA, as the product of economic globalization to a certain stage, objectively conform to the development of international industrial division. Although the majority of developing countries still find it difficult to reach a high standard in environmental protection, labor rights, intellectual property rights, and other aspects, TPP, TTIP, TISA bring more than challenges from the view of further participation in economic globalization and expedition of self-growth.

4 Investment and Trade Rules: Wane and Wax in Global Economic Governance System

For some time, the rules of trade under multilateral trading system are the cornerstone of global economic governance system. In various types of free-trade agreements, tariff reduction and elimination of non-tariff barriers are often the core contents of negotiations. This situation is now changing. Compared to the past free-trade agreements, TPP and TTIP pay more attention to investment in liberalization and elimination of behind-the-border barriers. Meanwhile, economies accelerate negotiations on investment agreements. Investment liberalization has become an important part in foreign economic strategies worldwide. All of these reflect the momentum of pattern adjusting in global industrial division, which means as follows: with the extension of industrial chains, a transnational corporation is no longer satisfied with funding an economic entity but attaches more importance to effective allocation of resources in it, which is the only way for the corporation to prevail in the fierce competition. Because of the intensification of economic globalization, such momentum is likely to grow during the 13th Five-Year Plan period, when, therefore, in the global economic governance system, investment rules might overweigh trade rules and gradually become the cornerstone whereof.

D International Energy & Resource: Profound Reform in Distribution, Tension with Slight Leniency in Supply-demand Relation

1 USA's Shale Gas Revolution: To Transform Supply Domain of International Energy & Resource

The United States of America has made significant breakthrough in shale gas and in the technology of shale oil exploration and extraction, with continuous and rapid rise in the output of shale gas, shale oil, and other oil and gas resource, which resulted in the USA entering the stage of large-scale commercial development. In 2012, the output of natural gas in the United States of America reached 24.1 trillion cubic feet, and it became the world largest producer of natural gas, overtaking Russia. According to the prediction of the Department of Energy, in 2020, the output of crude oil and natural gas in the United States of America will be, respectively, 9.55 million barrels per day and 29.1 trillion cubic feet, up 47.1% and 20.7% compared to 2012; crude oil imports will go down to 5.79 million barrels per day in 2020 from 8.43 million barrels per day in 2012, the lowest level since the financial crisis; net imports of shale gas will rise to 1.93 trillion cubic feet in 2020 from

1.51 trillion cubic feet in 2012, with the overall energy self-sufficiency rate up to 93.5%, on a rise of 10% compared with that in 2010.

Overall, the United States of America has established its position in global energy supply territory. Meanwhile, some developing countries with abundant energy resources will increase their export of related products to turn their resource advantages into economic and development ones, which will change the flow of global energy resource and main energy channels. As the energy supply in the United States of America, the world largest energy consumer, grows, its crude oil imports from the Middle East will fall, which will lead to part of oil and gas resources in the Middle East to enter the European market and backlog Russia's market share. Under the context, the importance of Suez Canal, Strait of Bosporus, and the Bab El-Mandeb will decline, which were earlier used to transport the oil and gas exported from the Middle East to Europe and the United States of America. International Energy Agency estimates that in 2035, the crude oil trade volume of the three places will, respectively, account for 11%, 2%, and 11% of the total volume of global trade, down 3%, 2%, and 3% as opposed to that in 2010. At the same time, the importance of the Strait of Hormuz and the Strait of Malacca will increase as they will be used to transport oil and gas exported from the Middle East to Asian channels. International Energy Agency estimates that in 2035, the crude oil trade volume of the latter two places will, respectively, account for 50% and 45% of the total volume of global trade, up 8% and 13% as opposed to that in 2010.

2 *International Energy Demand Shift Focus onto Emerging Economies and Asia*

During the 13th Five-Year Plan period, emerging markets and developing countries will continue their rapid industrialization and urbanization, with their demand for energy resources maintaining steady growth, accounting for higher proportion in global energy consumption. According to International Energy Agency, from 2011 to 2020, energy consumption in non-OECD countries increased at an average annual growth rate of 2.5%, obviously higher than that in OECD countries, at 0.23%; in 2020, the former will account for 62.9% of global energy consumption, up 5.4% as opposed to that in 2010.

From a regional view, Asia will become the area with highest rate of rise in energy consumption. International Energy Agency predicts that the energy consumption of non-OECD countries in Asia will grow at an average annual rate of 3.2% from 2011 to 2020, which is significantly higher than that in Africa, Latin America, and Eastern Europe. China will utilize more than half of energy consumption share in Asia, with increasing expanding gap between supply and demand, and might become the world's largest oil importer in 2020s. Moreover, India's energy consumption will also show a rapid upward growth, with increasing growth in the demand for coal consumption, and it might become the world's largest coal importer in 2020s.

3 Supply-demand Pattern of International Energy and Resource:
  Mostly Tight but a Bit Loose

From the perspective of demand, during the 13th Five-Year Plan period, global economy is expected to maintain moderate recovery, industrialization and urbanization of emerging economies and developing countries to accelerate to grow, and global energy resources demand to continue to increase. In terms of supply, the shale gas revolution in USA has increased global fossil energy supply; together with the rapid development of global solar, wind, and other new energy, global energy supply is able to meet the demand. Generally speaking, in terms of both factors of supply and demand, the tight balance between supply and demand of global energy during the 13th Five-Year Plan period will not be fundamentally changed but expected to mitigate a bit, compared to the time before the financial crisis. In this regard, energy price rise is anticipated to be on a slump. According to International Monetary Fund, in 2019, the global average crude oil and natural gas spot price baselines in 2019 were US$89.4/barrel and US$10.8/ million British thermal units, down 14.2% and 3.6%, respectively, from 2013.

II Influence of International Environment Changes on China

After the international financial crisis, the interaction between China and the world economy has been significantly adjusted. The world needs to adapt to a more powerful China, and so does China. During the 13th Five-Year Plan period, the changes in the international environment have brought both opportunities and challenges to China's economic development. Overall, it is necessary to better grasp new opportunities in the interaction between China and the world, properly respond to new challenges, and initially create an external environment conducive to China's transformation, development, and peaceful rise.

A Chances from International Environmental Changes for China

1 Continuous Economic Globalization: Still Big Chance for
  China's Growth

As a developing country with a large population, China still faces the protruding problems of imbalance, disharmony, and unsustainability, mainly detailed as follows: economic development of urban and rural area needs to be balanced, potential of domestic market to be developed, independent innovation capability and enterprise management to be improved, and shortage of natural resources to be covered. In such context, economic globalization provides China with great opportunities to display comparative advantage, participate in international competition and division, make full use of resources from domestic and foreign markets, further establish and improve open economy, and accomplish the goal of building a moderately prosperous society. To be more specific, firstly, it is conducive to implementing a new round of opening to the world, so as to promote reforms and force domestic underlying systematic reforms; secondly, it is good for China to utilize international market size to expand and stabilize exports and continue to promote economic growth and employment increase; thirdly, it is beneficial for China to introduce foreign advanced technology and equipment, talents, and management experience to promote domestic technical progress and industrial upgrading and transformation; fourthly, it makes it easy for Chinese enterprises "to go out" to carry out international cooperation in energy resource development, expand channels for energy resource supply, transfer outward excess capacity, and allocate resources on the global scale.

2   Flouring of Emerging Industries and Technology to Bring New Chances for China's Industrial Transformation and Upgrading

Despite that a relatively complete industrial system has been developed in China, the problems still stand out, like agriculture with unstable position of foundation, industry big but not strong, and service lagging behind. To accelerate industrial upgrading is the strategic task that will decide the overall transformation of economic development mode. At present, all countries expect much from the emerging industry and technology. The new energy, cloud computing, 3D manufacturing, gene diagnosis, and repair have made continuous breakthrough, and service outsourcing and service industry investment have been rapidly developing, which provide a new opportunity for China's industrial restructuring and upgrade during the 13th Five-Year Plan period. In its entirety, the emerging industry is still at the initial stage, which is conducive to China keeping abreast with the new round of global industrial restructuring, seizing the commanding heights of future industry development, narrowing its gap with the developed countries, and changing its unfavorable status in global division pattern. Emerging technology market has a broad prospect for its great potential in application development, which means a great opportunity for China to find new economic growth sectors and to transform and upgrade traditional industries. Service outsourcing and service industry investment are becoming a new focal point in global economic and trade cooperation, which also provides a new way for China to establish new open economic system on the basis of expanding the opening up of service industry.

3   Changes in International Energy Domain: Gives China Leeway in Allocation of Resources Worldwide

For a time, China's external dependency on main energy resources had been on a rise, among which the external dependency on oil increased from 26%

at the beginning of 21th century to 58.3% in 2013, and that on natural gas was close to 30%. To steadily obtain energy resources from overseas market at reasonable price guarantees China's energy and economic security, as well as multilaterally and bilaterally deepens economic and trade relations and regional economic cooperation with relevant parties. After the shale gas revolution in the United States of America, global energy layout has turned on a new look. The Middle East, Central Asia, Russia, and other important energy resource exporters count more on China's market for support. As heteronomy of China is on a slump, China's cooperation with relevant countries has shifted from "based on wishful thinking" to "upon consensus". It not only helps to enhance the insurance of China's energy security, but brings China more latitude to perform in international economic and political arena as well, which provides an opportunity to expand the development of China outward and promote the construction of the Belt and Road. From another aspect, with the gradual self-sufficiency in energy of the United States of America, the world largest consumer of energy, the tight relation between supply and demand of energy at a time was therefore relieved to subdue prices, which helped reduce the costs of energy resource import into China.

4 Evolution of World Economic Pattern: Further Enhances China's International Influence

During the 13th Five-Year Plan period, the overall pattern of the world economy will remain at the momentum of South Up and North Down. Such momentum will promote the transformation of global governance system and international economic order into a more fair and reasonable direction, continuously increase the shares of developing countries in international trade and investment, as well as bring great opportunities for China to further enhance its international influence and maintain its own interests in development. According to a conservative estimation, China's imports and foreign investment during the 13th Five-Year Plan period will reach up to USD10 trillion and USD500 billion, which will vigorously lead the development of other economies. Some countries and regions will rely more on support from and cooperation with China, which lays the foundation to uplift China's influence and its right of say in international affairs. Meanwhile, as for developing countries, their status in the world economy will lead to the enhancement of their status in global governance system. It will increase China's decision-making power in international organizations and accelerate the shift of its attitude toward international governance rules – from active participation and passive acceptance in the past to active guidance and bilateral interaction. The establishment of BRICs Development Bank and emergency reservoir help China play a more important role in the reforms of global monetary and financial system to promote the accelerated internationalization of renminbi.

B Main Challenges to China from International Environmental Changes

1 Adjustment of World Economic Growth Pattern Raises China's Pressure on Improvement of Quality and Efficiency

China has become the world second largest economy, without fundamentally changing its extensive mode of development as high input, high emissions, high pollution, low quality, and low efficiency. It is extremely critical for China to improve the quality and efficiency of development during the 13th Five-Year Plan period, with concern to the profound adjustment of world economic growth pattern, continuous low growth rate, unstable and uncertain factors, as well as the weakening of its advantage in traditional competition in participation in economic globalization. In the past years, China's export growth rate had slowed down to the single digit, to 7.9% both in 2012 and in 2013. From the perspective of trend, due to factors such as the adjustment of debt consumption patterns of the developed countries in the United States and Europe and the intensification of international competition, the past development methods have become unsustainable. Even if the world economy will maintain a moderate recovery, it does not mean that the external impetus for China's growth can be as powerful as the time before the crisis. It is highly pressing to advance strategic adjustment in economic structure and optimize the proportion between supply, demand, regions, and elemental input. At the same time, in the complicated external environment, China will encounter increasingly more pressure to establish a comprehensive concept on quality and efficiency, solve the structural and systematic problems that have existed for a long time, and foster new advantage in international competition and cooperation.

2 Global Industrial Distribution Changes Exert Complex Impact on China's Industrial Transformation and Upgrading

After the international financial crisis, developed countries actively promoted reindustrialization, while the emerging economies and developing countries accelerated the industries with comparative advantages, which brought new changes to global industrial layout. Simultaneously, China continued its industrial transformation and upgrading and strengthened its competitive relations in industrial development with developed and developing countries. On the one hand, China's labor and land costs went on a concentrated rise, traditional competitive advantages in its manufacturing industry tended to weaken, and the development of some labor-intensive industries, especially in low-end manufacturing sector, began to move into low-income countries. All of these changes led to the strengthening of China's relations with developing countries in related fields. On the other hand, China accelerated the development of strategic emerging industries and fostered new international competitive advantages concentrated in technology, brand, quality, and service, which intensified its competition with developed countries in new energy, new materials, energy-saving, environmental protection, and high-end manufacturing. In 2012 and 2013, in new energy sector, such as photovoltaic components, China had serious trade disputes with Europe and the United States of America. In the upcoming period, China will encounter more strong competitors and disturbance from trade protectionism. China will come across new challenges in dealing with competition and cooperation with countries in industrial development.

3 Profound Reforms in International Economic and Trade Rules Raise Threshold of China's Access to Economic Globalization

Since China acceded to WTO, it has been actively involved in economic globalization, with increasing uplift of impact and right of say in the existing multilateral trade system, which makes it the biggest beneficiary in economic globalization. The United States of America, via TTIP and TPP, has reshaped global economic and trade rules, which will result in the upgrade of the standards of international economic and trade rules. Because of system mechanism, management mode, factor endowments, and other problems, it is more or less hard for China to fulfill TPP and TTIP standards in market opening, environmental protection, and intellectual property right protection, as well as to surmount the high threshold in its continuous involvement in economic globalization. China might face lengthy negotiations or may encounter various pre-conditions set by the United States of America if joining TPP or TTIP, or otherwise suffer from increasing loss related to trade diversion if things continue this way. By estimation, if China joins the TPP or TTIP, its foreign trade exports and imports will be, respectively, reduced to more than USD120 billion or USD100 billion. Of course, we should also see that some of the provisions in TPP and TTIP, like those on the opening of tertiary industry and improvement of investment liberalization, accord with China's construction of the new system of open economy. It is crucial for China to make good use of reversed transmission of pressure to accelerate system reforms and innovation mechanism and narrow the gap between present situations with high standards.

4 Adjustment of Geopolitical Layout Upgrades Difficulty of China's Maintaining and Realizing Interests in Development

For a time in the past, in the context of world multi-polarization in politics, China had experienced rapid development in economy as well as had impact on global and regional affairs. During the 13th Five-Year Plan period, the world multi-polarization is still the major trend, but new changes take place in geopolitical patterns, along with the growing tendency for relevant countries to prevent and curb China's development. It grows increasingly difficult for China to maintain and realize its own interests in development. Concerning the peripheral regions, the United States of America implemented the strategy of returning to Asia-Pacific regions which resulted in more instability in the peripheral geopolitical environment for China and more complicated territorial disputes between China and relevant countries. It not only affected the proper and timely solution to relevant specific issues, but also inevitably shrank the external room for China's development, which had an adverse impact on its implementation of foreign trade and investment cooperation as well as the strategy of free-trade zones. From regional perspective, the relevant parties will continue the fierce gambling in Northeast Asia, South Asia, and Central Asia. The hot issues may arise from time to time, with possible occurrence of calamities without any reasons. Globally speaking, on the one hand, China has obtained more and more overseas interests; on the other hand, the ethnic, religious, and territorial conflicts are difficult to end in West Asia, North Africa, and Eastern Europe. To set up the image as a responsible country and safeguard its own interests requires growing wisdom from China.

III Strategic Choice to Deal with International Environmental Changes

During the 13th Five-Year Plan period, China is still in strategic circumstances. Profound changes have taken place in the connotation and condition of the strategic circumstance under the influence by external environment conditions. On the one hand, China is still facing opportunities, challenges, risks, difficulties, as well as unstable and uncertain factors; on the other hand, China's position in global political and economic pattern will continue to rise, so will the ability to shape the external environment. Therefore, it is necessary to be accurately aware of the interaction between external and internal changes, to actively create and maintain a favorable environment for development, to shift the foothold of growth into the improvement of quality and efficiency, and to accelerate the streamlining of socialist market economic system and transformation of economic development mode. In this way, China will promote its sustained and healthy economic development as well as maintain and realize its benefits.

A Constructing New System of Open Economy

Based on the strategic focus of "The Belt and Road" construction, China shall accelerate the pace of going-outside and build a new system parallel to the industrial division system led by developed countries and change the unfavorable situation embedded with the existing system of labor division, in order to improve the efficiency of developing open economy. It is also advisable for China to increase its opening up to the West, accelerate the interconnection in infrastructure construction with the neighboring countries and regions, and expand the communication with the border inland areas, with a view to streamline its layout of opening up. Based on the transformation of mode of foreign economic development, China shall speed up fostering the new international competitive advantage centered by technology, brand, quality, and service, improve its position in international division and value-added capability in international industrial chains, push on the transformation and upgrading of foreign trade, and enhance the comprehensive efficiency of utilizing foreign funds. Taking China Shanghai Free-Trade Zone as the pilot, China shall explore the implementation of foreign management mode of pre-establishment national treatment and negative list, expand access of foreign investment to tertiary sector, reform mechanism of foreign investment management, and deepen the reforms of management system of foreign trade.

B Implementation of Innovation Driven Development Strategies

The innovation-motivated development strategies are detailed as follows. First, China shall fully implement inclusive policies like additional tax deduction for enterprise research and development to set up innovation platform for emerging industrial entrepreneur, with a view to catch-up with the advanced countries in new generation of mobile communications, integrated circuits, big data, advanced manufacturing, new energy. and new materials, as well as to orient the future industrial development. Second, China shall expedite the reforms of science and technology system, strengthen the dominant position of enterprises in technical innovation, encourage enterprises to set up R &D institutions, and lead the build-up of collaborative innovation alliance among production, learning, and research sectors. Third, China shall increase the government's investment in basic research, cutting-edge technology, social welfare technology and major common key technology, improve public service platform for science and technology, and streamline the implementation mechanism of major special technical projects. Fourth, China shall strengthen the protection of intellectual property rights and relevant application and value science popularization and scientific moral cultivation. Last but not least, China shall intensify the talent development planning and coordinate major talent projects.

C Enhance Domestic-Demand-Driven Growth

Consumption as the starting point to expand domestic demand can be carried out by elevating consumption ability via increasing household income; improving consumption policies; publicizing consumption focus; purifying consumption environment; expanding service consumption in retirement, health, tourism, and culture; and promoting information consumption. As investment is the key to stabilize economic growth, it is of importance to speed up investing and financing system reforms, promote investment diversification, optimize investment structure, as well as intensify afforda-ble housing projects, agriculture, major water conservancy projects, railway to Midwest China, energy saving and environmental protection, and so-cial undertakings. In addition, it is vital to implement in depth the national strategies differentiated by regions, including prioritizing the development of the western areas, comprehensively revitalizing the northeast rust belt and other old industrial bases, vigorously promoting the rise of the central region, and actively supporting the transformation and upgrading of econ-omy in the east area.

D Comprehensively Promote Economic System Reforms

In accordance with the unified deployment of 18th CPC National Congress and the Third Plenary Session of the 18th CPC Central Committee, China is supposed to comprehensively promote the reform of the economic sys-tem, balance the relationship between the government and the market, high-light the decisive role of the market in allocation of resources, and display the role of the government in macro-control, market supervision, and pro-motion of sustainable development. Next, China ought to uphold and im-prove the fundamental economic system, advance state-owned enterprises to streamline modern enterprise systems, support healthy development of non-public economy, and actively develop mixed ownership economy. Fur-thermore, China shall speed up the perfection of modern market systems; establish fair, open, and transparent market rules; and improve the market determination pricing mechanism. In addition, China shall also expedite the reforms of the financial and taxation system and advance the harmony between the mechanism of central and local financial resources and pow-ers of authority of office. Moreover, China ought to deepen the reforms of financial systems, develop multi-level capital markets, and continue to push for market-oriented reforms of interest exchange rates.

E Active Participation in Global Economic Governance

It is important for China to make good use of the platform of G20, en-hance its ability to create and guide topics in international conferences, and express its views on global economic governance at summits. China shall continue to support and maintain multilateral trading system, deepen eco-nomic and trade cooperation with developed economies, expand economic and trade cooperation with emerging markets and developing countries, as well as coordinate regional and sub-regional cooperation. China shall also adapt to the new situation of economic globalization and the new changes of international economic and trade rules, and more actively participate in ne-gotiations on multilateral trade systems, regional free trade and investment agreements, new issues and new rules. In addition, China shall promote the development of free-trade zones based on cooperation with peripheral countries, intensify and upgrade that of the concluded free-trade zones, and speed up the ongoing negotiations on free-trade zones. Last but not least, China shall advance reforms of international monetary systems, fully participate in governance on global issues, as well as heighten its influence and right of say in formulation of international economic and trade rules and standards.

Notes

1 See *Strategies for Economic Comprehensive Growth*, released by Japanese government in June 2013.
2 According to statistics from IMF.

Bibliography

CPC Central Committee's Decision on Deepening Reforms of Numbers of Major Issues (instructive edition), Beijing: Chinese People's Publishing House, 2013.
Government Work Report, Beijing: Chinese People's Publishing House, 2014.
Government Work Report (instructive edition), Beijing: Chinese People's Publishing House, 2014.
Hu Jintao. *Report to the Eighteenth National Congress of the Communist Party of China: Firmly March on the Path of Socialism with Chinese Characteristics and Strive to Complete the Building of a Moderately Prosperous Society in All Aspect*, Beijing: Chinese People's Publishing House, 2012.
IMF. *World Economic Outlook, April 2014: Recovery Strengthens, Remains Uneven*, IMF,2014.
Report to the Eighteenth National Congress of the Communist Party of China (instructive edition), Beijing: Chinese People's Publishing House, 2012.
UNCTAD. *World Investment Report 2013*, 2014.
United Nations. *World Economy Situation and Prospects*, 2013.
World Bank. *Global Economic Prospects*, 2014.
WTO. *World Trade Report 2013*, 2014.
100 Q&A in Tutoring the Study on Decision of CPC at the Third Plenary Session of the 18th CPC Central Committee, Beijing: Party Building Books Publishing House, 2013.

3 Changes of Prospect in Economic Globalization and China's Solutions in 13th Five-Year Plan

In order to realize the goal for the Two Centenary Goals [note: the two goals are to complete the building of a moderately prosperous society in all aspects by the centenary of the CPC (founded in 1921) and to build China into a modern socialist country that is prosperous, strong, democratic, culturally advanced, and harmonious by the centenary of the People's Republic of China (founded in 1949)], the 13th Five-Year Plan period is critical to the New 35 Years (2014–2049). During the 13th Five-Year Plan period, to adapt to the new situation of economic globalization and make achievements in such strategic circumstances for China's development mean to comprehensively intensify reforms and expand opening- up, as well as to lay the foundation for the new open economy mechanism with high openness, standards, and qualify of development. Historically, economic globalization means a crucial period for opportunities. Those who hold this opportunity will be able to make "overtaking at the bend". However, the last financial crisis changed the game strategy of the great powers. For example, the United States of America took the short-term strategy of quantitative easing and expansive exports, medium-term one of promoting the re-industrialization, re-innovation, and re-employment, and the long-term planning of building with developed economies a new rules system after the border rules, including high-standard free-trade areas, high-standard investment, and service trade liberalization, as well as neutral competition. These will change the multilateral framework of economic globalization and lead the international environmental group rules to shift to regional exclusiveness, local protectionism, and conglomeration of politics and military. The majority of emerging economies and developing countries are facing with the plight of marginalization. During the 13th Five-Year Plan period, how to deal with the turbulence of global rules is a big problem for China. Whether the international economic environment will provide China with opportunities or challenges, whether China will act as a responsible country or a marginalized one, whether China will seek the full confrontation or open cooperation, China shall make strategic choices and set out solutions to deal with. China's attitude toward reforms shown at the Third and Fourth Plenary Session of the 18th Central Committee of the CPC is detailed as follows: to implement open cooperation strategies beyond the zero-sum game, to grasp the important period of strategic opportunities, to turn the challenges of global high-standard free-trade areas and the rule changes into the pressure and impetus for promoting and deepening of the new round of high openness, high-standard and high-quality reforms, so as to achieve the Two Centenary Goals and the great rejuvenation of the Chinese nation.

I To Adapt to New Situation of Economic Globalization in the 13th Five-Year Plan

A Basic Characteristics of Economic Globalization

One of the characteristics of economic globalization is that the global economy presents openness-driven, market-driven, and innovation-driven economy.

To be open-driven is the basic feature of economic globalization. Since the 1990s, in the bilateral and multilateral open protocols and open policies, many countries have commonly adopted liberalized measures of reducing tariffs, canceling non-tariff rules, expanding access to service sectors, and promoting facilitation of trade and investment measures. All of these conducts advanced the rapid development of international exchange, cooperation, and competition; enhanced mutual interrelation and interdependence in economy and society between countries all over the world; and improved the economic benefits of the countries and regions that actively participate in economic globalization.

To be market-driven is the operational criterion of economic globalization. Since the 1990s, all the developed and developing countries and those in transit have generally promoted and intensified marketing reforms. The advocate of state intervention of Keynesianism was turned into the proposition of the market's decisive role of the new liberalism: that of establishing a highly centralized planned economy into market-directed economic system reforms, and that of implementing import-substitution-based industrialization development strategy into export-oriented one. In this regard, the world economy shall see a rapid rise.

To be innovation-driven is the driving force of economic globalization. Since the 1990s, the open and marketing reforms have fully released the huge dividends of globalization; accelerated global imitation and diffusion in knowledge accumulation, technical innovation, and human capital investment results; reduced the differentiation in performance of development between countries worldwide; and promoted contribution of technical progress and productivity growth to economic growth. Especially being fueled by the first digital technical revolution and the second digital technical progress,[1] globalization is undertaking the mode conversion from global division to Internet division.

The second feature of economic globalization is the "double-edged sword" effect. Historically, economic globalization was always accompanied with conflicts in international politics, economy, and military as well as frequent occurrence of banking currency crisis. The first economic globalization (1870–1913), caused by the sharpened contradiction between the conservative and emerging powers, finally led to the two world wars. Learning from the lesson of ending of the first economic globalization, the international community managed to focus on world peace and development and avoided the outbreak of the third world war. However, the economic globalization is still confronted with frequent occurrence of crisis in the world economy, banking, and currency. For example, the Vietnam War in late 1960s and the dollar crisis and stagflation caused whereby in early 1970s and the two times of occurrence of oil crisis directly resulted in the collapse of Bretton Woods System and interruption of world opening process.[2] In 1990, under the impetus of global marketing reform and opening-up, the world economy once again entered the era of modern economic globalization. However, after the outbreak of the international financial crisis in 2008, the economic globalization showed uncertainty at the prospect of whether to move forward or to split away.

The third feature of economic globalization is that the main propeller of the opening process is not necessarily the biggest beneficiaries from opening dividends. For instance, the United Kingdom, by virtue of the technical and industrial advantages in the first industrial revolution, promoted the first economic globalization in human society.[3] However, when the world second industrial revolution occurred, it overvalued the overseas investment and expansion by prioritizing the construction of the Great British Empire over the investment in technology and industry reserved from the second industrial revolution. The comprehensive national strength of Britain thus went from a prosperous start to a wane due to the hollowing-out of industries in Britain, whereas the United States of America and Germany got on a rise by seizing the golden time of economic globalization for economic growth.

B *Phases of Modern Economic Globalization since 1990*

The first stage of modern economic globalization was from 1990 to 2001. Most countries and regions, by actively participating in economic globalization, won global dividends. Among them, the United States of America and other developed economies obtained the greatest share. For example, the GDP of United States of America accounted for about 26.1% of global GDP in 1990, and up to 32% in 2001, with an average annual increase of about 0.5%. Meanwhile, China, India, and other emerging economies also went on a rapid rise. According to the analysis of OECD scholar Angus Maddison in *On the Long-term Performance of China's Economy*, China's GDP growth rate per capita was significantly higher than the world major countries and regions at that time.

The second stage was from 2002 to 2008, the time of unreasonable global prosperity propelled by bubbles in financial and real estate markets of

United States of America. Its GDP was on a slump, from 32% in 2001 to 23.8% in 2012 of global GDP, because of the three events that occurred in 2001, which are as follows.

First, the bursting of world IT bubbles marked the end of the longest period of prosperity of new economy in the history of the United States of America. It led the declination by 53% of global direct investment as opposed to that in the previous year. However, the United States of America was reluctant to carry out a new round of economic adjustment but greeted a new round of bubbles in financial and real estate markets, which exacerbated hollowing-out and virtualization of its economy and the irrational global prosperity. At that time, the global economy grew at an average annual rate of 4.5%, on a rise by 1% compared with that of 3.5% in 1990.

Second, the outbreak of the "9/11" incident made the United States of America turn their attention to global wars against terrorism. In the era of economic globalization, the vigorous promotion of its values and political systems exacerbated the conflicts between world civilizations.

Third, China's formal access to the WTO speeded up its economic revitalization.[4] The purposes for China to join WTO include actively participating in economic globalization, expediting the compliance of its system with current international rules and standards, as well as enhancing the ability to involve in international division and exchange. The expression that occurred most frequently at that time in the speeches of all departments, regions, and enterprises in China was "the wolf is coming". It was 15 years since China applied for its access to the WTO. It was the period for China to actively respond to the "wolf shock" and to intensify its reforms. After a long period of preparation and positive response, China entered the prime time of economic development. According to Table 3.1, China's GDP increased from USD1.64 trillion in 2003 to USD8.23 trillion in 2012 on the basis of market exchange rate; while according to Table 3.2, China's GDP increased from ID4.12 trillion to ID12.47 trillion.

The third stage of modern economic globalization arrived posing dilemma since 2009. Whether to continuously promote the open-drive, market-driven, and innovation-driven economic globalization, or to avert to regional

Table 3.1 GDP on the basis of exchange rate of USD from 2003 to 2012 (Unit: trillion US dollar, %)

	2003	2004	2005	2006	2007	2008	2009	2010	2011	2012
World	37.59	42.29	45.73	49.54	55.88	61.34	58.08	63.41	70.37	71.67
USA	11.09	11.80	12.56	13.31	13.96	14.22	13.90	14.42	14.99	15.68
China	1.64	1.93	2.26	2.71	3.49	4.52	4.99	5.93	7.32	8.23
Brazil	0.55	0.66	0.88	1.09	1.37	1.65	1.62	2.14	2.48	2.25
India	0.62	0.72	0.83	0.95	1.24	1.22	1.37	1.71	1.87	1.84
Russia	0.43	0.59	0.76	0.99	1.30	1.66	1.22	1.52	1.90	2.01

Source: World Bank DI Database.

Table 3.2 GDP on the basis of purchasing power from 2003 to 2012
(Unit: trillion Geary-Khamis dollar, %)

	2003	2004	2005	2006	2007	2008	2009	2010	2011	2012
World	49.28	53.12	57.31	62.72	67.94	71.84	72.10	76.64	81.35	85.89
USA	11.09	11.80	12.56	13.31	13.96	14.22	13.90	14.42	14.99	15.68
China	4.12	4.66	5.36	6.24	7.33	8.22	9.05	10.12	11.30	12.47
Brazil	1.37	1.48	1.58	1.70	1.85	1.99	2.00	2.18	2.29	2.37
India	2.01	2.23	2.52	2.84	3.21	3.41	3.73	4.18	4.54	4.79
Russia	1.34	1.47	1.70	2.13	2.38	2.88	2.73	2.96	3.20	3.37

Source: World Bank DI Database.

exclusiveness, local protectionism, and corporate alliance in politics, economy, and military – the world major powers shall make clear choices.

C Development Prospect of Modern Economic Globalization

In the first stage of modern economic globalization, the liberalization of trade and investment worldwide was vigorously promoted. At that time, the global openness was still based on competition and cooperation between real economies, and the global governance system and the institutional framework established after World War II were still able to adapt to it. However, when the economic globalization evolved to financial and monetary liberalization,[5] systematic risks and institutional risks appeared, completely different from liberalization of trade and investment. When virtual economy was infused with the increasingly growing global openness, the rise of systematic and institutional risks in global finance and currency was caused by the lack of system for global financial governance and financial supervision, the lack of global macroeconomic policy coordination mechanism, and the lack of mechanism to restrict the beggar-thy-neighbor and protectionism. The result was to deal a direct blow upon the Great Delta region that possessed the most perfect global marketing economy system, the most mature interior governance structure, and the strongest capacity of controlling and transferring systematic risks. In addition, it also directly caused the developing countries to forcibly suffer from a severe and lasting negative effect, which shall eventually endanger the prospect of economic globalization.[6]

II Taking Opportunities from Transition of Global Rules in the 13th Five-Year Plan

A World Economy in Changes in Global Rules, Order, and Pattern

After the financial crisis, some new changes took place in world economy, such as TPP, TTIP, Bilateral Investment Treaty 2012 (BIT2012), TISA, Japan-EU Economic Partnership Agreement (EPA), and Competition

Neutrality Principle.[7] One of the common characteristics of these changes was that developed countries led a new round of reforms in high-standard rules to reshape the future structure of global economy. The U.S. Vice President Joe Biden believed that with historical significance, TPP and TTIP provided opportunities for the United States of America to mold global economy and to strengthen its leadership in the world.[8] The second feature was that the changes of global rules were mainly based on what the United States of America would like to set up. Those who received it could still enjoy the open interest, and those that did not would face the marginalization risk. The third feature was that the governance of the USA would become the model of global governance rules, with the potential of leading international economic orders to the situation of benefiting oneself at others' expense, leading to lack of coordination and falling apart. In this regard, the localization, corporation, and the regionalization of the global situation would aggravate contradictions and differences between developed countries and emerging economies and possibly darken the long-term prospect of the world growth rather than brighten it.

Concerning the transition of global economy rules, it was put forward at the third Plenary Session of the 18th CPC Central Committee that China was supposed to adapt to the new situation of economic globalization, expedite the cultivation of its new advantages in participation and orientation of international economic cooperation and competition, adhere to the rules of world trading system, expand implantation of the strategy of free-trade zones on the basis of peripheral countries and regions, develop global network for high-standard free-trade area, expand the opening-up of inland and border areas, and form the new pattern of opening-up at all aspects. Upon the joint efforts of China and the international community, the Bali Package Agreement was concluded on December 7, 2013. It was the first multilateral trade agreement since the establishment of WTO, including the positive progress in trade facilitation, agriculture, cotton, and development.[9]

B USA Dominates Transition of Global Economic Rules

1 Promotion of TPP and TTIP

Nominally, the United States of America shall build the model for a world standard free-trade area (FTA), globally advocating the principle of fair competition. Substantially, however, the United States of America shall turn its own rules into global standards and even stipulate regulations for reforms of global governance in the future.

2 Advancement of BIT2012 and TISA

The former shall be incorporated in the negative list management, preestablishment of national treatment, and other terms. The latter requires all service sectors, including the new service that may arise in the future, shall equally treat foreign investment. It is ordered to cancel all kinds of requirements for establishment of joint ventures and the restriction on the stockholding ratio for foreign capital and its business range, and it is forbidden to withdraw the new opening-up measures upon its implementation. Nominally, the United States of America shall build the model for high standard of liberalization in investment and service trade. Substantially, however, the United States of America shall highlight its advantage in asymmetric rules for its investment and services to enter the global markets.

3 Formulation of Competitive Neutrality Principle and Other International New Rules

It can limit the government's ability to utilize preferential policies to prioritize state-owned enterprises over private enterprises. At the same time, it can also vigorously promote the release of higher standard new rules in terms of labor and employment, environmental governance, intellectual property protection, government procurement, competition policy, state-owned enterprises, and industrial policies. The characteristic of competitive neutrality principle is the transformation from the previous promotion of trade and investment liberalization to the present fair competition rules centered on behind-the-border competition policies.

4 Promotion of Adjustment of Global Rebalance

According to the annual report in 2009 of US-China Economic and Security Review Commission (USCC), the source of this crisis was the global economic imbalance. China and the United States of America should bear half of the responsibility. To this end, the United States of America pressurized China to assume more responsibility for global rebalance and make more contribution to lead world economy out of recession by increasing domestic demand and consumption, expanding imports and opening-up, as well as enhancing the appreciation of renminbi and reforms of non-trade sectors. Therefore, a possible perspective was proposed as follows: when the developed countries stepped out of crisis, the emerging economies might run into plight of adjustment. The year of 2014 was likely to be a turning point in such a scenario.

C Impact of Transition of Global Rules on China's Development

1 China: Still in Phase of Strategic Opportunities without Existence of Opportunities

The United States of America and Japan, members of TPP, the GDP and trade volume of the total 12 ones of TPP accounted for over 40% of the global; the United States of America and Europe, members of TTIP, the GDP and trade volume of which, respectively, accounted for half and one-third of the global; the ongoing negotiation of EPA between Japan and EU also involved about one-third of global economies; However, the above agreements excluded the participation of China, but the three other countries among the four largest economies.

According to the perspective of Philip Stephens, United States of America is replacing the postwar multilateralism with preferential trade and investment agreement between like-minded countries (allies) and casting aside the multilateral trade agreement. Without the support of the United States of America, multilateral orders will further fall apart leading to the disintegration of globalization; China, as the biggest beneficiary of the liberal order, will become the biggest loser of globalization.[10] At the same time, some China scholar also suggested the removal of Americanization, which means to establish such a new world order where all countries, large and small, rich and poor, can be respected and protected in terms of important interests on equal basis.[11]

So, does the Sino-US relation only follow the traditional routine of conflict and confrontation between conservative and emerging powers? Is it in compliance with the benefits of China, the USA, and the whole world for China and USA to continue with the all-out confrontation and thus lead globalization to fall off? Can both countries develop mutual trust and cooperation? Just as Xi Jinping, General Secretary of Communist Party of China, put forward, "the United States of America and China need to strengthen dialogue, increase mutual trust, make cooperation and control differences and constantly promote the new relationship for great powers in between".[12] Therefore, a new relationship between the United States of America beyond the zero-sum game and promotion of economic globalization through cooperation are key to winning the current strategic circumstances.

2 Whether China Has Opportunity to Join TPP?

It is generally believed that TPP is a tool used by the United States of America to contain China. Only upon the stipulation and system establishment of TPP could China possibly accede to TPP. At that time, the United States of America would claim much more than China's estimation, which would have comprehensive impact on China's system, industry, and employment. Another view states that to join TPP and participate in rule formulation can reverse transmission of pressure on China to make reforms. A research group of National Development Research Institute of Peking University applied CGE model, taking the year of 2013 as the base period, and calculated the data for the advantages and disadvantages of access to TPP. The study found that if the existing negotiating member countries, excluding China, join TPP, then China's export growth rate would go down by 1.02% than the estimated growth rate in 2013, and the GDP growth rate will be down by 0.14%. However, if China acceded to TPP, its export growth rate would go up by 3.44%, import growth up by 5.58%, and GDP by 0.68%.[13] According to a working paper by John Walley from National Bureau of Economic Research (NBER) of USA, China's participation in TPP would have different impacts on itself in various sectors under different cost elimination. On the one hand, China's production shall go up by 3.816% under whole trade cost elimination, by 1.967% under non-tariff barriers elimination or by 0.59% under only tariff elimination. On another hand, China's welfare would go up by 1.125% under whole trade cost elimination, which would lead to the rise of welfare of other member countries.[14]

TPP caused increasingly significant loss to China's economic and trade development. For example, the Rules of Origin, the "spinning frontier" put forward by the United States of America, required that the spinning, weaving, cutting, and tailoring of all the textile into the market of USA must be completed in the territory of TPP. Some Chinese textile and garment enterprises were forced to move value-added activities to Vietnam and other TPP negotiating countries. On the other hand, the real barrier for China's entrance to TPP is that the United States of America might propose against China's rigorous special standards and conditions, just like Article 15 of the protocol on China's accession to the WTO. It is predicted that China's negotiation for accession to TPP will be more difficult than that for accession to WTO.

3   The 13th Five-Year Plan: Turning Point of Global Rebalance

The year of 2014 saw the turning point for global economy growth from being at "double rates" (the economy of USA, Japan, and the EU on a slump, but emerging economies on a normal-growth path) to being at "reversal double rates" (the economy of USA, Japan, and the EU in recovery, but emerging economies in declination). The reason for the declination rate of emerging economies was imputed by some experts to its internal structure and system flows, whereas some others quoted the external factors, like the USA ending the quantitative easing (QE), which caused the outflow of capital and developed into external shock. In fact, the economic revitalization of the United States of America, Japan, and the EU was at the expense of the economic bubbles in emerging economies.

First of all, global imbalance mainly came from inherent contradiction of globalization,[15] namely, the lack of effective supervision and governance despite the globalization dividend. To this end, the United States of America, with global hegemony and financial and monetary privilege, aspired to monopolize globalization dividend even at the expense of a bubble. One bubble occurred in the period from 1990 to 2001 in the IT sector, and another one from 2002 to 2008 in the financial and property market. They both exacerbated global imbalances[16] and brought to the United States of America the industrial hallowing-out and economic virtualization. However, the United

States of America accredited the crisis to the out-of-control of globalization and unfair competition from China and India and requested China and other emerging economies to bear part of the responsibility for the crisis and burden of the cost of rebalance adjustment.

Second, as for the developed economies of the United States of America, Japan, and the EU, one of their measures of rejuvenating economy was quantitative easing and expanding exports. It gave birth to a new round of global inflation, asset bubbles, and protectionism and resulted in the rise of capital inflows of emerging economies, skyrocketing of asset prices, appreciation of currency, and increase of imports. Once the QE policy of the United States of America was cast aside, the balance between bubbles would be disequilibrated, thus directly affecting the macroeconomic stability of emerging economies.

Furthermore, in order to get rid of the economic and industrial hollowing, the United States of America implemented the adjustment of reindustrialization, re-innovation, and reemployment by means of trade protectionism and contradiction transfer outward, which exacerbated the plight caused by shrinkage of external demands, rise of costs, mounting of the pressure on ecological environment, and intensification of political and social contradictions. It showed that the global economy was in a new cycle of adjustment. In the 13th Five-Year period in China, if China could not comprehensively intensify reforms and opening-up, it would possibly fall into a new development predicament.

III The 13th Five-Year Plan: To Comprehensively Intensify Reform and Opening-up for New Round Change in Global Rules

A The 13th Five-Year Plan: To Start New Reform and Opening-up

Comrade Xi Jinping pointed out that the reform and opening-up policy was key to determine the fate of contemporary China and to achieve the Two Centenary Goals and the great rejuvenation of Chinese nation. Comrade Deng Xiaoping also mentioned in the 1980s, "the significance of reform is to lay a good foundation for sustainable development for the next decade and the first five decades in the next century. Without reform, there will be no sustainable development in the future".[17]

Presently, China's reform and opening-up policy has reached an important turning point. In the past 35 years, through the unremitting efforts of the members of Chinese Communist Party and the Chinese people, China's reform and opening-up policy has made prominent achievements in development and has thus become the world second-largest economic power and largest foreign trade power. However, it is difficult for the system, mechanism, development strategies, and structure, which have proved right in the past 35 years, to support the development in the next step. Standing at the new historical starting point, China shall explore the new system, new strategy, and new structure to cross the middle-income trap, for the purpose of realizing the Two Centenary Goals and rejuvenating the Chinese nation.

First is to establish a new system pattern consistent with the new round of high standard of reform. In the new period, based on drawing on capital, technology, and talents, China shall pay more attention to attraction of systems, namely, the introduction of norms of modern marketing economy system in adaption to China's specific national conditions, development, and value systems. Through institutional innovation and pilot practice, China shall gradually develop the socialist marketing order and modern governance structure with Chinese characteristics.

Second is to establish a new open pattern consistent with the new round of high standard of opening-up. In the new period, China should better deal with the coordinated development relations between "three aspects of opening up", "two general situations", and "internal and external opening up".[18] It is advisable for China to direct the priority and strategic focus of opening-up to the tenor of the Third Plenary Session of the 18th Central Committee of the CPC, in order to build the new open economic system, form the new pattern of all-round opening-up, as well as foster the advantages in China's involving and leading action in international cooperation and competition.

Third is to establish a new development pattern consistent with the new round of high-quality development. In the new period, China shall shift from the pursuit of economic growth and GDP to improvement in growth quality and livelihood protection; from "economic development is of overriding importance" to "the planned and coordinated development of economy, society and ecological civilization is the absolute principle"; and from encouraging exports and attracting foreign business and investment to expanding domestic demand and implementing economic internationalization strategies. Besides, it is also important to plan and coordinate the relations between short-term stable growth, medium-term structural adjustment, and long-term institutional changes. To address many such problems, China must keep its development at a certain growth rate – as a scientific one in compliance with economic principles, a sustainable one in compliance with natural rules, as well as an inclusive one in compliance with social laws.[19]

B The 13th Five-Year Plan: Problem-solving Period for New Round of Reform and Opening-up

The 13th Five-Year Plan is the crucial period linking the past and the future 35 years. The old systems, strategies, and structures in the past 35 years, which are inadaptable to the future development, shall gradually exit out of the historic arena, while the new systems, strategies, and structures in the coming 35 years oriented to the future development shall be explored and established. It is a profound change that China shall experience now after 35 years since the reform and opening-up in December 1978. It will be a radical transformation full of difficulties for individuals, families, nation, and the whole country.

First, by 2020, decisive results shall be achieved in the all-round intensified reforms in important areas and crucial segments; law-based governance shall make great progress; and the early and pilot implementation of replicable and transferable institutional innovation shall be stimulated to achieve stage progress. These shall provide institutional and legal guarantee for the development of the future 35 years.

Second, by 2020, a well-off society shall be completed in all aspects, and the GDP and real income of urban and rural residents per capita shall be double the target for 2010. This will provide important material and technical basis for China to "overtake at the bend" and become the world's responsible, open, and innovative power with high individual income.

Third, the year of 2020 shall be a strategic opportunity to develop in the future. China, as the beneficiary of economic globalization, shall continue to promote the openness of multilateralism and regionalism; accelerate the implementation of free-trade zone strategies to gradually form a globally oriented network linking high-standard free-trade areas based on the surrounding; as well as adhere to the rules of world trade system, actively participate in international governance reform, and take the responsibility as an amenable power.

C Focus and Starting Point of Intensifying New Round of Reform and Opening-up in the 13th Five-Year Plan

1 Focus of Intensifying Reform and Opening-up in 13th Five-Year Plan

First of all, it is not appropriate for China to continue export-oriented economic system. Since the reform and opening-up, China has developed and improved its export-oriented economic system by encouraging exports and attracting foreign business and investment through continuous practice in the system innovation and reforms. As for renminbi, for a long time, its exchange rate, interest rate, tax rate, price, currency decisive system, as well as relevant policies on industry, fiscal taxation, finance, and regions, have been simulated and directed by encouraging exports and attracting business and investment. In the past three decades, China has addressed the bottleneck restraints caused by the shortage of foreign exchange, capital, and supply, and created the "Chinese development wonder" in a short time. China has introduced the marketing of economic factors, burdened pressure from foreign competition, and propelled the transformation of system from planning economy to marketing economy. China has carried out the process of learning by doing in compliance with the nature of path dependence of reforms, enlightened hundreds of millions of people to be knowledgeable of modern development results, and explored a development path of Chinese characteristic socialism integrated with international experience and China's practice by expanding opening-up and intensifying reforms. However, China is not supposed to continue its export-oriented economic development strategy, though successful in the past, as it is a strategy for a small country. If China continuously implemented it, the contradictions and conflicts between China's economy and world economy would become more acute. Therefore, it is of paramount importance for the blueprint of China's reforms in the future 35 years to construct a new open economic system during the 13th Five-Year Plan period.

Next, China shall not implement imbalanced development strategy anymore. Since the reform and opening-up, China has implemented the strategy to firstly "let minority get rich" and then to "realize common wealth"; to firstly consider the vision of developing the eastern coastal areas and then the mid-west areas; to firstly develop economy and then to realize the coordinated development of economy, society, and ecology. As for the priority of opening-up, China implemented the imbalanced open strategy of firstly expanding the opening-up toward the Western developed countries and then expanding that toward the transit countries and regions, like the former Soviet Union, East Europe, and other developing countries. Such imbalanced development strategy has made great success in the initial development and in the later opening-up, but in the meanwhile it has brought the contradiction and problems on imbalance, disharmony, and discontinuity of development. Therefore, to develop the new open pattern at all respects during the 13th Five-Year Plan period matters much for the vision of the opening-up in the future 35 years.

Furthermore, China shall stop the industrial structure to join international division on the basis of low costs. Since the reform and opening-up, China has established global competitive advantages of the element of low-cost structure, large-scale production mode, and simple imitation of technology through the migration of rural surplus labor of more than two hundred million people to non-agricultural sectors and cities. In the global context of prosperous economic globalization, China actively participated in multinational companies in terms of global work order division or product internal division system and built the processing trade production system through Original Equipment Manufacture (OEM) in manufacturing. However, external demand shrank due to the slowdown of global growth and trade friction and protection became acute because of the overall rise of prices in domestic and overseas elements. All these showed that it was infeasible for China to continue its industrial and trade structure based on low cost, low price, and low end, which it had been following for the past 35 years. Therefore, fostering China's new advantages in participating and leading international cooperation and competition during the 13th Five-Year Plan period is crucial to the development in the future 35 years.

2 Staring Point of Intensifying New Round of Reform and Opening-up in the 13th Five-Year Plan

First, China shall set up a legalized high-standard open economic policy system and simulation direction at all aspects on the principle of fairness and discrimination. In terms of instruction of resource allocation, China shall overvalue neither exports nor imports, neither "leading inside" nor "stepping outside", neither industry, tertiary, or agriculture. The reasonable and effective layout for resource allocation decided by marketing mechanism shall come into being.

Second, China shall follow the pivotal strategy of expanding domestic demand. It is advisable for China to set up the long-term system to advance domestic consumption and investment rise and attract imports and foreign investment growth, with a view to construct an open economy system with complementary advantages, cooperation and interaction, benign competition, mutual benefit, and win-win situation between China's economy and world economy.

Third, China shall speed up the implementation of economic internationalization strategy. By extending the effort to build a new open economy system from inside China's territory to cross the border or beyond the border, a new pattern of all-round opening-up shall be developed. By vigorously promoting internationalization in talents, capital, industries, markets and cities, and capital market internationalization, the world's most outstanding talents, enterprises, and quality factors shall be absorbed to cultivate China's new advantages in participation and instruction in international cooperation and competition.

Fourth, China shall expedite the modernization of national governance systems and governance capacity, and gradually develop into an open power with decision right for global prices, formulation right, responsibility-undertaking right, as well as the capacity of converse period regulation.

Fifth, China shall plan and coordinate the strategies of "stepping outside", "leading inside", and localization to develop its new advantages in an open and innovative international cooperation.

D 13th Five-Year Plan: Displaying China's Role as Accountable Power in Advancing Economic Globalization

First, to promote global open economic development is the solid basis to enhance multifaceted international cooperation. It was decided at The Third Plenary Session of the 18th Central Committee of the CPC that China would globally set up high-standard free-trade zone network, which were the key words at the session. In the high-standard free-trade zone, a new open economy system would be set up on the basis of the principle for a more standardized, more transparent, and more fair marketing economy, and systematic standards would be set up in accordance with the development and national conditions of China. The target for the free-trade zone network was to set up all-dimensional international cooperation systems, including the upgraded edition of Cross Economic Cooperation Framework Agreement (CEPA) or Strait Economic Cooperation Framework Agreement (ECFA) in the Four Regions Across the Strait, upgraded edition of Free Trade Area between China and the Association of Southeast Asian Nations (ASEAN), China ROK Free Trade Area, China Japan ROK Free Trade Area, Asia-Pacific Free Trade Area, the free-trade zone for South-South shared development, as well as other different types of free-trade areas of Sino-America, Sino-EU, Sino-India, and Sino-Russia, for the ultimate purpose of forming a new all-round open pattern.

Second, to promote global inclusive development is an important condition to maintain world fairness and justice. From the perspective of world history, whether developing countries have equal access to the process and shared results of development rather than a few advanced countries exclusively having development opportunities and achievements, is one of the bases to determine whether the international order is inclusive or exclusive. In the case of main developed countries unwilling to take more responsibility, while developing countries lack the say and governance capacity, China is playing an important role. China shall bear the responsibility of global public goods supply to match its own strength and promote global inclusive development.

Third, to promote global balanced development is the fundamental guarantee for realization of world peace and development. Now there are two views on balanced development: one is the global imbalance and rebalance measured by open economy. In February and April of 2011, a package of global economic imbalance, including the private, public, and external sectors, was proposed at the Meeting of Secretary of the Treasury and President of Central Bank of G20. One of the deficiencies of such method is that it is difficult to measure the product internal division or work order division in economic globalization environment. Therefore, a wrong judgment occurred that developing countries were the source of global imbalances, as the current accounts of developed countries often generally present deficit while that of developing countries surplus. Another one is that from the perspective of development, it can be found that the gap between the developed and underdeveloped, rich and poor, urban and rural continues to expand in the global environment. In this regard, China, as a responsible power, shall help the least developed countries and regions to get rid of poverty; respect the protection of human rights, property rights, and the rights to development in different conditions of culture and system; and provide more public innovation and technical transfer service on the basis of protection of intellectual property rights.

Fourth, China shall promote globally sustainable development. At present, the developed countries have ushered in the era of service economy and knowledge economy. In possession of professionals and technology of low-carbon, the developed countries enjoy a high-quality life with high-carbon and high-energy consumption, but demanding developing countries to shoulder more responsibility for low-carbon development and to pay higher price for low-carbon technology. In this connection, China shall vigorously propel energy conservation, emission reduction, green transformation, and low-carbon on the basis of development, especially sustainable development, by means of comprehensive economic and technical cooperation.

E The 13th Five-Year Plan: To Construct New Pattern of All-round Opening-up

The construction of key areas of new pattern of all-round opening-up shall be implemented during the 13th Five-Year Plan period. First of all, China shall set up a comprehensive transport network system linking sea, land, and air to expedite the construction of multifaceted communicative channels between China and Central Asia, West Asia, North Africa, South Asia, Southeast Asia, and Northeast Asia; timely advance the construction of multifaceted communicative channels between China and Africa, Latin America, Oceania and Arctic; and finally build up multifaceted communicative channels between China and the Great Delta comprising USA, Japan, and Europe to form a new pattern of all-round opening-up. Next, China shall develop international network and production system for global investment, global production, global export, global services, and global cooperation, as well as enhance its efficiency in flow of commerce, material, capital, human resource, and information to develop the system of cross-border production and trade supply chains. Furthermore, China shall fully deepen the open mode of financial integration like Shanghai-Hong Kong Stock Connect and Shenzhen-Hong Kong Stock Connect. In this context, China shall establish a new system for financial openness based on financial deepening and opening-up, renminbi internationalization, capital account opening, and reforms in exchange rates and international payment balance.

The construction of cooperation mechanism of new pattern of all-round opening-up shall be constructed during the 13th Five-Year Plan period. It was proposed at the Third Plenary Session of the 18th CPC Central Committee that,

> the establishment of China Shanghai Free Trade Pilot Area is a significant initiative of the central leading body of CPC to promote the reform and opening up in the new situation. It is important to actually develop and manage it and to explore new ways and accumulate new experience for the intensification of reform and expansion of opening up.

Visibly, Shanghai pilot area has met the requirements of the new round of domestic high-standard reform and opening-up, adapted to TPP, TTIP, and other transformation in global rules, as well as made trial practice oriented to global high-standard FTA network. It is of great significance as it will promote the internationalization, modernization, and legalization in China's economy at a higher level, greater range, and wider areas. Whether the pilot experience and modes of Shanghai and other places can be duplicated and publicized in central and western regions of China is related to the overall situation of the construction of the all-round open economy system. China shall follow the measures as follows: first, based on attracting capital, talents, and technology from foreign countries, China shall pay more attention to system introduction and deepen system reform, capacity building, and talent exchange and cooperation between the eastern coastal developed areas and the central and western areas in China. Second, China shall establish cooperation mechanism between the pilot areas in Shanghai and in the central and western areas, for example, to strengthen the cooperation between Shanghai free-trade zone and Ningxia inland open economic pilot area. In the process of building Shanghai International Trade Center, China can turn the Ningxia inland open economic zone into the platform for cooperation and development of Ningxia and Shanghai, as well as establishment of both economic and trade relations with the Arabic regions. Third, in the construction of Shanghai International Financial Center, International Trade Center, International Shipping Center, China shall give priority to the pilot area to expand trade, investment, and industrial cooperation with emerging economies. For example, China shall strengthen the cooperative platform between the western regions and the eastern coastal areas of Shanghai, Tianjin, Guangdong, Fujian, and other places; develop all-round cooperation with West Asia, Central Asia, South Asia, Africa, and Latin America; establish the new South-South cooperative mode of "shared development", green transformation, mutual benefit, and win-win; as well as lead the western areas to further opening-up and scientific development.

Notes

1 Presently, there are all kinds of description of the characteristics of the current world science and technology revolution, such as the second machine revolution, the third industrial revolution, the fourth industrial revolution, the second digital technology revolution, etc.
2 Domestic and foreign scholars commonly agree that the first economic globalization of human society took place in 1870–1913. The biggest controversy is about the second one from 1950 to 1973, the period of separation and confrontation between the two world economic camps of socialism and capitalism. The third one refers to the period of modern economic globalization since 1990.
3 In 1842, Britain began to abolish manufactured product tax rates and reduce import tax rates. This achieved free trade in 1860, but Britain returned to trade protectionism after 1913. In 1860, after the signing of Cobden-Chevalier Treaty, European countries began to provide mutual most-favored-nation treatment and import tariff concession; but after 1880, Germany, France, Italy, Russia, and other countries implemented protective tariffs on agricultural and

manufactured products. After 1890, a dual tariff was developed in the trade treaty system, namely, to impose non-treaty countries' high import tariffs and the treaty countries low ones. In 1913, the whole Europe resumed trade protectionism. During this period, the United States of America has been wavering between trade protectionism and liberalization. An investigation showed that the growth of American industrial protection was below the accepted level from 1879 to 1904, and much lower than that of its cotton textile industry protection. A. G. Kenwood et al. *Growth of the International Economy* (Beijng: Economic Science Press, 1996).

4 Angel Gurria, Secretary of Organization for Economic Cooperation and Development said,

> when historians review our times, they can find that none of the other countries' economic development can be as remarkable as China's rise. However, when they further widen the historical horizon, they may see that it is not a rise but a revival".

See "Preface" (by Angel Gurria) of *Long Term Performance of Chinese Economy*, Angus Maddison Shanghai People's Publishing House, 2008.

5 Martin Wolf believed that the majority of the elite did not correctly understand the consequences of the reckless financial liberalization; when the risk occurred, the disastrous consequences often presented collapse of economy, surge of unemployment, and sharp increase in public debts. See *Failing Elites Threaten Our Future, Financial Times*, January 14, 2014.

6 For years, international trade scientist Bhagwati has been encouraging to promote global trade and investment liberalization, in the view that open and market-oriented reforms would enhance the global economic benefits. However, he has been cautious and doubtful about propelling global financial liberalization.

7 GDP and trade volume of the 12 members of TPP accounted for about 40% of the world aggregates. The agenda of TPP negotiations included tariffs, intellectual property rights, competition, government procurement, environmental protection, regulatory barriers, labor rights, and so forth. TTIP negotiations began in June 2013, covering the market access, government procurement, investment, services, regulatory consistency, intellectual property rights, state-owned enterprises, and so forth., with trade volume accounting for one-third of the world trade volume and GDP for half of the global GDP, involving a population of more than 800 million people. The Japan-EU Economic Partnership Agreement negotiations officially launched in March 2013, with economic volume accounting for about one-third of world economic output upon its establishment.

8 Joseph Biden, *Financial Times*, March 4, 2014.

9 Zhang Lin, "Where Will Governance of International Trade Rules in Post-Bali Island Period", internal manuscript, Institute of World Economics and Politics of Chinese Academy of Social Sciences, January 6, 2014.

10 Philip Stephens, *Financial Times*, October 10, 2013.

11 An English review on de-Americanization was published by Xinhua News Agency on October 13, 2013. The White House of USA later held a special meeting to discuss the political implications of such article by China's official news agency.

12 Xi Jinping, "Speech at the Press Interview with Obama", *People's Daily*, June 9, 2013.

13 See "Sino US Economic Dialogue", Research Group of National Development Research Institute of Peking University, meeting report, 2013.

14 See Chunding Li, John Whalley, working paper of NBER of USA, No.18090, May 2012.

15 Zhang Yansheng, "Cause and Measurement of Global Economic Imbalance, Responsibility of Rebalance between China and USA", internal manuscript, December 2011.
16 The current account deficit of America continued to increase since 1990, accelerated nearly on an annual rise by USD100 billion after 2001, and exceeded USD800 billion, the historic record, in 2006.
17 Xi Jinping, "Speech at the Second Collective Learning at Political Bureau of the CPC Central Committee", December 31, 2012; "Correspondence of General Office of the CPC Central Committee", Issue No. 1, 2013.
18 Deng Xiaoping had made three important conclusions: firstly, the three aspects of opening-up. Deng Xiaoping said,

> as for the opening up to the outside world, some people still remain unclear in thought that it is only opening up to the west. In fact, we are open to the three aspects: First is towards the western developed countries, where we attract foreign investment and introduce technology. Second is towards the Soviet Union and Eastern European countries. Third is towards the developing countries in the third world.

(See Deng Xiaoping's speech at the Symposium of Central Military Commission, November 1, 1984, *Collected Works of Deng Xiaoping,* Volume III, P98–99). Secondly, the proposition on "the two general situations". Deng Xiaoping said,

> to speed up the opening of the coastal areas so that the mast land whereof with a population of hundred million can rapidly develop and lead mainland to better develop, matter much for the general situation, where the mainland shall show consideration. In turn, at certain time, the coastal areas shall be asked to contribute much to help the mainland develop, which is also in the general situation. At that time, the coastal areas shall also be subject to such situation.

(See Deng Xiaoping: "Accelerate Development of Tibet Based on Ethnic Equality", June 29, 1987, *Collected Works of Deng Xiaoping,* Volume III, P246). Thirdly, the opening-up inward and outward. Deng Xiaoping said, "the opening up includes two contents, the internal opening up and the external opening up". He also said, "the internal opening up is reform, which is a comprehensive one, including economic, political, science and technology, education and other industries".
19 See the announcement for meeting of Political Bureau of the CPC Central Committee.

Bibliography

Andrew Nathan, Andrew Scobell. "The Sum of Beijing's Fears: How China Sees America", *Foreign Affairs*, September/October 2012.

Angus Maddison. *Long Term Performance of Chinese Economy*, Shanghai: Shanghai People's Publishing House, 2008.

Chunding Li, John Whalley. *Working Paper of NBER* No.18090, May 2012.

Elvin,G. John Ikenberry. "Getting Hegemony Right", *The National Interest*, Spring of 2001.

Mark Elvin. *The Pattern of the Chinese Past*, Stanford: Stanford University Press, 1973.

Mark Leonard. "Why Convergence Breeds Conflict", *Foreign Affairs*, September/October 2013.

Martin Wolf. "Failing Elites Threaten Our Future", *Financial Times*, January 14, 2014.

Petersen Institute for International Economics. *Internal Report*, 2013.

Philip Stephens. *Financial Times*, October 10, 2013.

Research Group of National Development Research Institute of Peking University. "Sino US Economic Dialogue", *Meeting Report*, 2013.

Robert Gilpin. "Hegemonic War and International Change", *Conflict After the Cold War: Arguments on Causes of War and Peace*, Ed. Richard K. Betts, Third Edition, New York: Pearson-Longman, 2008.

"White House Holds Meeting to Discuss Political Implications of China's Official News Agency's 'De-Americanization' Article", *Xinhua News Agency*, October 13, 2013.

Xi Jinping. "Speech at the Press Interview with Obama", *People's Daily*, June 9, 2013.

Zhang Lin. "Where Will Governance of International Trade Rules in Post-Bali Island Period", *Internal Manuscript of Institute of World Economics and Politics of Chinese Academy of Social Sciences*, January 6, 2014.

Zhang Yansheng. "Cause and Measurement of Global Economic Imbalance, Responsibility of Rebalance between China and USA", *Internal Manuscript*, December 2011.

4 Basic Concepts of Economic System Reform during 13th Five-Year Plan Period

Economic system reform is the basis for healthy development of China's economy during the 13th Five-Year Plan period and even for a long time in the future. Based on the requirements for development strategy and conditions for institutional reform, it is highly important to focus on the four aspects to promote reforms during the 13th Five-Year Plan period: firstly, loosening regulation of production factors including land, interest rate, and exchange rate to stimulate a new round of market-oriented reforms; secondly, reconstruction of national capacity to advance government reforms; thirdly, replenishing social security funds to coordinate the improvement of overall social security system with reforms of state-owned enterprises; fourthly, boosting residents' disposable income to intensify the income distribution reform.

During the 13th Five-Year Plan period, economic development enjoys a good prospect and a big space as favorable conditions, such as great market capacity, high national savings rate, and improved infrastructure, which still continue to work. In addition, the aspiration of the public and government at all levels for prosperity and development remains strong. However, factors hindering the development are also accumulating. For instance, the contribution of demographic dividend to economic growth will gradually disappear due to premature aging population. Besides, we are faced with numerous problems consisting of weak technical support for economic growth, insufficient domestic demand, prominent resource constraints, a burdensome environment, and ever sharper social contradiction. If those obstacles cannot be successfully overcome, it will be difficult to achieve the goals of the 13th Five-Year Plan, which will make the development afterward more arduous. Therefore, only by further deepening institutional reform can we break down the obstacles that hinder the development, and only then can the strategic targets of the 13th Five Year Plan be realized, and then the Chinese economy return to the sound and fast development track. Based on the needs to develop strategies and to create conditions for institutional reforms, it is highly important to focus on the four aspects to promote reforms during the 13th Five-Year Plan period: firstly, loosening regulation of production factors including land, interest rate, and exchange rate to stimulate a new round of market-oriented reforms; secondly, reconstruction of national capacity to advance government reforms; thirdly, replenishing social security funds to coordinate the improvement of overall social security system with reforms of state-owned enterprises; fourthly, boosting residents' disposable income to intensify the income distribution reform.

I Focus on Loosening Regulation of Production Factors to Stimulate New Round of Market-oriented Reforms

In the past 30 years, China has successfully promoted the market-oriented product reform, laying necessary institutional foundation for release of economic vitality. However, market-oriented reform is not complete, as the resource allocation of production factors, the material bases for the production, such as land and mineral products, are excluded from the market-oriented reform. For that reason, the market plays a limited role in the optimal allocation of resources. For instance, the current mandatory land planning control not only negatively affects the normal development of the residential sector – the industrial pillar that could have promoted consumption upgrade – but constitutes a major obstacle to the economic expansion in some areas as well. In recent years, as heatedly argued, even though prices of resource products are mostly determined by the market and spared from influences of the price formation mechanism, prices of resources, an important part of production costs, are still subject to government regulation. Since most mineral enterprises have non-market access to mineral resources, prices of natural resources are heavily distorted. This not only reduces allocative efficiency, causing serious unequal distribution and political corruption, but becomes the root cause of intensified social conflicts as well. Therefore, to promote growth and to enhance social justice, efforts should be focused on loosening control over production factors to bring in a new round of market-oriented reforms.

A Reform of Land System

Land is the most fundamental production factor. However, currently, China's land system is still under the planned economy state, which is accentuated in the program of construction land franchised by local governments under the mandate of the central government. Relevant problems including unclearly determined property rights of farmlands in rural areas and the imperfect land circulation system are all derived from the planned economy. The long-term existence of these problems has not only seriously set back the implementation of major development strategies such as "urbanization", "expansion of domestic demand", and "optimization and upgrading of industrial structure", but also constitutes major latent risks that may jeopardize social instability. Therefore, based on the reformation logic of economic system, as well as drawn on the practice of land system in other developed countries and the land reform experience in some parts of our country, we need to push forward market-oriented reform of the land system in a gradual way. In the near future, we aim to break the government monopoly in the supply of urban construction land in order to optimize the circulation system of land use rights, to improve the land requisition system, and to deepen reform of current urban land use system. In the long run, we will strive to promote the diversification of urban and rural land property rights and to realize market-oriented allocation of land resources.

1 Deepen Reform of Urban and Rural Land Use System at Early Stage of the 13th Five-Year Plan Period

Firstly, we will abolish central government's quantitative control over land supply. Currently, the central government's quota-based control over urban construction land is contradictory to the market-oriented concept that market plays a fundamental role in resource allocation. Though it is agreed that government needs to adhere to the "red line of 1.8 billion mu (120 million hectares)", we should achieve the goal through land use planning and tax leverage rather than through quantitative control, a typical method of planned economy. Besides, land reserve system should not be abused to make profits, but should be used to serve public projects as originally planned. Secondly, we will carry out market-driven reform of rural collective construction land. In the principle of "same land, rights and price", rural collective construction land will be promoted to directly enter the market. Besides, we will step up the establishment of a unified market of urban and rural construction land, and formulate the circulation mechanism of rural residential land, so as to allow the free circulation of homesteads in rural areas subject to the legal criteria for area distribution of "one housing land for one household". In addition, we will establish trans-regional land use system to facilitate long-distance, large-scale replacement of construction lands between rural and urban areas, to alleviate the short supply of urban construction land, and to guarantee remote rural areas a fair share of value-added benefits in industrialization and urbanization, so as to ensure that residents will be bound to their lands between urban and rural areas, or between different regions. Thirdly, we will improve the compensation mechanism for land expropriation. We will strictly define the boundary between public welfare land and commercial construction land. In terms of land expropriation, we will timely grant full-amount compensation to collective economic organizations and farmers in the principle of "same land, same price". We will increase compensation standards of the expropriated public welfare land and provide farmers whose land has been expropriated with the same social security benefits as rural residents to ensure that their long-term living standards will not decline. For disputed compensation and resettlement cases of land expropriation, we will establish the coordination and arbitration system to settle disputation to encourage the public to participate in land expropriation and promote procedural transparency. Besides, we will explore the replacement of rental system over expropriation system in public welfare land. In the conversion of collective rural lands to public welfare land, the governments shall change the practice from one-time buyout to rental payment, with rental fees annually paid to farmers' organizations or to farmers, based on price level and local fiscal capacity.

2 Accelerate Institutional Reform of Land Property Rights at the End of the 13th Five-Year Plan Period

Diversification of land property in rural areas should be promoted at national, collective, and individual levels. The land developed and utilized under the unified national planning shall be requisitioned, developed, and reserved through land reserve institutes. In villages where collective economy develops vigorously, the existing operating system can be maintained, but land ownership in the legal sense shall be restored to "collective" ownership. Lands suitable to be owned by farmers (including homesteads) shall be reallocated based on actual rural population, the property rights of which shall be clearly defined as individual ownership. Reform of property rights of urban lands shall be conducted based on different usage purposes and classification like the land for real estate, industrial use, and administrative use. The ownership of real estates including residential, industrial real estate, and commercial real estate shall be clearly assigned to actual users. The ownership of industrial land shall be defined as either state-owned or individual-owned by referring to actual users. Administrative and military land shall be classified as state-owned. In such consideration, the purchasing expenditure of urban construction land from farmers shall be paid to them in line with market prices. Since the users of all types of real estate lands have made one-time land-transferring payment to governments for 70, 50, or 40 years, the users can freely choose to rent or purchase the land in the determination of land ownership. If they choose to rent the land, they can re-sign rental contract or purchase the property according to local price after the expiry of the old lease contract without paying real estate taxes during the rental period; if they choose to purchase the property, they need to pay real estate tax without paying repayment fee of land purchasing.

B Reform of Financial System

Market-oriented reform in financial sector is relatively backward. On the one hand, there still exists strong governmental intervention in areas where market should have played a fundamental role, thus distorting the allocation of financial resources. On the other hand, in some areas prone to market failure, effective governmental intervention is insufficient to compensate for market imperfections. We will speed up the reform of financial market, promote the diversification of financial intermediaries, reduce the overall access threshold of multilevel capital market, and effectively satisfy the financing needs of various economic entities so as to enhance the allocation efficiency of financial resources.

1 Loosen Market Access Limitation in Financial Sectors

At present, one of the financial factors hindering China's economic development is the limited number of small and medium-sized banks. It is hard to fundamentally change the loan-borrowing problems for small and medium-sized enterprises in the long run. The hierarchical system of a few giant state-owned banks – the leading financial intermediation system – is too complicated. Serving similarly as administrative institutions, these banks are low in efficiency and high in risk. Therefore, it is necessary to loosen market access limitation and develop a large number of small and medium-sized joint-stock commercial banks and micro-credit institutions, cooperative financial organizations in local areas to meet the financing needs of "agriculture, farmers and rural areas". Only by taking such actions can we genuinely promote competition, improve overall efficiency of the financial industry, and increase the allocation efficiency of financial resources to ensure a healthy development of the real economy.

2 Relax Regulation over Financial Products

We will reduce administrative intervention in the issuance of stock and bond and improve the marketization degree of securities issuance. Outside the exchange market, we will develop counter market, property rights trading market to diversify the capital market and to provide companies unable to meet the listing requirements with direct financing platform. We will moderately develop innovative financial products and risk hedging tools. In addition, we will optimize and adjust economic structure through multilevel development of the capital market, and accelerate the development of bond market, especially local government bond market and corporate bond market, to build an effective financial supporting system for urbanization.

3 Abolish Control over Financial Product Pricing

We will accelerate the market-oriented reform of deposit interest rate by centering on the marketization of monetary and bond interest rates. Besides, we will increase transactional subjects in the monetary market, diversify transactional products, and enhance the effectiveness of Shanghai Interbank Offered Rate as the benchmark interest rate. We aim to cancel control over deposit interest rates by gradually weakening the role of deposit interest rates. We also strive to realize independent pricing for financial institutions, and to provide depositors with more choices for financial institutions.

C Reform of Natural Resource System

The saying "land is the mother of wealth" derives from the fact that capital and labor cannot create wealth without natural resources. In China, per capita share of available resources is below the global average, and therefore resources become all the more valuable. However, as resource development companies have non-market access to resources and market evaluation mechanism to determine prices of resources, an important factor of costs is desperately insufficient, and predatory exploitation of mineral resources and serious overdraft of ecological resources are commonplace in today's China. Property rights of other non-mineral resources are not clearly determined as well. For instance, it is still unclear who owns the property rights of which kinds of hydropower resources – the central or the local government. Problems such as underestimation of water and electricity rates, "preemptive acquisition of land", and "mandatory tax collection" (local governments levy taxes on companies after the completion of programs) are all closely related to the unclear definition of property rights. It is obvious that the existing natural resource system exerts an inverse regulating effect. Therefore, during the 13th Five-Year Plan, we will carry out the reform of resource system based on "ownership determination, market-oriented approach". Thus, in areas where market should play a decisive role based on the clearly determined resource property rights, resources price formation mechanism shall be established.

1 Promote Reform of Resource Property System

Clear property ownership is the prerequisite for the marketization of resources. China should also learn from international experience to clarify the property ownership of all kinds of mineral resources and water resources, and to regulate relevant rights and obligations. By doing so, we aim to protect the rights and interests of resources owners, to raise the efficiency of resource development, to promote social fairness, and to preserve environment in places where resources are abundant.

The initial ownership of mineral resources should follow the principle of "first occupied, first owned". To determine the ownership of mineral resources, such as those natural resources that permanently attach to land without mobility, we shall follow the aforementioned principle. Since China has established the state-owned system of underground mineral resources, the focus of ownership determination is to divide the ownership of those mineral resources, that is which resources shall be assigned to the central government, and which shall be assigned to local governments, including rights allocation among sub-provincial governments. From the perspective of ecological environment protection and optimal allocation of resources, resources buried within a certain administrative region shall belong to the corresponding local government; resources buried across different administrative regions shall be jointly shared by adjacent regions and the government at a higher level. Initial property rights may be transferred or leased. Based on it, price, tax, and payment system for state-owned resources will be established.

Unlike mineral fuels that have a fixed storage location, water is liquid. Groundwater, surface water, as well as surface water within the same watershed are interacting with each other. Therefore, determination of the initial property rights of water resources shall be based on the universal "shoreline ownership principle". Water resources within one administrative region shall belong to the local government. Water resources across different administrative regions will be jointly shared by governments alongside the river and the government at a higher level. For rivers across different provinces like the Yangtze River, the Yellow River, and the Pearl River, their property rights should be shared by the central government and provincial governments. Revenues from water development shall be jointly shared between the central government and local governments, of which a larger share should go to local governments. The central government's ownership of water resources is mainly manifested in its rights to make unified planning and distribution of water resources (including the mechanism of "water dispatching prior to electrical dispatching") as well as the rights to collect and allocate water fees.

2 Market-Oriented Resource Prices

We will establish the payment use system and trading system of mining and water resources based on the clearly determined property rights. Mining rights refers to the exploration and development rights of mineral resources. Governments should transfer, lease their mining rights, and determine related fees through competitive market-oriented methods including public bidding or auction. On the basis, a secondary market for mining rights will be established to further enhance the efficiency of resource allocation.

II Focus on Reconstruction of National Capacity to Advance Government Reforms

Though the reform and opening policy has been implemented for more than 30 years, "the relationship between government and the market" is still the core issue in the reform of China's economic system. The coexistence of "ultra vires" and "absence" of the government remains the main obstacle to further promoting the market-oriented reform of the economy. In other words, the root cause that hinders the marketization of China's economic system is the lack of a modern government that serves market economy. Hence, we must vigorously promote the government reform by focusing on enhancing the government capacity at all levels.

A Enhance Governmental Efficiency by Clarifying Rules of Governmental Organization and Operation

1 Establish Rules of Governmental Construction and Operation Based on Requirement of Market Economy

We will build a modern government by breaking the notion that the government is almighty. Unless it involves public interest, or market fails to function in certain areas, governments should neither make nor approve an investment. All governmental agencies should be established and authorized in accordance with the law and with government's decision-making, and regulation implementation should conform to the law. Law also regulates conditions and methods for government to directly intervene market. We will strive to reverse the situation of overlapping responsibilities and mutual containment between different departments. Different departments should not be measured by their sizes but by their well-defined duties and functions. Meanwhile, public participation will be introduced to strengthen the supervision and check mechanism of governmental activities, and to further enhance the fairness and operability of public policies.

2 Establish Modern Supervisory System Based on Market-Oriented Economy

So far, China has not witnessed supervisory and regulatory practices in the modern sense. Poor social supervision has been accentuated once and again in social accidents, including "poisoned milk powder" and "mining accidents". Effects of economic regulation hardly got recognition from the public. In recent years, monopolistic industries have become the target of public criticism due to their "low efficiency and high income". The "market-oriented reform" of public services characterized by the sale of state-owned assets and the auction of chartered rights is in full swing; however, there is a lack corresponding regulatory system to supervise the reform. Compounded by the rising price of public facilities, public distrust toward the government has accumulated in some areas. In market-oriented economies, supervision is the most fundamental function. The modernization of supervision and regulation in China should start with the establishment of independent supervisory business and decision-making system so that supervisory and regulatory bodies can independently and effectively conduct regulation and supervision. We will, on the basis of respecting technical and economic characteristics, and financial responsibility of the industry, set up a hierarchical supervisory system that is fully functioned, with duties reasonably divided. Supervisors should publicize their operational and decision-making information to the public. We will establish a new type of consumer organization to truly ensure openness, transparency, and public participation throughout supervision, and form the check and balance mechanism toward supervisors.

3   Construct Diversified Social Public Services System

The government should also delegate, authorize the rights to social groups, and give full play to the self-management capacity of social organizations. Quantity and quality of the basic public services should be upgraded through market-orientation, including contract outsourcing, franchising, issuing public service vouchers, and granting subsidies to private sectors if they make investments in public projects. First-class public services will be provided by the market. We will significantly improve the emergency management and accountability system to better cope with public health, and social security emergencies to intensify the integration of grass-roots resources, to strengthen urban and rural community services system, and to improve the new community management and services system.

B   Adjust Governmental Fiscal Conduct with the Aim of Promoting Equalized Public Services

Government fiscal conduct is the material basis of governance capacity. As China has entered the club of middle- and upper-income countries, equalized basic public services is the necessary condition for overall quality improvement and an important sign of social fairness and justice. We expect relevant progress in the following aspects:

1   Shift Focus of Fiscal Function

In order to meet the strategic objectives of the 13th Five-Year Plan, we will adjust the focus of the fiscal functions accordingly. We will further increase investment in basic public services by raising expenses in education, health, medical services, social welfare, poverty relief, and social security. We will raise subsidy standards, expand the coverage of social security, effectively lower the pressure of consumption on low-income groups, and stabilize their consumption expectation to create favorable conditions for expanding domestic demand; We will enhance efforts in increasing investments in the protection of resource and environment, and focus on strengthening capacity to abate pollutions in rivers and lakes so as to lay a good foundation for sustainable development.

2   Adjust Financial Relationship between Central and Local Government Based on Reasonable Division of Rights

It is necessary to shift upwards the expenditure responsibility of basic public services including education and social security, from grassroots government to the central or provincial governments so as to alleviate the financial burden on grassroots governments. It is essential to authorize local governments, especially provincial governments with corresponding fiscal legislative power, including lawmaking rights and tax credit rights, to realize equalized public services. We need to streamline the transfer payment system and strengthen the reform of tax refund and value-added tax-sharing system. We will expand the coverage of general transfer payment program and reduce and standardize special transfer payment programs. Besides, we will expand the scale of formulated capital distribution to form a standardized, transparent, predictable transfer payment system across the central and provincial governments.

3 Deepen Budget System Reform

It is necessary to establish a new modern budget management mechanism characterized by separated and balanced rights throughout budget development, implementation, and supervision. The expenditures of the central government and various departments shall be examined and approved by the special committee of the People's Congress. The transfer payments shall also be reported to a special committee. Approval shall be made after necessary debates or hearings. We will appoint a third-party institution to conduct the performance assessment of the special transfer payment.

III Focus on Replenishing Social Security Funds to Coordinate Improvement of Overall Social Security System with Reforms of State-Owned Enterprises

According to the requirement of establishing and perfecting the market economic system, reform of state-owned enterprises is far from completion, and the state-owned economy has advanced too much and retreated too little under the layout adjustment strategy of "the advance and retreat of state-owned economy in some areas". Besides, state-owned economy has further strengthened its monopoly in the guise of providing "public welfare" services. There are many mistakes in SASAC's (State-owned Assets Supervision and Administration Commission) positioning and management of state-owned enterprises. Our long-term aim is to make sure state-owned assets shall be shared by all the people. However, many factors constitute obstacles for us to achieve that goal. In addition, the gap of social security system is getting larger than ever. As a result, we will focus on replenishing social security funds with state-owned assets. We will make sure state-owned assets serve the public interest in the real sense as required by the market-oriented reform, by the concept that state-owned assets are shared by all the people. Only by doing so shall we facilitate the perfection of the social security system and improve people's livelihood, and will potential demands be released. In broader sense, it will help to promote urbanization, stimulate enterprise innovation, and bring about transformation of economic development mode.

A Rationally Position and Define Logic Boundary of State-Owned Enterprises

State-owned enterprises in the real sense should only exist in links of the production of public goods and quasi-public goods where market fails to function or fails to provide public welfare services. From this point of view, current state-owned enterprises and their governing department are transitional entities. During the 13th Five-Year Plan period, the reform of state-owned enterprises does not simply mean reducing the number of state-owned enterprises. Apart from that goal, we aim to significantly reduce the capital and market share of state-owned enterprises and to expand the space for the development of private economy. We will rationally position the functions of state-owned enterprises, determine the logical boundary of state-owned enterprise, gradually phase out state-owned enterprises in competitive areas in the near and medium term, and transform them into mixed ownership companies with diversified equities. For state-owned enterprises in monopoly areas, we will classify them as monopolistic business or competitive business, split competitive business as soon as possible, and strengthen governmental supervision in nature monopoly industries. We will also step up market-oriented reforms in industries where natural monologue characteristics fade out due to technological progress and the transformation of market structure. Eventually, we aim to transform state-owned enterprises into non-profit entities constrained by public laws and establish an effective government structure.

B Replenish Social Security Funds with State-Owned Capital Withdrawn from State-Owned Enterprises

As people's enterprises, "state-owned enterprises" are not supposed to dispose all profits. Instead, they should turn some profits to the government as investment in social security. This move can effectively fill in the gap of social security fund, increase effective supply of basic public services, and significantly reduce tax burden for low-income groups. Besides, it can effectively limit the investment scale of "state-owned enterprises", reduce investment errors, and finally perfect the social security system. Thereby, three specific methods are proposed as follows:

1 Turn in Profits of State-Owned Enterprise to Supplement Social Security Funds

In principle, all the profits of the "state-owned enterprises" should be turned in to national finance. If state-owned enterprises need capital to develop business, competent departments need to make an examination before government allocates the money. Only a fool will hand over his or her hard-earned money to others without caring for loss or gain. The self-financing system is only applicable in the initial stage of the reform of state-owned enterprises.

After 30 years of the reform of state-owned enterprises, it is necessary to restore the original characteristics of "state-owned enterprises". For that purpose, we must accelerate the operational budget reform of state-owned capitals by raising the profit handover ratio of state-owned enterprises from current 5%–10% to 50% or more. All the profits turned in shall not be utilized within SASAC, but to be used to replenish the social security fund.

2 Allocation of Liquidated State-Owned Assets

During the "13th Five-Year Plan", we will continue to promote "state-owned enterprises" restructuring. Regardless of reform forms, through either implementation of mixed ownership or the overall transfer of property rights, all or some of the realized assets of reformed state-owned enterprises shall be appropriated to social security system.

3 State-Owned Shares to be Held by Social Security Fund

In the future, after the shareholding reform of "state-owned enterprises", state-owned shares shall be held by the social security agencies. For listed state-owned enterprises where state-owned shares occupy the biggest proportion, their state-owned shares shall gradually be held by social security institutions as well.

C Reposition Functions of State-Owned Assets Supervision and Administration Commission

The orientation of reforms in "state-owned enterprises" determines that SASAC is a transitional entity. However, even during the transitional period, the function of "SASAC" needs to be repositioned. To abandon the role of "mother-in-law and boss", SASAC shall change the management method of state-owned assets characterized by "state-owned assets preservation and appreciation". During the "13th Five-Year Plan", we will push forward the transformation of shareholding system in state-owned enterprises by focusing on "cost-revenue" relation of the liquidated state-owned assets and finalize the duties and evaluation criteria for SASAC. To achieve that goal, SASAC shall develop a comprehensive budget system covering both liquidating and operational budget system of state-owned assets. In addition, as guardian of state-owned assets, SASAC shall effectively lower payroll standards and restrain professional consumption behavior in state-owned enterprises.

IV Focus on Boosting Residents' Disposable Income to Intensify Income Distribution Reform

Lassalle once argued the main task of the socialist movement is to realize equalized distribution. Marx criticized that contention by stating that distributional relation is the other side of productive relation, and the irrationality of capitalist distribution fundamentally lies in the unreasonable private ownership of the means of production. In China, the gap between the rich and the poor is among the largest one across the world, and unequal distribution is extremely prominent. With ever-increasingly serious social contradiction emerging during the 13th Five-Year Plan period, strategic goals of economic development can hardly be achieved unless action is made to curb that momentum. In the reform of income distribution, the key to increase residents' disposable incomes lies in reasonable adjustment of the distribution of residents' property incomes as well as breakthrough in the reform of property rights system. Only by doing so can people truly share the fruits of economic growth and resident's income growth keep up with overall economic growth. The three aspects mentioned will help improve current national income structure. In particular, coordinated reform of state-owned enterprises and improvement of social security system is fundamentally important in terms of significantly reducing social security payment, raising social security standards for middle- and low-income groups, and turning those true owners of state-owned assets. Meanwhile, the following measures should be taken to push forward income distribution reform.

A Make Strict Restriction on Compensation Package of Executives in State-Owned Enterprises

In recent years, compensation package for the management, especially for the executives in China's state-owned enterprise management, is matching with that in large companies and giant multinational companies in developed economies. However, the risks assumed by managers at the state-owned enterprises and private enterprises are quite different. Against the basic principle of labor capital market, unreasonably high compensation in state-owned enterprises is a kind of misappropriation of public welfare. Hence, it is imperative to strictly limit compensation package for the executives in state-owned enterprises. We will establish rewards and punishment system in light of the characteristics of state-owned enterprises and make on overall reduction of compensation package standards.

B Push Forward Property Rights Reform of Natural Resources

As mentioned earlier, in China, unclearly determined property rights of natural resources not only lead to huge waste of resources but also facilitate embezzlement through private grants of mining rights among some people, which, as a result, has become the hotbed for power corruption and unfair social distribution. Besides, owing to the unclearly determined property rights, revenues of state-owned natural resources are inappropriately occupied by the central government and central enterprises, forming the income gap in different regions. Therefore, during the 13th Five-Year Plan period, mechanism reconstruction will be centered on the establishment of a rational sharing system of public resources revenues.

C Moderately Reduce Macro Tax Burden

Firstly, we need to establish a scientific and effective budget management system to strictly control financial budget and to ensure a reasonable reduction of macro tax through institutional methods. On such basis, we will moderately lower macro tax by centering on structural tax reduction. Meanwhile, we will reduce tax burdens on companies and residents to boost residents' disposable incomes. Besides, in order to streamline the taxation system for adjustment of personal income distribution, we will launch the reform of personal income tax by establishing a mixed personal income tax system that combines comprehensive declaration and classified deduction. We will establish and perfect property tax system to strengthen positive adjustment of distribution of incomes and social wealth.

D Promote the Market-Oriented Reform of Interest Rates, Improve Supervisory System of Capital Market

Under the control of China's government, deposit interest rate has been lower than the inflation rate for a long time. This is a statutory deprivation of the interests of the depositors (mainly the residents). In order to safeguard the legitimate interests of depositors, to guarantee reasonable growth of residents' property incomes, and to truly improve the quality of state-owned banks, it is necessary to promote the market-oriented reform of deposit interest rates by allowing the market supply and demand to determine the relation between deposit and loan interest rates. In addition, we will consummate the supervisory system of capital market through rules improvement, strict enforcement, and expansion of public participation to effectively supervise capital market, to restrict excessive speculation in the capital market, to improve quality of listed companies, to maintain the value-added function of capital market, and to protect the interests of small and medium-sized investors.

E Build Land Rights Protection Mechanism

As mentioned earlier, in China, since farmland is collectively owned, the government places various restriction on the disposal rights of farmland. In addition, currently, the management of urban construction land not only lacks flexibility, but it has evolved into a kind of governmental franchise, becoming a cash cow for local governments. As a consequence, farmers can hardly turn their possessed value-added assets to property incomes, which constitutes one of the reasons to push up real estate prices and push down disposable incomes of urban residents. In addition, we must loosen control over lands and make institutional changes in light of the development of socialist market economy with the aim of protecting land rights, optimizing distribution layout of residents' incomes, improving allocation efficiency of land resources, and promoting social harmony. In the long run, we will make sure supply and price of urban construction land will be independently determined between landowners and users under the government's city planning. Besides, in terms of the ownership rights and use rights of the rural farmland, we will guarantee buyers and sellers can directly make transactions according to law without governmental intervention.

F Promote Market-Oriented Reform and Develop Modern Supervisory System in Competitive Industries

The efficiency and price in monopoly industries are closely connected with the fair distribution of national incomes. Extremely high costs or high profits will over-occupy the public interests. In recent years, it has become a prevailing phenomenon that costs climb sharply and profits remain extraordinarily large in some industries. As consequence, we must advance the market-oriented reform in those sectors, expand market access requirements, lower entry threshold, and introduce social capitals into oligarchy areas that should have been highly competitive, including telecommunications, oil, and banking. We will see to it that price control system be flexible, namely, price control should be liberalized in highly competitive areas. We should speed up the establishment of a modern market economy-oriented supervision system to restrict high profits and unreasonable expenses of monopoly enterprises, and to curb the exploitation on consumers with the unreasonable rise of prices of products or services.

Bibliography

Bai Zhongen, Qian Zhenjie. "Distribution of the Elements of National Income: Story behind Statistics", *Economic Research*, vol. 3, 2009.

Economic Center at National Development and Reform Commission. "Research Report on China 2020: Trend and Strategy", 2011.

Liu Shujie. "On Modern Supervision Concept and China's Regulation Modernization", *Economic Review*, no. 6, 2011: 1–7.

Liu Shujie, Wang Yun. "A Study on Rational Adjustment of Residents' Incomes", *Macroeconomic Research*, no. 12, 2009: 11–16.

Mashiko Aoki, Wu Jianglian. *From Authority to Democracy: Political Economics in Sustainable Development*, Beijing: China Citic Press, 2008.

Wu Jinglian. "Let History Illuminate the Road of the Future: On China 's Reform on Market Economy", *Comparative Economic & Social System*, no. 5, 2009: 1–10.

5 Reform in Factor Markets in the 13th Five-Year Plan

Production factors, or factors for short, refer to the input for manufacturing products and providing services, including capital, labor, land, and resources. A complete market system includes not only the market of products or goods but also that of factors like capital, labor, land, and resource. China's reform in the product market has been a smooth process since the reform and opening-up, and now well developed. However, the reform of factor markets lagged behind, and the regulation over factor price led to the distortion of China's economy despite fueling the speedy growth of the latter. Therefore, market of factor prices reform is the focal and difficult point In the future reforms, centered by the realization of the marketing of fact prices. Chinese government laid great emphasis on such reforms at the Third Plenary Session of the 18th Central Committee of the CPC.[1]

However, the disputed and promoted factor market reforms, including that of finance, household registration, and land, have left on us the impression that "an empty barrel makes the biggest sound". There were many reasons for this. One of the important points was that those who implemented these reforms had poor knowledge of them, with neither any vision about the relations between the reform of factor market and that of goods market nor a general view for the analysis of the discrepancies seen and correlation between reforms of different factor markets. Only by intensifying the understanding about the reform of factor markets can we be tolerant of the negative reform bonus in a short time and anchoring force of policies before the reform bonus is realized in the long run, and thus to truly intensify the reform of factor markets. The following contents emphasize the three key questions. Why did the factor market reforms lag behind? Why do we need the factor market reforms? How shall we propel the factor market reforms?

I Reasons for Lag of Factor Market Reform and In-Place of Product Market Reform: Fulfilling Both Speedy Economic Growth and People's Living Needs at Low Costs

Presently, the product market reform is in place after several twists and turns. It was pointed out at the Third Plenary Session of the 12th Central

Committee of the CPC in 1984 that China's socialist economy is not equivalent to a planned economy but a commodity economy based on public ownership. The major problems of commodity economy and value laws broke away the bondage of the Left thought at the Third Plenary Session of the 12th Central Committee of the CPC, and fully started up the product market reform. The dual-track pricing system implanted in the 1980s, though playing the role of transit in the early time, led to the prominent problems of low efficiency in resource allocation and corruption in pursuit of seeking rent. In 1988, the central government proposed the initiative of "pass-crossing in pricing". To cross passes is a vivid metaphor to define the merging of the dual-track pricing system in a short time to adjust economy to balance with balanced price. The central government quickly declared to suspend the pricing reform, for the prices were unexpectedly far more out of control, although it was known previously that the form would be difficult to pass. After the failure of crossing such a pass, the dual-track pricing system of product market was gradually merged after rectifications until the resumption of relevant reforms in 1992. It was proposed at the Third Plenary Session of the 14th Central Committee of the CPC in 1993 to establish socialist market economy system. In this regard, the product market reform centered by pricing reform is fundamentally completed with the following details: first, the prices of most products are not decided by the government anymore. In 1992, China released the right of pricing for about 90% products by the government. This rate is higher now. Second, the main market players of most products were diversified and thus developed the balanced prices that were competitive but not monopolistic.

Although the reform of product market and the merging of dual-track pricing system were completed, the reform of factor market was lagging behind, and so was the property pricing reform, which was more complicated. There is still the dual-track pricing system for the coexistence of planned and market economy. Possibly, there are multiple reasons for the lag of factor market reform and for the product market reform to be in place. For example, compared to product markets, the vested interest groups in the dual-track pricing system of factor markets are stronger, which makes the reforms extreme slower. Additionally, the "pass-crossing in pricing" might easily fail, and the loose control over factor pricing might have butterfly effects, which shall exert more impact on China's economy and society. It will be risky to try such measure. Besides, the writer also believes that the essential reason for the reform of factor market and that of product market being out-of-sync is that such reform portfolio helps pursuing high-speed economic growth and fulfilling fundamental living needs of people at low costs. On the one hand, the reform of product markets bred the marketing product prices, which inspired the production enthusiasts of enterprises and increased the market supply of products. China thus turned from the seller's market with coupon-based supply for severe shortage of commodity in the early period of reform, to the buyer's market with affluent supply of goods in terms of volume and category. Upon key inspection by the Ministry of Commerce, it was found that of more than 600 kinds of goods, those with supply greater than demand were close to two-thirds and those with supply equal to demand were one-third.[2] On the other hand, the difficult operation of, and price control over, the factor market curbed the price of factors, thus reducing investment costs and greatly stimulating investment and exports, which developed the pivotal support for the high-speed economic growth.

Despite the discrepancy between different factor markets, the price regulation of all factors might stimulate overinvestment, as seen in the following paragraphs.

Firstly, for the capital market, interest rate regulation policies depressed loan rates and reduced capital costs. The economic growth theory and international experience show that the higher a country's economic growth rate, the higher will be the actual loan rate. From 1980 to 2010, China's actual GDP grow rate was 10%, while its actual loan rate was supposed to be approximately 7%. However, the actual loan rate under interest rate regulation was only 2%.[3] In comparison, in the corresponding period, the actual loan rate in Germany exceeded 8% that of the USA, Canada or France reach 5% or so, and that of Japan or Britain doubled as much as that of China. The actual loan rate of each of these countries was far higher than their economic growth rate. The interest rate regulation greatly reduced the capital costs of enterprises, especially state-owned enterprises, and provided stimulation for enterprise investment (Figure 5.1).

Secondly, for the labor market, low salary policy and household regulation system greatly reduced labor prices. In the context of demographic dividend, China's ample labor supply and deficiency in the negotiation system of labor markets led China to implement low salary policy for a long time.

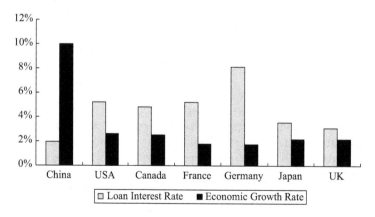

Figure 5.1 Actual loan rate and economic growth rate of China and major countries from 1980 to 2010.

Data source: calculation of data by World Bank.

Under the influence of low salary policy, China has obvious advantages in terms of labor prices, which greatly cut down the labor costs of enterprise investment. Take the salary of manufacturing workers, for example – the salary of Chinese workers is far lower than that in the USA, Japan, and OECD countries and even remarkably lower than other East Asian countries, Brazil, and other emerging economies. In 2002, the average hourly wage of a Chinese manufacturing worker was only USD0.6, which was equivalent of 2.2% of the average hourly wage of an American manufacturing worker and of 6.7% of the national average wage level of East Asian countries, excluding Japan. Later, with the enhancement of market regulation and further expansion of economic scale, China's labor costs increased. Despite this increase, China's manufacturing hourly wage was only 5.7% of that in the United States of America and 7% of the national average level of OECD countries.[4]

Thirdly, for the land market, the government, by virtue of its monopoly position in the land market, provided a great deal of cheap land for industrial usage, which encouraged people interested in enterprise investment. The land market in China is highly distorted. On the one hand, through the system of land acquisition, bid invitation, auction, and listing with Chinese characteristics, the government pushed the commercial land price and residential land price to a high level to get substantial revenue out of selling land. In 2013, China's total revenue of land remises amounted to RMB4.13 trillion, surpassing the previous high of RMB3.15 trillion in 2011; the land remise revenue was 32% of the national fiscal revenue and 60% of local government fiscal revenue. On the other hand, the price of industrial land remained extremely low due to the low cost of land acquisition, as well as the pressed-down land prices released in succession by local governments out of fierce competition between them to attract foreign business and investment. From 2000 to 2011, the price of industrial land increased from RMB451 per square meter to RMB807 per square meter, up 1.8 times; later, the price of industrial land fell to RMB670 per square meter in 2012 and RMB700 per square meter in 2013.[5] During the same term, the price of commercial land and residential land increased by 4.5 and 6.7 times, respectively.[6] These two aspects effectively stimulated the investment in real estate and industry, respectively.

Fourth, in terms of the resource market, the government brought down the cost of resource that was supposed to be borne by enterprises, and stimulated the expansion of investment of enterprises. For a long time, as the prices of water, electricity, natural gas, and other important resources inevitable for production of enterprises were controlled by the government, the resource costs that China's enterprises shouldered were much lower than international regulations. Take the price of water, for example, where an investigation by Global Water Intelligence in 2011 showed that the average price of water in 25 main cities in China was USD0.46 per cubic meter, while the international average price of water was USD2.03 per cubic meter, 4.4 times as much as that in China.[7] As for electricity prices, when production cost of power generation enterprises was on a constant rise, the price of electricity remained low. In 2007, the industrial electricity price in China was USD0.068 per kWh, equivalent to 72% of that of OECD countries, much lower than that of Japan, which was USD0.12 per kWh, and Britain, where the price was USD0.13 per kWh.[8] In terms of natural gas prices, in 2007, the industrial natural gas price of China was USD281.9 per GCV,[9] in OECD countries USD336.6 per GCV, France USD414.1 per GCV for 1.5 times as much as that of China, and ROK USD551.1 per GCV for twice as much as that of China.[10]

Fifth, in terms of the environmental market, Chinese local governments significantly attached more importance to economic growth than to ecological environment, which resulted in the enterprises polluting the environment at extremely low expense. A local government of one place, in order to quickly develop economy and prevail in competition with that of another place, could even acquiesce to the establishment and existence of high-pollution enterprises and even become the protector for enterprises responsible for high pollution. It made many laws and regulations related to environmental protection, which were passed by the Chinese government, practically perform no function. According to statistics, from 1998 to 2002, there were 387 major and extra serious environmental pollution accidents in China, but only 25 of them were investigated for legal responsibility. From 2003 to 2007, there were more than 90 major and dangerous environmental pollution accidents in China, but only 12 of them were investigated for legal responsibility.[11] Besides, different from the United States of America and other developed countries, China enforced the maximum amount of penalty against corporate environmental pollution and ecological damage behaviors[12] and considered the continuous illegal discharge of pollution to be a violation, which would punishable. Such provision greatly reduced the punishment that China's environment-polluting enterprises would face.[13]

The factor price regulation supports high growth as it can not only stimulate enterprise investment but also increase the international competitiveness of the products and significantly promote export growth. The fundamental reason for China to be mentioned as a "world factory" is that the low cost of production has created the price advantage of export products. The low prices of labor, capital, major resource products, and other production factors have provided export enterprises advantage of low costs, where the low labor costs play a significant role. From 2004 to 2010, China's unit output labor cost[14] was only 8.4% that of Germany, 11.7% of Japan, and 15.8% of the United States of America. Compared with Mexico, the Philippines, and other competitors, China's labor cost advantage was also remarkable. As for the processing trade mode of "putting both material purchasing and product selling at the oversea market", labor costs determine the final costs. Thanks to low labor costs, China has been rapidly raising its share in the international markets by vigorously developing processing trade and has become the world's largest exporter. Of its total exports, China's processing trade accounted for the increase from 5% in 1981 to 56.8% in 1996, and later around 50% for a long period. In and after 2006, such proportion was in declination, but remained as high as 42.1% in 2012.

Factor price regulation provided China's high investment with strong stimulation, created prominent cost advantage for its exports, and therefore resulted in dual-wheel-driven growth mode of high investment and high exports, which was the backbone for the high growth of Chinese economy. This emphasizes that there was a linkage mechanism between Chinese exports and investment. The rapid increase of exports promoted the further expansion of investment scale, consume the large productivity in investment expansion, and maintain considerable investment income, which sustained the high investment development mode. Especially when China joined WTO in 2001, low- and medium-end manufacturing industries were gradually shifted from developed countries and regions to Chinese mainland that provided cheap production factors; meanwhile, the international competitiveness of cheap Chinese products grew stronger, which gradually developed into export-oriented economy. China economy therefore made remarkable achievements as follows: in terms of world GDP, China's GDP accounted for an increase from 1.9% in 1980 to 11.3% in 2012. In 1978, China's GDP ranked tenth in the world. It ranks second now, and possibly up to the first in 2014, calculated according to purchasing power parity, exceeding America. Therefore, objectively speaking, given that the product market reform satisfies people's basic living needs, factor price regulation can support rapid economic growth. In accordance with the core idea of the Party's ruling for the people, it will enhance the stability of political power, with undeniable historical and periodical significance.

II Factor Market Distortion Leads to Severity of China Structural Distortion Caused by Imbalance of Income Distribution, Total Demand, and Consumption

To confirm the active role of factor market regulation does not mean that the growing costs can be ignored. In the context of the dual-track pricing system of the factor market, it is inevitably to meet with the problems of poor efficiency of resource allocation and possibility of corruption generated in rent-seeking. To make matters worse, the factor market regulation resulted in the imbalance of severe distortion due to structural imbalance of income distribution, total demand, and consumption.

1 Severe Structural Imbalance of Income Distribution

At present, China's income inequality is on a constant growth. Data from National Bureau of Statistics showed that the income Gini coefficient of China was only 0.29 in 1981, but quickly exceeded the international warning line of 0.4, maintained 0.47 for a long time, and reached its historic peak value of 0.49. In contrast, the mean value of income Gini coefficient of OECD countries in 2005 was only 0.31. Furthermore, two types of evidence indicate that the official income Gini coefficient has been underestimated: first, investigation results of some institutions show that China's income Gini coefficient is higher than that mentioned. According to the investigation results from the Institute of Social Science Survey of Peking University and National Survey Research Center at Renming University of China, China's Gini coefficient exceeded 0.5 in 2009. Survey and Research Center for China Household Finance of Southwestern University of Finance and Economics also pointed out that the Gini coefficient was 0.61 in 2010. Second, if the "hidden income" is taken into consideration, China's income inequality will be further increased. Research shows that with the "hidden income" included, the revenue of highest income group was 26 times as much as that of the lowest income group of the China's urban families in 2008, far higher than the officially announced figure of nine times. Owing to the acceleration of the income growth of low-income households in recent years, such figure actually reduced to 20.9 times in 2011, still higher than the officially announced figure of 8.6 times.[15]

The author summarized the causes of the growing income inequality of China into six main aspects: non-balanced development strategy, initial distribution imbalance, reversal regulation of second distribution, fortune-making without innovation, deformed development of real estate market, and intergenerational solidifying of gap between the rich and poor.[16] Among the six aspects, initial distribution imbalance is of paramount importance, while the factor market regulation is the key reason for initial distribution imbalance. At present, the initial distribution imbalance in China is severe. The proportion of the residents' disposable income accounted for GNI (gross national income) dropped from 63.2% in 1993 to 50.6% in 2007, while that of the enterprise and government revenues accounted for GNI, respectively, increased from 19.8% and 20% in 1993 to 24.6% and 24.7% in 2007. From 1996 to 2006, the proportion of the disposable income of national resident department of most OECD countries accounted for GNI was between 72% and 80%.[17]

So, how does the factor market regulation lead to initial distribution imbalance? The income of Chinese urban residents comprise of wage income, net operating income, property income, and transfer income; the income of rural residents is made up of wage income, family operation income, property income, and transfer income, among which transfer income is non-factor income, and the rest are factor income. For a long time, most of Chinese residents' income was derived from factor income. Data from National Bureau of Statistics showed that the income of urban residents in 2012 accounted for 76.4% of the total residents' income, while that of rural residents accounted for 92.4%. The reason was that the resident department was the provider of capital, labor, and land; although factor price regulation was good for the government and enterprises to expand investment by virtue of low cost incentive, the income of residents' department would dramatically decline.

As far as capital market is concerned, interest rate regulation resulted in damage to household property income. Concerning the imperfection of China's financial industry and the shortage of more attractive resident-oriented investment channels than bank deposits, the proportion of Chinese residents occupied a high percentage of GNI. In 2012, the urban household capital in type of deposits of China reached 23.7%, while deposits of 10% of the poorest urban households accounted for 33.5%. In 2010, the household capital in type of deposits and cash of USA accounted for only 4.3%, and the deposits and cash of 10% of the poorest households of USA accounted for only 16.5%.[18] Interest rate regulation seriously depressed deposit rates, so the interest income of Chinese households was low. From 1996 to 2003, the actual deposit rate was up to 3%; the proportion of household interest income accounting for GDP was between 5% and 6%. From 2004 to 2012, the actual deposit rate plunged to −0.3%; the proportion of household interest income accounting for GDP starkly declined, down to 2.5% in 2009, while it increased from 45% to about 70% in the context of the proportion of household savings versus GDP.[19]

As far as the labor market is concerned, the labor market distortion led to the low-wage income of ordinary workers. The example of the salary of manufacturing workers showed that the wage income of Chinese workers was significantly low, lower than the United States of America, Japan, and other developed countries, and lower than Brazil, Mexico, and other emerging economies. The comparison with other countries brought us the findings that the proportion of Chinese workers' compensation versus GDP was also low, which reflected the fact that the wage income was low again. In 2011, the proportion of Chinese workers' compensation versus GDP accounted for 44.9%; while that of America reached 55.4%, with France, Germany, the United Kingdom, and Japan, respectively, accounting for 53.5%, 51.6%, 53.7%, and 50.6%.[20]

In terms of the land market, local government monopolized land acquisition rights and farmers were not entitled to dispose land. The local government did not provide enough protection and compensation in land expropriation for the rights and interest of farmers, which caused the poor revenue obtained by rural residents based on land contracting. The national investigation launched by Kong Xiangzhi in 2006 on the farmers who lost land showed that, on average, the farmers who were willing to take benefits from land acquisition were five times, on average, more than those who were willing to receive compensation.[21] The results of the survey by Ye Jianping and Tian Chenguang in 2013 also indicated that the compensation of landless farmers, on average, was RMB 17,000 per mu (RMB1,133.33 per hectare), with median value of RMB 12,000 per mu (RMB 800 per hectare), whereas the average price of confiscated land transferred by the local governments was RMB778,000 per mu (RMB 51,866.67 per hectare), with median value of RMB200,000 per mu (RMB13,333.33 per hectare).[22]

2 Drastic Balance of Total Demand Structure

Distortion of factor market is beneficial to investment and exports, but not to consumption. There are three major systems for it: first, low factor costs under regulation of the factor market, especially low interest rates, are conducive to investment stimulation. Second, low factor costs under regulation of the factor market, especially labor competitive advantage in low salary, enhance the international competitiveness of China's products and result in export growth. Third, the low factor income of residents under regulation of the factor market makes the disposable income low and eventually curbs residents' consumption.

Under the influence of the above three mechanism, severe imbalance arose in the structure of China's total demand is embodied in the ultra-high investment rate and extreme low consumption rate of resident sector. The investment rate increased from 35% in 2000 to 48.5% in 2011. In comparison, the average investment rate of the globe was only about 20%. Even upon overview of the history, the peak value of investment rates of all countries was prominently lower than China: that of OECD countries was only 26%; that of Japan, ROK, and Singapore, respectively, 38.8%, 39.7%, and 46.9%; the three emerging economies of Brazil, Mexico, and India, respectively 26.9%, 27.4%, and 38%. It has become an indisputable fact that China's investment rate has climbed to a high level, or there is a situation of overinvestment by more and more research institutions.[23] While the investment rate continues to rise, the consumption rate of the Chinese residential sector has been declining all the way, and has now fallen to the bottom line of international and historic data. The consumption rate of China's resident department reduced from 65% in 1970s, to 34% at present, much lower than the average global level of 60%. Undoubtedly, China's current total demand structure has stepped into severe imbalance mode. This is characterized by ultra-high investment rate and increases risks of overheated economy and excessive capital bubbles and production capacity, which weakens the continuity of economic growth. In addition, the ultra-high investment rate even "squeezed out" the resident consumption rate, which did not increase with the growth of economy. This will trigger social problems in the long run.

3 Structural Imbalance of Consumption: Overseas Consumption Replaces Domestic One

China's consumption demand resulted in the recession of consumption due to ultra-low disposable income, excessive preventive savings, as well as the consumption transfer from overseas market to domestic market. Statistics showed that the shopping expenses of China's outbound tourists exceeded one-third of the total consumption. Besides, consumption transfer could lead the outflow of fortune. China Luxury Brand Consumption Report 2014 presented that in 2013, the total market volume of global luxury products was USD217 billion, including local consumption of USD28 billion, overseas spending of USD74 billion, and Chinese luxury product consumption, which accounted for 47% of the total amount of global luxury product consumption.

The superficial reason for consumption transfer was the "external appreciation but internal depreciation" of renminbi. On the one hand, from the exchange rate reform in 2005 to the end of 2013, renminbi versus US dollar accumulatively appreciated 35.7%, which made renminbi cheaper in offshore shopping. On the other hand, China's CPI increased by 25% in the corresponding period. If we take into consideration the rise of housing prices, the increase of CPI would be more astounding. Therefore, compared with domestic consumption, renminbi could buy more foreign goods, which stimulated the enthusiasm of Chinese residents for overseas consumption.

The main reason for consumption transfer was the regulation of factor market. The regulation of interest rate and exchange rate, important components of regulation of capital market, commonly caused the tremendous amount of currency supply. The inflation stemming from it further weakened the domestic purchasing power of renminbi. Therefore, in the context of external appreciation of renminbi, residents would prefer overseas consumption through various channels.

The consequences of consumption transfer were seen in domestic enterprises struggling to survive and in curbed domestic consumption, instantiated by the positive value of CPI but constant negative value of PPI on and after March 2012. Furthermore, the wealthy owned more channels for outbound shopping than the poor. It sharpened the protruding social contradictions in the context of extreme disparity in fortune distribution in China, which would be against social stability.

III How to Intensify Factor Market Reform without Repeating Mistakes of "Pass-crossing in Pricing" and Prevent Collapse of China Economy

Fortunately, there is consensus about factor market reforms in the government, though with few agreements on the total reforms. Under the promotion of hard-earned consensus about reforms, the factor market reforms were enforced. However, we shall pay attention to the following aspects to ensure the intensification of factor market reforms and avoid collapse of China's economy and failure of reforms.

1 Factor Market Reforms: To Construct Complete Competitive Factor Market System Instead of Easing Pricing Regulation

An erroneous view was put forward that as long as the government relaxes price controls and allows free market pricing, the pricing of production factors can be market-oriented. A complete competitive market system is composed of four aspects: first, fair production factor trading market; second, a production factor price formation mechanism based on demand and supply in the market rather than on government instruction; third, market diversification to ensure that the market price is competitive rather than monopolized; fourth, clear property rights of production factors. At present, China performs well in terms of the first aspect, "fair production factor trading market", rather than of the remaining three aspects. If China only performed the second aspect, relaxing government's control over pricing, instead of making further reforms, a sophisticated competitive factor market system still could not come into being.

First, the market-oriented reforms refer to the marketing of competitive markets. Only diversified market players can ensure the market price to be a competitive one rather than a monopoly one. The market structure can be divided into four kinds: monopoly market, oligopoly market, monopolistic competition market, and fully competitive market. The prices developed in the former two kinds of market structures are not competitive market prices, but those developed in the latter two kinds are. As for factor markets, if the market players are in small number or even single, even if the government relaxes price control to allow free market pricing, a competitive market-oriented price in the true sense shall not be obtained. It deserves our special attention.

In the case of interest rate markets, the liberalization deposit interest rates are entirely the interest rate marketization. In other words, the deposit interest rate liberalization is not the last step in interest rate marketization reforms.[24] The premise for interest rate marketization is the establishment and improvement of a series of basic systems, including market player diversification, deposit insurance system, financial institution withdrawal system, and market-based nomination system of senior management personnel. The reforms in these basic systems are more complex and difficult, influencing more stakeholders' interests than simply opening up deposit rates. In particular, it is necessary to break the market access of banks and monopoly of state-owned banks in order to allow more private capital to establish private banks, especially large private banks, to promote market player diversification, and thus to promote the market-orientation of interest rates. Therefore, even if the interest rates are liberalized, interest rate marketization shall still go through a long way requiring far more than one to two years. Of course, only the opening up of deposit interest rate already had great impact on China's economy because the income of interest rate spreads accounts for a high share of the profits of state-owned banks, and the survival and development of state-owned enterprises and local government investing and financing platform also demand low-cost funds under financial repression.

Second, the clear property rights of production factors are the premise of factor price marketization, and the premise of the free flow of production factors for market transactions. On the contrary, the unclear property rights will make it hard to reflect the interests of owners and the external costs in factor prices. The property rights play a crucial role in the marketization of land and mineral resources. Concerning the factor of land, if the land ownership is unclear and the land use rights of farmers are not put into comprehensive practice, even if the local government is required to compensate the farmers whose lands are expropriated, equivalent of releasing price regulation as opposed to the regulation on compensation on the basis of land original use, it will still be possible for the local government to confiscate the land as the land owner. In the meantime, the farmers still have enough capacity for price negotiation, which will make the land price not truly market-oriented. As for mineral resources, the existing laws only generalize that the ownership of all mineral resources pertains to the nation, without clearly defining the right to use and to yield. Firstly, it resulted in the separation of the right to use mineral resources from the right to yield them. Only a handful of state-owned enterprises monopolized the right to use of mineral resources via free allocation and occupied the right to yield them that was supposed to belong to the whole nation. Secondly, it made the mineral resource enterprises bear only the direct cost of extraction instead of the indirect costs of environment governance and ecology compensation. If we do not make property reforms, but simply open up price regulation, most likely a few state-owned enterprises will continue to access mineral resources for free or at extreme low cost. Even so, they might still ignore the external effects like environmental pollution and ecological destruction, which finally would lead to the failure of completely market-oriented pricing of mineral resources.

2 Differentiate, Categorize, and Sequence Reforms of Factor Markets Rather than Generalize and Urge Them

According to the difficulty of reforms and possibility for a breakthrough, the factor market reforms ought to be categorized into three types, which need to be differentiated and sequentially advanced. It is unreasonable to attempt to accomplish the total reforms at one stroke.

The first type of factor market reforms is comparatively easier than the others because of its clear reform orientation, like market-oriented financial reforms centered by market-oriented interest rate, market-oriented exchange rate, and renminbi free convertibility. Superficially, such kind of reforms is hard to advance, as it influences the benefits of the powerful vested interest groups, including the government, state-owned banks, and state-owned enterprises. However, as opposed to other factor market reforms, just because it is the country whose benefits would be influenced, the reforms were promoted in a smoother way. The fundamental tenet of CPC is to serve the people whole-heartedly, just as the Party Constitution stipulates,

> the Communist Party only cares for the interests of the working class
> and the broad masses of the people, instead of its the special interests

of its own. The Communist Party put the interests of the people in the first place at any time..., doing everything for the masses, relying on them in tasks and carrying out the principle of 'from the masses, to the masses'.[25,26]

Based on the above logics, as long as prompt and resolute decisions are made, the first kind of reform can take the lead in success.

The second type of factor market reforms is comparatively difficult, mainly because the legal obstacles have resulted in unclear thoughts and immature pilot experience, especially in land market reform and resource market reform. The difficulty lies in that the reform of property rights is not straightened out in the interim term. Take the land market reform as an example; because of the ill-defined relevant laws, the rights of ownership and usage of land were not effectively implemented, which led to repeated violations of farmers' land rights. For example, the Land Management Law stipulated that "the rural land pertains to the collectives of farmers", and that "out of the needs of public interest, the country is legally entitled to claim land expropriation or requisition and make compensation". Concerning such provisions, the connotations of "collective" and "public interest" herein were once in obscurity. Thus, all levels of the government were able to expropriate land from farmers in the name of "collective" and "public interest". Take another example. The "property law" stipulated that "the right to use such collectively-owned land as cultivated land, house sites, land and hilly land allotted for private use, except for those mortgageable as prescribed by any law, may not be mortgaged". The financial function of the right to use the contracted land by farmers is restrained, which made the right to use land not available for fund-raising for agricultural production. Such reforms are related to the regulation and improvement of legislation, which is quite difficult.

The third type of factor market reforms, the labor market reforms, appears simple but is in fact the most difficulty.. The labor market reforms mainly include the reform of household registration system. As it involves great adjustment of the pattern of vested interest groups, the household registration system reform faces the resistance not only from local governments but also from the majority of urban residents. Such kind of factor market reforms is therefore the most difficult. First, the household registration system reform will add much more burden on local governments, who have not implemented incentive to promote it. Taking the household registration as the threshold, local governments can block the access of migrant workers to the urban and town public service system to reduce financial burden and utilize cheap labor to promote economic development. Upon the reform of household registration system, the government shall provide medical care, education, social security, and other public services for the newly registered residents and shall not have cheap labor, which is detrimental to local governments. Second, the reform of the household registration system will affect the interest of urban and town residents, with one of the most prominent problems in education. The children of the newly registered urban and town residents have to share the limited educational resources with those of the existing ones. Under the current enrollment quota allocation system of college entrance examination, the children of newly registered urban and town residents even directly "grab" the enrollment quota of those of the existing ones; meanwhile, the existing urban and town residents spare no efforts in preventing household registration system reform. Therefore, in advancing the reforms, it is necessary to further emancipate the minds of urban and town residents, top-level design by the central government, and have the central and local governments at all levels pay for the bill of reforms. Therefore, the household registration reform will be difficult.[27]

3 Impact of Factor Market Reforms: Not Enough to Lead to Collapse of China's Economy under Positive Development of Private Economy

To prolong factor market reforms is simply based on two aspects of considerations. The first one is that price control helps to reduce production costs to encourage investment and exports to maintain rapid economic growth, and the second one is if market reforms will lead to China's economic collapse. The first one has little significance now, as it has brought about serious economic distortion and unsustainable growth. The second one seems reasonable, especially when the current Chinese economy has ushered in sub-high growth with slow growth. China's economy has a characteristic, that is, when the situation is good, the authority prefers to summarize the experience, upgrade it into a new pattern, and lose the impetus to reform; on the other hand, when the situation becomes worse, the authority will be fearful of the impact of reforms on China's economy and will have no willingness to reform. Reforms are always much more declared than made. Under such logics, there will never be any chance for any reform to occur to the factor markets. Obviously, this is wrong. Therefore, it is necessary to clarify the second consideration that might delay reforms.

The reform bonus of the factor market reforms is to be found in the long run, and difficult to be seen in a short time or even likely to appear as negative dividend. The factor market reforms indeed impact China's economy, especially obvious in the state-owned enterprises. Take the interest rate marketization as an example. After such reform, China's actual loan interest rates will rise, so will the capital costs; and the investment activities of the whole society will be curbed. The author's research results show that after interest rate marketization, China's actual loan interest rate will increase from 3.66% to 4.59%, that is, by 25.4%. Under this influence, the production scale of the whole society will significantly shrink, with the total social capital stock falling by 10.3% and the total output declining by

7.2%.[28] After interest rate marketization, state-owned enterprises will bear the brunt. As they can get preferential loans, the actual loan interest rate that state-owned enterprises undertook from 2001 to 2009 was only 1.6%, while the market lending rate was 4.68%. If state-owned enterprises apply for loan at the market interest rate, they need to additionally pay the interest for RMB2.75 trillion, accounting for 47% of the net profit in the same period. Meanwhile, after the market-oriented reform of interest rate, the actual loan interest rate will further increase and the production scale of state-owned sectors may be quickly declined.[29] If the market-oriented reforms in the factors of labor, land, and resources are simultaneously carried out, the investment costs of enterprises, especially state-owned enterprises, will further increase. It is expected that the total output will reduce in a greater scale. Therefore, the impact of factor market reforms on China's economy is a force to be reckoned with.[30]

The simultaneous advancement of the reforms of factor markets and state-owned enterprises can maximize the reduction of negative bonus of reforms. The premise for factor market reforms to impact China's economy is that they are separately carried out while other conditions remain unchangeable. If they are not carried out separately but jointly with other aspects of reforms, it will actively develop the private economy and will not result in the collapse of China's economy. China's reforms include the reforms of economy system and the government[31] and legal system. The economic system reforms mainly include factor market reforms and state-owned enterprises reforms. If the factor market reforms are implemented in line with restraining monopoly of state-owned enterprises and actively developing the private economy, the impact of factor market reforms on China's economy will be limited. Take the interest rate marketization as an example. The loan interest rate after the reforms is higher than that before the reforms, which has an adverse impact on the state-owned enterprises that have obtained cheap loans. However, as for the private enterprises that can only obtain loans at high rate in the dual-track interest rate system, the acquired loan rate after the forms might be even lower than that before the reforms. Therefore, it means good news for such enterprises, especially for those excellent ones which can take higher factor prices.[32] In this regard, the development of private economy can reduce the impact of the interest rate marketization. For a long time, the important industries of electric power, telecommunications, oil, and finance have been monopolized by state-owned enterprises, though theoretically, the "new 36 articles (of provisions from Several Opinions of the State Council on Encouraging and Guiding the Healthy Development of Private Investment in 2010" and the "old 36 articles (of provisions from Several Opinions of the State Council on Encouraging, Supporting and Guiding the Development of Non-Public Economy, including Individual Private Economy in 2005)" have greatly improved the opening of monopoly industries to private economy. However, in fact, the prevalent existence of the "glass door", "spring door", and other hidden obstacles continue to hinder the access of small and medium-sized private enterprises.[33] To develop the private economy in a true sense, China is supposed to intensify the reform of state-owned enterprises, restrain the monopoly of state-owned enterprises, and create wide scope of development for private enterprises.

IV Conclusion

Concerning the total quantity of reform and opening up in the three decades, China has made brilliant economic achievements, though with distortion in its economic structure. Subjectively speaking, the structural distortion presented by the structural imbalance of income distribution and total demand in China's economy came from the factors of development mode, development stage, and international division, with historical necessity. However, China today is different from that in 1978. In 2013, China's GDP per capita was nearly USD7,000. Since then, China has ascended from a low-income country in the early period of reform, to be among the middle-income countries with the upper level and has started to keep abreast with high-income countries. As quoted by Mao Zedong, "the strong pass of the enemy is like a wall of iron, yet with firm strides, we are conquering its summit". Standing at the new historical stage, it is important for us to realize the following factors: the erosion against national sense of happiness due to the huge costs out of economic distortion; the orientation of development to national sense of happiness instead of merely growth; the most critical position of factor market distortion among various reasons for economic distortion, with the reform in factor market distortion being the key to address the distortion and to adjust the structure. In promotion of the factor market reforms, we have to build up a perfect competitive market system, distinguish and classify the reform of different factor markets, and correlate with the reform of state-owned enterprises. Only with these measures can we intensify the reform of factor markets, avoid repeating the mistakes of "pass-crossing in pricing", and prevent the collapse of China economy.

Notes

1 As put forward at the Third Plenary Session of the 18th Central Committee of the CPC,

> Establishing a unified, open, competitive and orderly market system is the basis for the market to play a decisive role in the allocation of resources. We must put in place a modern market system in which enterprises enjoy independent management and fair competition, consumers have free choice and make autonomous consumption decisions, products and factors of production flow freely and are exchanged on an equal basis.

It was also stated that China will "ensure that all economic sectors have equal access to the factors of production according to the law" by "improving the property rights protection system".

2 Zhang Zhuoyuan, 2008: "Thirty Years of China's Price Reform: Effect, Course and Prospect", *Red Flag Manuscript*, Issue No. 23.

3 For calculation method of theoretical loan interest rates, see: Chen Yanbin, Chen Xiaoliang, Chen Weize, 2014: "Interest Rate Regulation and Total Demand Structural Imbalance", *Economic Research*, Issue No. 2.

4 Foreign data quoted from the website of US Department of Labor, while Chinese data in 2010 quoted from Boston Consulting Group. 2011. "Made in America, Again: Why Manufacturing Will Return to the U.S.", Working Paper.

5 Data source: China Urban Land Price Dynamic Monitor.

6 Data source: China Urban Land Price Dynamic Monitor.

7 Source: "China Moving Forward with New Water-price Plan", *The Wall Street Journal*, January 3, 2014.

8 Source: Wang Qiankun, Hu Zhaoyi, Li Qionghui, 2009: "Comparison and Analysis of Electricity Price of China and Other Major Countries", *Electric Power Technologic Economics*, Issue No. 6.

9 GCV refers to gross thermal value, the unit of measurement of natural gas.

10 Source: Wang Qiankun, Hu Zhaoyi, Li Qionghui, 2009: "Comparison and Analysis of Electricity Price of China and Other Major Countries", *Electric Power Technologic Economics*, Issue No. 6.

11 Source: Qie Jianrong, "Non-act of the Government Is the Main Source of Environmental Crux," *Legal Daily*, November 15, 2011.

12 The law of Water Pollution Prevention provides that the maximum fine against the enterprises that cause serious water pollution accidents is one million yuan, and for air pollution accidents is 500,000 yuan.

13 In contrast, the Toxic Substances Control Act (TSCA) of the USA provides that to continue one day of an illegal act of enterprises will be regarded as a new one, and every time of an illegal act shall be fined below USD32,500, with no bottom line.

14 Because of the huge differences in labor productivity of different countries, the labor productivity changes with different tendency. The comparison of salary level cannot correctly reflect the true differences in unit labor cost in different countries. To this end, the International Labor Organization constructs the index of unit outcome labor cost. It reflects the relative momentum of a country's labor cost and labor productivity and applies to the international comparison on labor costs.

15 Source: Wang Xiaolu, 2010: "Distribution of Gray Income and National Income", *Comparison,* Issue No. 4; Wang Xiaolu, 2013: "Distribution of Gray Income and National Income (Annual Report of 2013)", *Comparison,* Issue No. 5.

16 Source: Chen Yanbin, "Institutional Reasons and Reform Ideas for China's Wealth Gap", www.ifeng.com, November 2, 2013.

17 Data source: Liang Ji, 2012: "International Comparison and Analysis of National Income Distribution Pattern", *Local Finance Research*, Issue No. 8.

18 China's data are calculated according to Aordo (2012), and that of the United States according to SCF (2010).

19 Data source: Nicholas Lardy, "To Promote China's Economic Growth with Interest Rate Liberalization", *21st Century Business Herald*, May 25, 2013.

20 China's data are calculated according to China Statistical Yearbook (2013), foreign data according to International Statistical Yearbook (2013), Japan's data according to the data in 2010.

21 Kong Xiangzhi, Gu Hongming, Han Jijiang, 2006: "Investigation Report on Status of Landless Farmers and Their Willingness for Expropriation Compensation", *Economic Theory and Economic Management*, Issue No. 7.

22 Ye Jianping, Tian dawn, 2013: "Status of Contract Pattern, Institutional Change and Policy Optimization in China's Rural Land Rights: Analysis of Survey

Data of 1956 Farmers in 17 Provinces", *Journal of Huazhong Normal University (Social Science Edition)*, Issue No. 1.

23 Li Daokui et al. (2012) found that China's actual investment rate was 15% higher than welfare maximization rate. Lee et al. (2012) calculated that China's current investment rate was 12% to 20% higher than the gold rate. Li Daokui, Xu Xin, Jiang Hongping, 2012: "Analysis of Welfare Economics China's National Economy Investment Rate, *Economic Research* Issue No. 9; II Houng Lee, Muraza Syed and Liu Xueyan, 2012, "Is China Over-Investing and Does it Matter?", IMF working paper WP/12/277.

24 On March 12, 2014, Zhou Xiaochuan, president of the Central Bank of China, pointed out that "the deposit interest rate liberalization can be realized in one or two years, which is the last step of market orientation of interest rate".

25 In the Communist Manifesto, Marx and Engels pointed out that in the past, all campaigns were led by a minority of people or for the interest of a minority of people. Now, the proletarian campaigns are an independent one led by the majority of people and for the interest of the majority of the people.

26 Adhering to the purpose of serving the people heart and soul is the highest value orientation of Communist Party of China. To realize the interest of the people with the support of the masses of Chinese people is the highest standard that measures whether CPC's routine, principles and policies are correct. A basic experience of CPC in its 90 years of struggles is to always keep in mind the purpose of serving the people wholeheartedly, closely rely on the masses, faithfully striving for benefits for the people and drawing inexhaustible strength from the masses of the people.

27 There are two key issues to be noticed about the labor market reforms. First, what is more critical and more profound than the welfare issue behind the household registration is the issue of fairness and intergeneration between people. Second, the ultimate goals of the labor market are to establish the nationwide free flow of labor markets to make all kinds of laborers able to vote even with their feet, able to migrate to any place at their will, and able to live or settle down at their will at any places of work, including Beijing and Shanghai. Such goals are available in almost all of the other countries, but far more than realistic for China. It requires great courage and imagination to make it come true. Premier Li Keqiang pointed out in the Report of the Premier in 2014 that "in the upcoming period, we should focus on solving the existing problem of 'three 100 million people', namely, to promote a relocated population of approximately 100 million agricultural people to settle in urban and town, to renovate rundown urban areas and villages in the cities that about 100 million people live, as well as to guide the urbanization of central and western regions with approximately 100 million people living nearby."

28 Source: Chen Yanbin et al. (2014).

29 Source: Sheng Hong, 2012: "Nature, Performance and Reforms of State-owned Enterprises", *Chinese Private Science and Technology and Economy*, Issue No. 6.

30 In promoting the factor market reforms, investing and economic growth may show a significant decline in the short term and thus affect social stability. However, the direction of reforms cannot be swayed, and the factor market reforms may not be prolonged because of any change or orientation. As for the social stability problems brought by advancement of reforms, we should give full play to the underpinning role of social policies and address it through appropriate social policies.

31 The focal points for transformation of the governmental functions from the "development-oriented government" to "public-service-oriented government" include the reform of local government performance evaluation system, the reform of financial system, the reform of administrative examination and approval system, and so on.

32 After investigation, Li Jianjun and Hu Fengyun (2013) found that the average financing cost of small- and-medium-sized enterprises via banks and other channels, on average, was 9.7%, and that via shadow credit markets, on average, 18.28%, which greatly exceeded the benchmark of lending rates. Li Jianjun, Hu Fengyun, 2013: "Development of Financing Structure, Financing Costs and Shadow Credit Markets of China's Small-and-medium-sized Enterprises", *Macroeconomic Research*, Issue No. 5.

33 Take oil industry as an example; the Technical Specification of Regulations of Refined Oil Product Wholesale Enterprises issued by the Ministry of Commerce provided that the registered capital for applying for establishing wholesale enterprises of refined oil products shall be no less than 30 million yuan and that the processing capacity for raw oil per time shall be more than one million tons. These provisions meant a really high threshold for small and medium-sized private enterprises to cross. The majority of small and medium-sized private enterprises can only fall into fierce, even cutthroat, competition in limited industries, with the development space being greatly compressed. Data showed that Chinese private holding investment in financial sector accounted for only 9.6%, that in the sectors of transportation, storage, and post only 7.5%, and that in the sectors of water conservancy, environment, and public facilities management only 6.6%. See Gu Shengzu, 2010: "Sound the Bugle for Private Capital into Monopoly Industries", www.people.com.cn, March 31, 2010.

Bibliography

Boston Consulting Group. "Made in America, Again: Why Manufacturing Will Return to the U.S.", *Working Paper*, 2011.

"Interest rate regulation and total demand structural imbalance", *Economic Research*, no.2, 2014. Chen Yanbin. "Institutional Reasons and Reform Ideas for China's Wealth Gap", *www.ifeng.com,* November 2, 2013.

Chen Yanbin, Chen Xiaoliang, Chen Weize. "Interest Rate Regulation and Total Demand Structural Imbalance", *Economic Research*, no. 2, 2014:18–31.

"China Moving Forward with New Water-price Plan", *The Wall Street Journal*, January 3, 2014.

Kong Xiangzhi, Gu Hongming, Han Jijiang. "Investigation Report on Status of Landless Farmers and Their Willingness for Expropriation Compensation", *Economic Theory and Economic Management*, no. 7, 2006:57–62.

Liang Ji. "International Comparison and Analysis of National Income Distribution Pattern", *Local Finance Research*, no. 8, 2012:4–10.

Nicholas Lardy. "To Promote China's Economic Growth with Interest Rate Liberalization", *21st Century Business Herald*, May 25, 2013(023).

Sheng Hong. "Nature, Performance and Reforms of State-owned Enterprises", *Chinese Private Science and Technology and Economy*, no. Z2, 2012:36–41.

Wang Qiankun, Hu Zhaoyi, Li Qionghui. "Comparison and Analysis of Electricity Price of China and Other Major Countries", *Electric Power Technologic Economics*, no. 6, 2009:27–30,42.

Wang Xiaolu. "Distribution of Gray Income and National Income", *Comparison*, no. 4, 2010.

Wang Xiaolu. "Distribution of Gray Income and National Income (Annual Report of 2013)", *Comparison*, no. 5, 2013.

Wei Hao, Guo Ye. "Unit Labor Cost of Manufacturing and International Comparative Study", *Statistical Research*, no. 8, 2013:102–110.

Xi Jianrong. "Non-act of the Government Is the Main Source of Environmental Crux", *Legal Daily,* November 15, 2011.

Ye Jianping, Tian dawn. "Status of Contract Pattern, Institutional Change and Policy Optimization in China's Rural Land Rights: Analysis of Survey Data of 1956 Farmers in 17 Provinces", *Journal of Huazhong Normal University (Social Science Edition),* no. 1, 2013:38–46.

Zhang Zhuoyuan. "Thirty Years of China's Price Reform: Effect, Course and Prospect", *Red Flag Manuscript,* no. 23, 2008:2–7.

6 Environmental Conditions and Trend Characteristics of China's Economic Development during the 13th Five-Year Plan Period

The 13th Five-Year Plan period is a crucial phase for China to build up a moderately prosperous society in all respects, to comprehensively intensify reforms, as well as to become world's largest economy and be among high-income countries. Besides, it also sees China accelerate the transformation of its economic development method and update and sublimate development pattern. Generally speaking, China remains in the period of development strategic opportunities, and its economic growth maintains continuous good momentum into the last phase of rapid economic growth. However, the connotation and the meaning of period of opportunity is changing, and all kinds of problems, including those hidden ones during rapid economic growth period, are gradually becoming prominent, increasingly restraining China's economic growth. With the foundation of socioeconomic development growing solid and development prospect becoming steady, the development environment is becoming increasingly severe and the restraints increasingly stringent. On the one hand, thanks to the release of dividends of comprehensively deepening reform, enhancement of urbanization and domestic demand potential, rise of potential of domestic demand, formation of self-innovation dividend and new regional growth poles, as well as the new impetus for the world economy to go into a new upward cycle, China will maintain a relatively fast growth rate. On the other hand, China's economic growth environment or conditions are becoming severe, and its economic growth is entering a new stage because of the reduction in number of production factors, weakening advantage of traditional international competition, de-globalization momentum in world political and economic pattern, and changes of major countries' attitudes toward China. With economic growth changing from high or ultra-high rate to medium-high or sub-high rate, China will reach a critical stage in becoming world's largest economy and be among the high-income countries. As economic development mode changes and adjustment of economic structure accelerates, especially that of industrial structure, industrialization will enter middle and late stage, industrial structure will change from secondary industry basis to tertiary industry basis, and demanding structure will shift from investment dominance to consumer orientation. In addition, urbanization will change from being labor-oriented to consumer-driven acceleration, and productivity layout will approach to frame forward. We should speed up the policy of "going outside" and transform from products export to capital export to usher in the new pattern of economic opening up in all respects. In response to new environment and features, we should formulate targeted and prospective strategies, policies, and measures. We can consider drawing up the medium-long plans spanning the 13th Five-Year Plan period and the phase in which China becomes medium-high-income country, extending the 13th Five-Year Plan period to 2030. To this end, we should avoid the step deceleration strategy of "sustainable and stable growth", but implement the strategy of industrial structure adjustment driven by innovation and upgrading, the strategy of new consumer-oriented urbanization, the foreign economic strategy that pays equal attention to exporting commodity and going outside, as well as the strategy of proactive resource-saving and environment-friendliness.

I   Strategic Positioning and Historical Mission during 13th Five-Year Plan Period

Overall, the 13th Five-Year Plan period is the crucial phase for China to build up a moderately prosperous society in all respects, to comprehensively intensify reforms as well as to become world's largest economy and be among high-income countries. Besides, it also sees China accelerate the transformation of its economic development method and update and sublime development pattern.

1. Sprint Stage to Become World's Largest Economy

In 2010, China's economic output overtook that of Japan, and it became world's second largest economy next to the United States of America. As currently China's population is several times as much as that of the United States of America and income per capita of the former is only one-ninth of the latter, to achieve the strategic objective of China's income per capita to be equal to that of medium-developed countries in mid-21st century, its economic output must exceed that of the United States of America to become world's largest economy by 2030. However, it is not China's subjective objective to have its economic output exceed that of the United States of America. It is inevitable a by-product or stage objective result in its development. According to our preliminary prediction, China's economic output will exceed that of America from 2020 to 2025, and it will become world's largest economy. In the baseline outlook, China is expected to become world's largest economy by 2021. In optimistic scenario, China is expected to realize such objective by 2019. In pessimistic case, China might achieve it

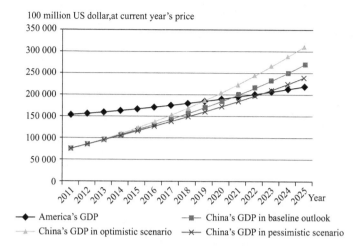

100 million US dollar, at current year's price

Figure 6.1 Comparison of total GDP forecast between China and the USA.

around 2023. Whatever it will be, the next eight to ten years, especially the 13th Five-Year Plan period, will be the sprint stage for China to gain such position (Figure 6.1).

2. Critical Stage to Rank among High-Income Countries

Upon crossing over the dividing line defined by the World Bank as a distinction of lower-income countries and middle-income countries, in its grouping of middle-income countries, China successfully ranked among the upper-middle-income countries in 2010. We are facing with important opportunities and unprecedented challenges as we rank among upper-middle-income countries. Historically, many non-Western countries, except Japan, ROK, and other countries, successfully ranked among the middle-income or even upper-middle-income countries after the world wars. However, these countries fell into the medium-income trap instead of becoming high-income countries as they had wished. In accordance with our forecast, China will successfully go through the middle-income stage around 2025, and on its way to becoming one of the high-income countries. In the baseline outlook, China is expected to become high-income country by 2024; in optimistic scenario, it will be a high-income country in 2022; in the pessimistic case, it will be one of the high-income countries around 2028. Therefore, the next ten years or so, especially the 13th Five-Year Plan period, will be the key phase for China's to cross the line for middle-income countries. Whether China can avoid the so-called medium-income trap and succeed in becoming a high-income country depends on the economic growth from now until the 13th Five-Year Plan period (Figure 6.2).

(USD,at current price)

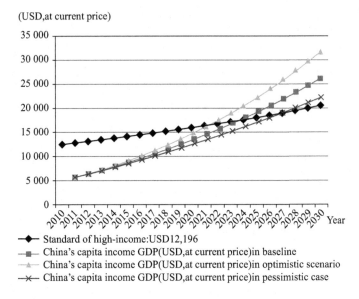

—◆— Standard of high-income:USD12,196
—■— China's capita income GDP(USD,at current price)in baseline
—▲— China's capita income GDP(USD,at current price)in optimistic scenario
—✕— China's capita income GDP(USD,at current price)in pessimistic case

Figure 6.2 Momentum forecast of China's GDP per capita.

3. Sublimation Stage in Transformation of Economic Growth Method and Reconstruction of Growth Pattern

In a sense, the middle-income trap means that the transformation of de-velopment impetus and that of growth system and pattern. Whether China can leap across the middle-income trap depends on whether it can success-fully transform its development impetus mechanism, which depends on whether it can establish sound mechanisms conducive to development pat-tern transformation and economic structure adjustment. China's original development model has played a positive role in its development in the early stage and works as driving force for it to become a middle-income country from a low-income one. However, with comparatively strong characteristics of kick-off stage and obvious limitations, the growth model cannot meet the needs of economic growth at its upgrading stage anymore. To mold the upgraded economy, we must explore its upgraded model. Specifically, whether industry pattern can upgrade from current labor-intensive basis to capital- and technology-intensive basis, whether industrial structure can transit from secondary industry-oriented to coordinated development of secondary and tertiary industries, whether the demand structure can trans-form from export- and investment-driven to equally focus on investment and consumption, and whether economic social development model can change from the one featured with unbalanced structures between regions and between urban and rural areas to the one with balanced and coordi-nated development between regions or urban-rural areas are factors that will decide whether China can keep sustainable and stable economic development in the next few years and whether it can avoid the middle-income trap. To achieve such transformations, we need to intensify reforms and unleash larger dividends deriving from reforms. Therefore, the 13th Five-Year Plan period is undoubtedly critical for China to comprehensively deepen reform and opening-up, promote transformation of growth mode, upgrade economic structure, advance economic growth restructuring, and build the upgraded economy. In this regard, currently, the 13th Five-Year Plan period may be more important than any other period. Thus, it was critically practical and profoundly important to study and formulate the 13th Five-Year Plan.

II Conditions and Opportunities of China's Economic Development during 13th Five-Year Plan

With the release of dividends of deepened reforms and enhancement of urbanization and domestic demand potential, the foundation of China's economy and social development is becoming increasingly solid and the growth prospect increasingly stable. However, due to the weakening of traditional comparative advantages and reversal of external conditions, the development environment is becoming severe and development path is experiencing twists and turns. Generally speaking, as it is still in an important period of strategic opportunities, China will maintain strong momentum and enter the last round of economic boom period around 2025 during the 13th Five-Year Plan period. However, changes are taking place in connotation and meaning of opportunities, with all kinds of problems becoming further prominent. On the one hand, as working-age population growth rate becomes considerably slow, savings and investment rates tend to go down. Improvement in the speed of productivity rate becomes obviously reduced by virtue of factor redistribution between sectors and technical catch-up. On the other hand, human capital accumulation and institutional innovation have improved quality of factor input and efficiency of factor utilization, while the enhancement of R&D capability has brought about industrial optimization and upgrading. Promotion of urbanization has expanded domestic demand, and regional gradient developments have created new growth poles, which have made China's economy maintain a rapid growth.

A *External Conditions of China's Economic Development during 13th Five-Year Plan Period*

As the world economy has ushered in a new prosperity cycle, the economy of the United States of America has been in a sustained recovery with formation of new growth points. In addition, for China and neighboring countries, export competitiveness has been weakened with formation of new energy supply sources. All of these are undoubtedly beneficial factors for China.

1 World Economy: Hopefully in New Boom Promoted by Low-Cost Energy

From the perspective of traditional extended period, industrial diffusion effect from first and second waves of information technology revolution has been dwindling, with new breakthrough and development urgently needed. During the 13th Five-Year Plan period, industrialization wave of third information technology revolution might take shape. From the angle of new technical revolution, diffusion effect of shale-gas revolution starts to appear and possibly brings about new prosperity. During the 13th Five-Year Plan period, as America's shale technology continues to diffuse to neighboring countries, the development of shale technology will step into large-scale commercialization in Canada, Australia, and Russia, which will result in enhancement of energy supply security and stabilization in energy price. Just as the deregulation in 1980s led to supply-side economic revolution and prosperity of Jugular cycle, shale gas revolution will possible ease global inflation pressure – that is, it will bring down the rising costs, or cost-down boom in a sense. Though the prosperity from diffusion effect of shale gas revolution is limited, if it is coupled with information technology revolution, it is still possible to bring significant supply-push prosperity of Juglar cycle.

2 Development of Emerging Industries: Probably Generating New Economic Growth Points of World Economy

Major breakthroughs are likely to be made in many technical fields, such as new-generation information technology, biotechnology, new energy, and new material. It takes certain time to turn technical breakthrough into industrialization. The so-called third industrial revolution is still in planning. It is premature to expect breakthroughs in it and achieve industrialization. During the 13th Five-Year Plan period, third informatization will mature and develop further, which will promote the formation of the emerging advantageous industry and new economic growth points. The latest trend of information industry characterized by Internet, cloud computing, and deep application of information technology presents the third wave of informatization after the first and second informatization, respectively, marked by the advent of computer and Internet of Things. In the next five to eight years, during the China's 13th Five-Year Plan period, the world will overall be in the diffusion effect of the third informatization wave, which possibly will eventually drive the world economy out of slump and into an upward recovery mode. China possesses technology and marketing advantages in

Internet of Things and cloud computing, which is an important development opportunity.

3 Developed Countries: Gradually Revive Driven by Technical Breakthroughs, Hopefully Generate New External Demand

In previous Juglar cycle boom, developed countries were in a stage of external diffusion effect of new technical revolution, while developing countries had advantages of labors and resource and undertook industrial shift from developed countries by outsourcing and forming obvious catch-up effect, which narrowed the gap between developed and developing countries and resulted in the rise of developing countries and decline of developed countries. At the present stage, developed countries are still at the original position – initiator and leader of innovation and new technical revolution – while developing countries learn from and imitate them in technology. It is predicted that during the 13th Five-Year Plan period, promotion and application of shale gas technology in developed countries may drive their economy into pick-up tendency and possibly result in a faster economic growth than that of developing countries. That may provide large marketing demand for China's commodity in original division labor system.

B Internal Conditions of China's Economy during 13th Five-Year Plan Period

1 Intensifying Reforms to Release Unprecedented Institutional Dividends

The practice has proven that reform and opening-up are important impetus for China's long-term, sustainable and rapid development. In the past 30 years, the five major reform waves in three phases brought three long-term booms, respectively, in the 1980s, 1990s, and the 21st century. Decision by the Central Committee of the Communist Party of China on Major Issues Concerning Comprehensively Deepening Reforms was adopted at the Third Plenary Session of the 18th Central Committee of the Communist Party of China. According to the decision, we have promoted reforms in economy, politics, culture, social and ecological systems, as well as defense, military construction, and party construction ("5 + 1 + 1") instead of the previous economic system. We pay more attention to implementing systematic, integrated, and coordinated reforms instead of the original single reform. The comprehensive deepening of reforms greater than any previous reforms in depth and width will release unprecedented reforming dividends. New reform dividends as well as the resulting dependent innovation dividends will take place of the gradual weakening dividends of population, resource, and globalization and become the new drive for China's economic sustainable and rapid development in the future.

2 Improvement of Production Factor Quality Increases Labor Productivity

Generally speaking, the change in China's labor supply-demand relation has led to reduction of incoming labor force, rise of labor's wage, increase of costs, and rapid weakening of comparative advantages of traditional labor-intensive industries. Meantime, with the aging of population, the ratio of population over 65 years old has increased. As China is moving into an aging society, savings rates tend to decrease and formation of capital gradually slows down. On the other hand, quality of China's production factor is improving, investment in human capital increasing, and educational level of workers enhancing. At the same time, as the equipment e rapidly takes place of labors, the intensification of capital will continue and constantly raise China's labor productivity.

3 Independent Innovation Generates New Industrial Competitiveness and Total-Factor Productivity

Impetus and capacity of technical innovation is continuously strengthening, social innovative environment is taking shape, and accumulative effects of self-dependent innovation are being formed. All of these will vigorously push forward China's prospective strategic new industrial development and industrial competitiveness. Meanwhile, the integration of continuous breakthroughs of technical innovation with institutional innovation will become an important factor to advance the increase of total factor productivity after labor reallocation and technology introduction effects.

III Difficulties and Challenges in China's Economic Development during 13th Five-Year Plan Period

A External Difficulties and Challenges in China's Economic Development during 13th Five-Year Plan Period

During the 13th Five-Year Plan period, there are both favorable and adverse factors for China's economy development in the international environment. Generally speaking, the adverse factors are increasing, while the favorable ones are decreasing. International environment becomes increasingly severe, and China's development restraints become increasingly rigid. In particular, the exclusive new regional trade pattern, the changes or transition of attitudes of leading countries toward China, the harassment of the neighboring countries to China's sea areas, and the potential risks of energy supply pattern are unfavorable factors that the international environment exerts on China during the 13th Five-Year Plan period brings about great uncertainty.

1 World Political and Economic Pattern: Economic Globalization Slows Down But International Competitiveness Intensifies

In view of external environment of China, it continues to compete with developing countries regarding transnational labor-intensive areas, while the competition with and replacement of developed countries has fully taken place in capital- and technology-intensive sectors. During the 13th Five-Year Plan period, with the continuous growth of China's economic competitiveness, the relations between China and developed, developing, and neighboring countries continue to change. China will probably usher in the most rigid international environment. It is inevitable for China to confront complicated challenges and attacks from developed countries and emerging economies in export of technology-intensive, capital-intensive, and labor-intensive products.

(1) RELATION BETWEEN CHINA AND DEVELOPED COUNTRIES: COMPETITIVE
  DISPLACEMENT OVER REGURGITATION FEEDING EFFECT

Owing to the changes of labor supply-demand relation, accumulation of capital accumulation and technical progress, and displaying of superimposed effects, China will expedite its transformation from labor-intensive industry to that of capital- and technology-intensive one. China's exports are transforming from the pattern of resource-consumption and rough process to deep-processing with high technology. China's competitors are thus gradually shifting from developing countries to developed ones. Essential changes are taking place in the relations between China and developed countries, from the original basis of complementarity to the coexistence between complementarity and replacement, and even to the new period of replacement dominance. Since the international financial crisis in 2008, developed countries, led by America, put forward a series of medium-long strategies to reinvigorate national economy and boost domestic demand, with relation of competitiveness or anti-competitiveness with China. As China's enterprises expedite their pace of going abroad, it is repaying developed countries in restructuring of infrastructure and traditional industries, but generally speaking, with greater replacement effect than repaying effect. It is more and more obvious for China be one of the developed states in capital-intensive and technology-intensive sectors, so is it obvious that the developed countries will make anti-competitive practice against China.

With China's further development, essential changes have taken place in its position in world economy, which will affect the relations between China and world's leading countries. Major changes will appear in the basic attitudes of the leading countries toward China. It is possible a worse conflict happens between China and the USA than the US-Japan trade friction in 1980s. Concerning the different economic cycles between both countries, America's economy might step into propriety, while China will be trapped in low growth because of conversion of growth drive in the next five years or so. The wax and wane of power comparison will lead to adverse impacts on China, with competition and frictions more intense than those of US-Japan trade in 1980s, but evidently different from US-Soviet confrontation, which is possible to recur in trades between China and USA. Leading countries will continue to adopt strategies of anti-competition, exclusion, and containment against China. Since 2008, the United States of America has implemented re-manufacturing, which in some sense is anti-competition against China. In addition, they currently put forward the new trade system arrangement with exclusive features to exclude China out of world trade. For example, they established the regional trade organization, TPP and TTIP, with higher standards and stricter requirements, and even targeted terms to directly squeeze China out and start regional anti-competitiveness that is against globalization. As China competes with all countries in all industry chains at present stage, these countries with developing or developed economy consider China as their public enemy. Developed countries are keen to build new trade barriers through regionalization for extensive response, which makes the restraints to China's development become increasingly serious.

As the camp of emerging economies is growing, the relations between the emerging market economies tend to be double-edged. On the one hand, the later emerging economies are bound to compete with traditional ones in exporting products. China will be the first to suffer from such situation. On the other hand, the transfer of industries between emerging markets will form the division of labor between upstream and downstream industrial chains. China will also join it to accelerate its "going outside" process. During the 13th Five-Year Plan period, the later emerging states compete with China in the following three aspects. First, the low-cost emerging economies compete with China in labor-intensive products, focusing on labor-intensive industries due to the limits of educational years of working-age population and industrial supporting capacity. They compete with China in labor-intensive industries. Second, the competition resulted from non-traditional competitive forces, such as transfer of industries based on politic factors, which has led some industries or technology that could have been transferred to China to be transferred to other countries under the influence of human factors. Third, the emerging markets compete with China's market in production factors such as resource and energy. During the 13th Five-Year Plan period, the competition and replacement policies of the later emerging economies against China are in line with China's industrial transfer policies, which develop complicated relations between China and the later emerging markets.

B Difficulties and Challenges of China's Economy during the 13th Five-Year Plan Period

1 Agglomeration Change of Labor Supply and Demand Relations Weakens Traditional Comparative Advantage

As China's Lewis turning point is coming. labor supply and demand relations are changing from infinite supply via labor to finite supply via labor. As labor cost continues to increase, China quickly lost its competitive advantages in labor-intensive industries. Meantime, as ratio of aging population increases, China is stepping into an aged society. The saving rates thus tend to decrease, while capital costs are on a rise. On the one hand, compared with the later emerging economies, China's advantages in labor-intensive industries are evidently reduced. On the other hand, compared with the developing countries, China's cost advantages in capital- and-labor intensive industries are obviously weakened.

2 Rise of Environmental Restraints Provides More Challenges for Supply of Resource and Energy

The occurrence of haze further highlights the severity and urgency of environmental problems. During the 13th Five-Year Plan period, the environmental restraints against economic development are on a rise and, to a certain extent, correspondingly reduce the potential growth. At the same time, with the sustainable development of China's economy, if there is no significant breakthrough in energy conservation and utilization, the external dependence on resource and energy will continue to increase. In the context of increasingly complicated international environment, especially when geopolitical situation fluctuates, the increasing uncertainty in China's oil production, procurement, and transportation grows.

3 Economic and Financial Risks Increase Macroeconomic Uncertainty

Owing to the imbalance between financial system reforms and economic development, the financial system compatible with China's rapid economy growth and specific low-cost expansion model has not been timely established. As a result, risks have been accumulated in financial sectors, including local government financing and off-balance sheet business of "shadow banking" of commercial banks. In the process of rapid economic development, traditional indirect financing system centered by banks is rapidly expanding in the context of its high growth. Meanwhile, direct financing in emerging transformed markets is restrained from congenitally deficiency and has not been fully developed in time, which has led to the constant rise of liability ratio of the whole society. In addition, the reform and development of real estate market is not well converged, with the welfare housing and market-oriented housing systems lacking appropriate transitional and convergence of institutional arrangements. Furthermore, the sharp imbalance exists between distribution and accumulation of wealth. All of the abovementioned led to bubbles to some extent in real estate markets. If the leverage ratio further rises, new asset bubbles might occur. However, deleveraging and deforming might cause a sharp decline in economic growth and affect the sustainable and stable economic growth. In a sense, economic and financial risks have been major and certain factors that restrict economic development and macroeconomic regulation.

4   Social Problems and Other Non-Economic Factors Grow

Although contradictions have been accumulated during China's rapid economic development, they are often covered by rapid growth or solved by the resulted dividends. With the slowdown of China's economic growth, some problems might come out in the wash and become restraints against intensification and stabilization of economic development. Of particular note, the deepening of public mental tolerance on income distribution and environmental problems declines or regresses, and the public expectation to higher income constantly increases in the future. At the same time, the pursuit of quality life has made the new generation migrant workers' attitudes toward work greatly different from their predecessors, which also has negative effects on supply of production factors and economic development environment.

IV   Trend & Features of China's Economic Growth during the 13th Five-Year Plan Period

A   Post-industrialization Shift from Medium to Later Stage

In line with the changes of labor supply-demand relations and other comparative advantages of resource endowment, China will slow down its economic growth rate but expedite its economic restructuring. Meanwhile, China's economy will enter the later stage from the medium one of industrialization.

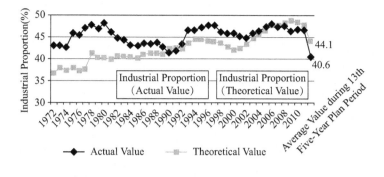

Figure 6.3 China's industrial proportion during 13th Five-Year Plan period: actual value and theoretical value.

1 Industrialization Develops from Medium to Later Stage

China's industrialization is now in the transition from medium to later stage. The proportion of high-processing industry tends to rise, so does gradually of the tertiary industry. The factor input transforms from mainly relying on quantity expansion to quality promotion, with investment rate gradually on a slump and the consumption rate on a steady rise; this led to expedite optimization and adjustment of factor, industrial, and demand structures (Figure 6.3).

2 Adjustment of Industrial Structure from "Made in China" to "Created in China"

At present, there is certain specificity in China's industrial structure, which is a higher proportion of secondary production than the tertiary industry. On the one hand, in the context of globalization, the proportion of China's secondary industry rises, thanks to the tremendous transfer of labor-intensive industries from developed countries to China; on the other hand, the access regulation on China's service industry, especially on production service industry, remains strict, so does that on financial service, logistics service, and cultural and creative industries, which objectively has lowered the proportion of the tertiary industry. Along with the changes of labor supply-demand relations, the external transfer of labor-intensive industries, and transition of industrialization growth phases, China's industrial restructuring will be further accelerated in the next five to eight years, in particular, the industrial structure will be gradually adjusted, the proportion of the secondary industry will be stabilized and gradually reduced, and the proportion of the tertiary industry will steadily increase. At the same time, the external transfer of labor-intensive industries can propel China's transition from the previous center of manufacturing to that of designing and manufacturing, namely, from "made in China" to "created in China".

3 Combined Mode of Production Factors Changes from Labor Resource-Intensive to Capital- and Technology-Intensive

In accordance with the changes of labor supply-demand relation and resource supply in China, the transition of combined mode of production factors and structure of supply will become the irresistible trend of economic restructuring during the 13th Five-Year Plan period. The upgrading from labor-intensive industries to capital- and technology-intensive industries and the transformation from high energy-consuming and resource-consuming industries to energy-saving and emission-reduction industries will be the two major directions for adjustment of combined mode of production factors in China. It is necessary for China to timely reform the retirement system and adjust the family planning policy, so as to stabilize long-term supply of labor factor. It is important for China to speed up construction of vocation-oriented education and training system and increase the investment of human capital in order to cultivate more high-quality labor force and skilled workers. It is advisable for China to stabilize saving rates and source of capital formation to maintain the capital contribution rate to long-term economic growth. It is suggested that China build a unified urban and rural construction land market, allow the rural collective construction land to be entitled to transfer, lease, share, as well as implement the same entry into capital markets, and enjoy same rights and prices as state-owned land is entitled to do, so as to ensure the reasonable supply of land resource on the premise of guaranteeing the economical and intensive utilization of land resource. It is imperative to reform the resource property rights system and environmental protection system to promote the economical and intensive utilization of land resource. China should strengthen foreign cooperation in the field of energy resource, improve the availability of strategic resource, and establish stable supply mechanism for external resources and energy and ensure constant supply of main resources. China should also take new competitive advantages formed in its capital- and technology-based industries to encourage equipment manufacturing and electronic information industry to develop in foreign countries. Furthermore, China should reinforce environmental protection standards; strictly control industrial access criteria; promote remolding, upgrading, and external transferring of high energy consumption and high pollution industries; and lead China's industries to develop from high energy consumption and high pollution to resource conservation and environment-friendly sectors.

B Intensification of Urbanization Leads to "Freeze-Frame" of Productivity Distribution

China has developed into the middle stage of urbanization. In the next five to eight years, China's 13th Five-Year Plan period, urbanization will show a pattern of "two speed advancement", with the quality of urbanization on a constant rise, which will lead China to come to the critical later stage of urbanization. At the same time, with the gradual advancement of urbanization and the initial establishment of regional urban cluster system, China's pattern of industrial spatial agglomeration will gradually take shape, with the main spatial framework of economic development being basically ascertained.

1 Urbanization: Two-Speed Advancement and Intensification

Urbanization provides the greatest potential for expansion of domestic demand and creates the upgraded version of economic growth. It has been a consensus to actively and steadily promote urbanization, with the key to be aware of the basic mode and driving characteristics of China's urbanization and to choose the focal points for promotion, including the following two aspects.

(1) INDUSTRIAL DEVELOPMENT ACCELERATES MIGRANT WORKERS AND RELATIVES TO SETTLE DOWN IN URBAN AREAS

At present, the absolute number of the working-age population in China has begun to decrease, and the time of large-scale outward rural labor migration in the central and western China has passed, which on and off caused trouble for the coastal areas to recruit labor. Changes in the pattern of labor supply and demand relation have promoted and will continue to promote the cities and towns, especially coastal areas, to further adjust the conditions of residency for migrant workers and their families to settle down and enhance the attractiveness of local enterprises to migrant workers. It is foreseeable that the migrant workers and their families who have been moved out of rural areas will be more rapidly settled down in urban areas with the implementation of urbanization policies.

(2) CONSUMPTION UPGRADE SPEEDILY DRIVES URBANIZATION

With the rapid development of China's economy for more than 30 years, its national income per capita has been on a constant rise, up to USD 6,000, which makes it rank among the middle- and higher-income countries of. Because of China's urban-rural dual structure, its urban-rural economic and social development is obviously not synchronized with residents' consumption. The rural household consumption is roughly equivalent to just one-third of urban households, about 10 to 12 years later than the urban household consumption. In the next ten years or so, rural living standards and consumption will enter a significant upgrade phase. However, the upgrade of housing consumption will be no longer like it was in the past, which was to rebuild or expand the rural houses, but which now is to buy commercial houses in cities and towns, especially county towns, and immigrate there. It is predicted that the urbanization of population will be accelerated due to the increase in residents' income and consumption.

2 *"Citizen-Oriented" Society Basically Takes Shape*

As urbanization is advancing in depth, the city clusters and urban system are basically established to be roughly synchronized with industrialization. Currently, China's urbanization rate is 52% measured on the basis of labor force, 35% measured on the basis of registered population that totally benefits from public services, and around 39 to 40% estimated on the basis of urbanization concept of production mode for registered and whole-family transferred populations. In line with the changes of labor supply-demand relation and local labor competition, the criteria for citizenization of migrant workers becomes increasing loose, with citizenization of migrant workers and their families, as well as the first rich population in rural areas, speeding up. In the next five to eight years, during China's 13th Five-Year Plan period, urbanization rate of labor force is expected to remain at 0.8% to 0.9%, but the population urbanization rate is expected to increase to more than 1%. The structure of social residents will accelerate the transition from the current pattern of half farmers (migrant workers) and half citizens to a citizen-oriented society. The citizen-oriented society will be further shaped around 2020.

(1) CITIZENIZATION OF RURAL MIGRANT WORKERS

Citizenization of migrant workers is the last and the most difficult part of industrial development to promote urbanization. Citizenization of migrant workers is only suitable for migrant workers who have stable work and living conditions in the city. It is estimated that all local governments will adapt to the labor supply-demand relation and further reduce the threshold of urbanization, including the settling down, social security, children's enrollment, and affordable housing of migrant workers, in order to accelerate the citizenization of local migrant workers.

(2) CITIZENIZATION OF RURAL MIGRANT WORKERS' FAMILIES

As there is still a considerable number of migrant workers who do not have stable work and living conditions in the city, their best choice is to purchase their own houses in their original domicile to solve the citizenization of their parents and children. With the advancement of urbanization, it will be relaxed in the basic rights guarantees, including the county construction land indicators, rural housing, and homestead. Besides, the cost of urbanization for the families of migrant workers will significantly reduce. Furthermore, the families of migrant workers who have been into, or not yet into, cities will turn their living state from "migration" to "citizenship".

Urbanization of the first rich population in rural areas is an irresistible trend in recent years and plays an important role in urbanization of rural population. With the development of rural economy and farmers' living standards, more and more rural people will move to the cities and towns, especially to the county, including professional contractors, private entrepreneurs, and other first rich group of people.

3 Productivity Distribution and Urbanization System Tend to "Preliminary Freeze-Frame"

The advent of changes in labor supply-demand relation and the slowdown in economic growth mean that the next ten years or so will see China's last period of high-speed growth, and also that it will be the stage of freeze-frame for China's economic growth. After entering this stage, the basic framework of the productivity distribution and urbanization system will be basically stabilized. If there is no other significant discovery in resources or other aspects, the national productivity distribution and national traffic trunk framework will be basically shaped. Also, the position and rank of a place in the whole country, the scope and functional zones of the urban built-up areas, and the road frame and infrastructure of the city will be generally determined.

C Formation of New Foreign Economic Pattern: Transition from "Commodity Output" to "Capital Output"

Along with the change of China's economic development and global industrial chain pattern, China will transform from the stage of commodity output to that of capital output. The "going out" strategy will also develop into the third phase, with the overseas investment on a gradual rise. At the same time, following the continuous expansion of imports, trade surplus will be narrowed down step by step, with the balance of payments approaching basic equilibrium.

1 Commodity Output: Upgrading, Updating, Growth of Service Trade

In line with the change of labor supply-demand relation, the intensified restraint of resource and environment, the world economy adjustment, as well as the boom of newly emerging market countries, China's foreign trade will usher in a new stage of development. On the one hand, the change of China's comparative advantage will promote the upgrade and shift from traditional labor-intensive products to capital- and technology-intensive products; on the other hand, with the progress of service industry, the service trade export will also speed up in the following aspects:

1   Products upgrade from labor-intensiveness to technology-intensiveness. Owing to the wage hike, RMB appreciation, rising resource price, and intensified environmental restraints, China's comparative advantage and competitiveness in traditional labor-intensive industries will tend to decline. Additionally, some later emerging market economies are continuously incorporated into the global division system, especially the production chain of relatively low-end labor-intensive products. It is expected that in the next three to five years, China might fundamentally lose competitiveness in traditional labor-intensive industries. Currently, seven categories of labor-intensive industries account for about 15% of China's export trade, which is likely to gradually drop to 8% or even 5% in the following five to eight years. After taking into full consideration the comparative advantage of China, the low-cost advantage of later emerging market countries in labor-intensive industries, as well as the experience of Japan, South Korea, and other countries in their development, it is estimated that China will import capital- and technology-intensive industries with relatively high value-added progressively in the coming years, so as to upgrade and update the export-oriented mode.

2   As for growth of service trade, the deficit is reduced and expected to turn into surplus. Service trade has currently been in deficit in China. In line with China's manufacturing industry upgrades and service industry's development, the competitiveness of China's service industry will tend to increase, and so will the export of China's service trade gradually. From the perspective of comparative advantage of China's current service industries, China has certain comparative advantage in cultural education, medical treatment and public health, high-tech service, and other sectors. Therefore, the outlook of service trade is quite optimistic. Through the concerted efforts made by all parties concerned, China's service trade is promising to make remarkable headway, which will gradually change the current deficit in service trade, thus achieving the basic balance of service trade with a slight surplus so as to make up for the possible impact possibly resulted from the continuous shrinkage of trade surplus in China's products.

2 Capital Output "Going Outside" into the Third Phase

Under the influence not only from China's resource endowment and comparative advantage but also from the competition of later emerging market countries at present, China is in the transition from commodity output to

Table 6.1 Stages and features of "going outside" of China's enterprises

	First stage	Second stage	Third stage
Industrial and commercial enterprises	Labor contracting, contracted construction projects (CSCEC, Sinotrans, etc.)	Resource development, (China Minmetal, Chinalco, Sinosteel, etc.)	Direct investment in factory establishment, M&A investment, (Lenovo, Huawei, etc.)
Service industry	Immigrant remittance, "Going outside" of banks	Follow-up service, development Bank, etc.	Full service, investment company, etc.

capital output. If the upgrading and updating of product output is a significant feature of China's foreign economy, such transition will be another major change. For some time in the future, China's enterprises' "going outside" will show a momentum of rapid and vigorous development (Table 6.1).

1   The "going out" of industrial and commercial enterprises enters the stage of direct and merger and acquisition (M&A) investment. The major progress and change of the "going out" of China's enterprises in recent years is to walk into the phase of large-scale development, which has generally gone through three stages as a whole. The first stage is dominated by labor contracting, which mainly includes the contracting of foreign large construction projects. In the past 30 years of reform and opening up, China has accumulated abundant experience in infrastructure through massive construction, which has now made it take the lead worldwide in terms of capability of constructing roads, bridges, and tunnels. Moreover, under the background of abundant labor resource, China has a certain comparative advantage in foreign contracted projects. The second stage is dominated by resource development. In the new century, along with the advance of China's economy at a super high speed and the continuous increase of China's consumption of energy resource, China's self-sufficiency of energy resource has been falling, with external dependence on a rapid rise. At the moment, all the external dependence of China's iron ore, copper, aluminum, and oil are over 50%, and the "going outside" to develop and exploit the energy resource has become a new task for China's enterprises. In recent years, China's metallurgy, oil, and food enterprises have got access to Australia, Latin America, North America, Russia, Middle East, and North Africa to tap resources, which has become a major feature of the "going outside" of China's enterprises. The third stage is dominated by direct and

M&A investment, which is the latest trend since China's financial crisis. For one thing, accompanied by the upward pressure on overcapacity in China, its manufacturing enterprises have invested in the establishment of factories and green fields in Latin America, Africa, Middle East, and Eastern Europe. For another, China's large enterprises have entered developed countries for M&A investment. Influenced and interfered by political and other non-economic factors, M&A investment of China's enterprises in developed countries has been in twist and turn, so has the direct investment in developing countries, which goes smoother than the former but is still confronted with all kinds of obstacles and difficulties.

2   The "going outside" of finance and other service industries has been in the stage of follow-up service. Slightly different from that of industrial and commercial enterprises in some focal points, the "going outside" of China's financial institutions and other productive service industries has also gone through three stages. The first stage of the "going outside" for financial institutions was fundamentally featured with immigrant remittance, which could be traced back to the earliest output of China's labor, the establishment of Bank of China, and the development of oversea business. The second stage was presented by the establishment of service counters in the international financial centers to follow-up the development trend of world banking, which was similar with learning-oriented behaviors. It started since China's reform and opening-up when the state-owned banks established representative offices and other branches in international financial centers in Hong Kong, Singapore, London, New York, and Tokyo. The third stage was marked by the follow-up service provided by China's financial institutions and other productive service industries in recent years following the "going outside" of China's enterprises. The third stage really combined with the "going outside" of enterprises and restored the substantive business-oriented one. It can be expected that in the coming years, especially during the 13th Five-Year Plan period, as China's enterprises "go outside", financial institutions and other productive service industries will accelerate their pace to "go outside".

V   Conclusions and Recommendations

The 13th Five-Year Plan period is the crucial phase for China to build up a moderately prosperous society in all respects, to comprehensively intensify reforms as well as to become world's largest economy and be among high-income countries (Table 6.1). Besides, it also sees China accelerate the transformation of its economic development method and update its development pattern. Generally speaking, China remains in the period with development strategic opportunities, and its economic growth maintains continuous good momentum into the last rapid economic growth. However, the connotation and meaning of period of opportunity is changing, and all kinds of problems including the hidden ones during rapid economic growth period are gradually becoming prominent, increasingly restraining China's economic growth.

Overall, with the release of dividends of deepened reforms and enhancement of urbanization and domestic demand potential, the foundation of China's economy and social development is becoming increasingly solid and growth prospect increasingly stable. However, as weakening of traditional comparative advantages and reverse of external conditions, the development environment is becoming severe and development path is in twist and turn. On the one hand, thanks to the release of dividends of deepened reforms, enhancement of urbanization and domestic demand potential, rise of potential of domestic demand, formation of self-innovation dividend and new regional growth poles, as well as the new impetus for the world economy to go into a new upward cycle, China will maintain a relatively fast growth rate. On the other hand, China's economic growth environment or conditions are becoming severe, and its economic growth is entering a new stage because of the reduction in number of production factors, weakening advantage of traditional international competition, de-globalization momentum in world political and economic pattern, and changes of major countries' attitudes toward China. The changes of international environment and domestic conditions will provide more possibility for China to be caught into the medium-income trap. In such context, China's economy will be presented as the acceleration of structural adjustment, intensification of urbanization, formation of new pattern of foreign economy, and occurrence of new periodic features. In response to the brand new environment and features, we should formulate targeted and prospective strategies, policies, and measures. To this end, we should implement the strategy of "sustainable and stable growth" by avoiding stepping slowdown, the strategy of industrial structure adjustment driven by innovation and upgrading, the strategy of new consumer-oriented urbanization, the foreign economic strategy that pays equal attention to exporting commodity and going outside, as well as the strategy of proactive resource-saving and environment-friendliness.

Meanwhile, we can consider drawing up the medium-long plans spanning the 13th Five-Year Plan period and the phase that China becomes medium-high income country; extending the 13th Five-Year Plan period to 2030. It is estimated that China's middle-income stage, where China steps into high-income stage, will cover the 13th and 14th Five-Year Plans. Before 2020, namely, the 13th Five-Year Plan period, the strategy of comprehensively building well-off society and detailed planning for decision of fully intensifying reforms will have been drawn up. If the 13th Five-Year Plan period only covers the five years from 2016 to 2020, on the one hand, the strategic role of 13th Five-Year Plan will be reduced and, to a large extent, will become the executive and action plan for the strategic goal of building well-off society in all aspects and the decision of comprehensively intensifying reforms; on the other hand, the target for China to develop into a high-income country, which is critical to China's development and modernization, will be led into a state of strategic gap for lack of special plans for it. Therefore, we propose to extend the period of 13th Five-Year Plan period to 2030, and draw up 13th Five-Year Plan and 2030 long-range perspective strategy, which are the medium-term and long-term planning that covers the 13th Five-Year Plan period and the upper middle-income phase. In time of making comprehensive efforts for the strategic goal of comprehensive building well-off society and the decision of fully intensifying reforms, we should make the same plans and early arrangements for China's development from the period of becoming a middle-income country to that of becoming a high-income country.

Bibliography

Research Group of Economic Research Institute of National Development and Reform Commission. "China's Choice for Economic Development Strategies of 2020", *Research Report*, 2011.

Research Group of Economic Research Institute of National Development and Reform Commission. "Research on Adjustment of China's Economic Structure during 13th Five-Year Plan Period", *Research Report*, 2014.

Song Li. "New Trend and Features of China's Economic Development", *Research on Central Enterprises' Layout and Structural Adjustment, Sub-project Research Report*, 2013.

7 Discussions on Problems of China's Urbanization during the 13th Five-Year Plan Period

From 1979 to 2013, China's urbanization rate achieved a rapid increase from 18% to 53%, with an annual growth exceeding 1% for more than 30 years, which was unprecedented in human history. Since 2014, China's urbanization has entered into a new phase of development, namely, from the old rapid growth phase in the past 30 years to a new relative slow phase with steadily improved quality. Therefore, the discussion on the development environment, speed, and urban-rural balance of China's urbanization in the 13th Five-Year Plan period is crucial both theoretically and practically.

I Development Environment of China's Urbanization during the 13th Five-Year Plan Period

Economic globalization and informatization are the main features of world economic development since the 1990s, especially after the new century. As for developing countries, economic globalization not only stands for advanced production technology and high-liquidity capital brought by international industrial specification but also symbolizes of the advent of a new economic era based on knowledge. The shortened technical innovation cycle results in lock-in effect of increasing returns and circulative accumulation, which indicates that the strategy of "introduction, imitation and export" is out of date. China's urbanization, in the context of such an international economy, is bound to undertake the double pressure that stems from traditional industry structure upgrading and economic globalization. Under the background of economic globalization, the enhancement of urban competitiveness becomes crucial. Meanwhile, the division among urban regions grows increasingly mature in the effect of economic globalization, thus creating a new urban hierarchy system and urban clusters. The urban spatial pattern in time of globalization presents a coexistence of diffusion and agglomeration. Cities find their own positions in global Industrial division. In such a development environment, China's urbanization is faced with both opportunities and challenges during the 13th Five-Year Plan period.

China's new round of international industrial transfer will promote urbanization in most areas. Coastal areas will take the lead in industrialization and urbanization and approach new economy of knowledge and technology-intensiveness. On the other hand, the central and western regions will undertake industrial transfer from eastern regions on the basis of gradient difference and take part in international specification to advance industrialization and urbanization. Industry structure upgrade, international industrial transfer, industrial chain extension, and restructuring are all essential factors to drive China's urbanization and affect its urban and rural economy.

In the information age, the allocation of production factors appears freer and more flexible, which gives rise to a fundamental change in urban functions. The brand-new land use pattern diminishes the restraint and impact from tradition industrial spatial pattern. Urban spatial structure switches from ring-patterned growth structure to network one, which makes the multi-function community the basic spatial carrier of the networked city. At the same time of urban-cluster-based development, we must be aware that world economic situation remains severe under the influence of financial crises. The recovery of developed countries remains sluggish, while latent risks in the overall rise of emerging economies still exist. Recently, the butterfly effect of financial crisis drove China's urbanization to some extent. In order to weaken the subsequent impact of financial crises, China has implemented the policy of pulling domestic demand, which will further speed up urbanization. At the same time, China's export-oriented economy is inevitably affected. The deterioration of economic situation in main export markets directly influences the operating conditions of China's enterprises and even causes the flow of migrant workers back to hometown. The rise of labor cost has led to the shortage of farmer labor in coastal areas and increased labor force for urbanization of inland rural areas to a certain extent.

Economic data show that China's economic output has constantly developed to a new height in recent ten years, overtaking Japan in 2010 and becoming world's second largest economy. In 2014, China's GDP surpassed RMB60 trillion and reached USD8 trillion and GDP per capita reached USD7,000 if converted by the average exchange rate. In addition, China's economic growth has made increasing contribution to world economy. Especially after the outbreak of financial crisis, world's major economies suffered from negative growth or stagnation and dragged the world economy downward, whereas China's economy maintained relatively high growth—increasing initially—and made significant contribution to world economic recovery. In the context of the present uncertainty in international economic situation, to boost domestic demand and integrate domestic economic resources to ensure sustainable growth are the pressing problems. Thankfully, China has recently made achievements in upgrade of industrial structure enhancement of basic industries and infrastructure, coordination of regional development, positive change of income distribution structure, transformation of economic development mode, and adjustment of economic structure. In view of industrial sectors, China has shown great performance in streamlining industrial productivity, optimizing product structure, and stabilizing and enriching service industries, especially modern service industry.

Moreover, urban social and economic development has reached a new height. First of all, urbanization has steadily improved. China actively promotes urbanization and guides rational and orderly flow of population to further strengthen urban infrastructure construction as well as advance urban overall carrying capacity. In 2009, China's urban population reached 621.86 million, accounting for 46.6% of national total population. Urbanization rates were 50% in 2010 and 53.3% in 2013. Secondly, new trends show up in urbanization along with expansion of urban scale. With the development of economic globalization, more and more cities are directly involved in international division and cooperation. Especially, the step-by-step implementation of the goal of constructing cosmopolitan cities intensifies China's opening-up to the outside world and promotes the development of the surrounding areas with expansive influence. Thirdly, rapid respond and adjustment by the governments of cities at prefecture level and above in view of the changes in the international and domestic economic situation ensure the steady growth of the fiscal revenue. The rise of fiscal revenue enables the city to make achievements in economy, people's livelihood, infrastructure construction, and service capabilities, which contribute to the benign circle of urban sustainable development. Finally, continuous development of the tertiary industry optimizes the industrial structure. Since 2009, the proportion of value of the tertiary industries accounting for GDP began to exceed that of secondary industry, accounting for GDP for the first time in cities at prefecture level and above, which proves the economy in urban areas is shifting from the industrial economy orientation to service industry orientation.

In addition to the favorable factors from the above-mentioned macroeconomy, China's urbanization is also facing difficulties in its further development during the 13th Five-Year Plan period.

First, continuous increase of income gap brings about the latent risk of falling into the middle-income trap. China's urbanization improves quickly with it is unprecedented economic boom since the economic transformation. However, such rapid economic growth and economic structure transformation do not leave sufficient buffer time for many hidden contradictions. At the beginning of reform and opening-up, China's urbanization rate was 17.9%. However, according to the prediction of *World Urbanization Prospect 2009* by the United Nations, China's urbanization rate will exceed 70% in 2045, that is to say, the rate will increase from 25% to 70% in less than 60 years. In contrast, the United States of America spent 90 years to complete the stage from 1870 to 1960, Japan 40 years from 1930 to 1970, and Brazil more than 60 years. As for China, a country with large population and vast territory, it is of great importance to achieve urban and rural structure adjustment in a short time. Sustained rapid economic development, fast change of urban and rural structure, and quick urban growth will give rise to problems such as lag of industrial structure adjustment, inequality of income, and ignorance of urbanization quality, which will result in income gap between urban and rural areas and that between different regions. Coordinated development of urban and rural areas is the premise for economic growth, and meanwhile the integration of dual economy of urban and rural areas should not impede the overall economic growth. Under such conditions, once the economy grows rapidly and urban-rural division aggravates, the entire economic system will face the latent risk of falling into the middle-income trap.

Second, we are confronted with the inhibition from unprecedented external ecological environment and resource restraints. With continuous influx of urban population, the demand for consumption of food, water, electricity, and energy is growing exponentially. China's urbanization is facing rigid restraints like the shortage of resources and fragile ecological environment. Water resource availability per capita in China is only one-fourth of the world average value and its distribution is extremely imbalanced. The south area is richer in water resource than that in the north, and in the urban areas there is more shortage of water than in rural areas, all of which restrict the economic development. Arable land area per capita in China is only half of the world average area. The dislocation of spatial distribution of water and land resource imposes restriction on land productivity growth. The water resource in the Yangtze River Delta and its south areas accounts for more than 80% of that in the whole country, while arable land areas only account for 38%. In contrast, the water resource in Huaihe River Basin and its north areas accounts for less than 20% of that in the whole country, while arable land areas account for 62%. This phenomenon is not only reflected in natural resources, but restraints of energy of coal, oil, and natural gas are also becoming increasingly prominent.

In addition, ecological environment problems in China's industrialization should not be ignored either. Soil erosion area has reached 38% of China's total area. Desertification land area continues to expand, with annual expansion rate of 2,460 square kilometers, accounting for about 27% of the total area. Grassland degradation, desertification, and alkalization increase year by year, accounting for one-third of the total grassland. Pressure on the environment caused by municipal solid waste, industrial wastewater, waste gas emissions, and climate warming is becoming increasingly critical. The explosive growth of urban population and the prosperity of city industry gradually put more and more burden on the ecological environment. Air, water, and noise pollution is increasingly growing. China's urbanization encounters unprecedented challenges from restraints of external environment and intensive use of resources.

Third, major changes in urbanization development patterns result in challenges for China. The urbanization in the past was a kind of extensive expansion mode centered by land, relying on price difference between agricultural and non-agricultural land, as well as extremely low resource cost to expand city built-up areas. However, a large number of rural migrant workers cannot make household registration in cities where they work for long term, nor can they enjoy local social security and public service even though they contribute enormous economic value at the same time. On the one hand, along with this urbanization mode, government obtains huge benefits from land finance as a consequence of fast growth in resource and factor input. On the other hand, because of restriction from household registration, social security, public services, and other institutional factors, human capital and labor remuneration have been inhibited, and the benefit ratio of resident sectors for rural migrant workers is on an obvious slump. Such phenomenon produced two kinds of effects. On the one hand, the contribution from consumption to economic growth continued to go downward in the past ten years, which gave rise to continuous structural imbalance. On the other hand, hundreds of millions of migrant workers' living conditions could not fundamentally change due to the endogenous mechanism drive by such urbanization mode, which does not meet the demand for establishing a people-oriented and harmonious society. Therefore, it is urgent to achieve great transformation of urbanization mode and implement a new people-oriented urbanization mode proposed at the central working conference on urbanization convened by the central government of China.

II Speed of China's Urbanization during the 13th Five-Year Plan Period

The urbanization rate was only 17.92% when China initiated its reform and opening-up policy in 1978, and it surpassed 50% in 2010. We predicted China's urbanization rate would reach 50% when undertaking a key project of the National Social Science Fund in 2004. The estimated results were later incorporated into the *Research Report* on *11th Five-Year Planning* published and edited by the National Development and Reform Commission. Many people did not believe the estimated results, since there is no precedent in history that a great power can achieve such progress. However, at the end of April 2011, the State Council announced the sixth national census data, which showed that China's total population in mainland was 1.34 billion in 2010, and 49.7% of the population lived in large and medium cities or small towns. If we take population urbanization rate as a sign of urbanization rate, it can be considered that China has basically reached an urbanization rate of 50% in 2010.

Now controversy still exists about whether China's urbanization rate has exceeded 50%. Different views mainly focus on the issue whether migrant workers with a number of more than 200 million should be counted as part of urban population. It is polite to say it is peri-urbanization and impolite to say it is pseudo-urbanization, because these migrant workers have not yet settled down in urban areas. However, this issue can be seen from the point of urbanization with Chinese characteristics. It cannot be concluded that migrant workers should be excluded from the process of urbanization just because they are not yet registered into urban social security system. From a broader perspective, it is also an important symbol of China's development mode, otherwise it would be difficult to explain China's rapid development over the past 30 years. In fact, in light of the indicator of gross enrollment rate of education, China's urbanization rate of 50% can be named as gross urbanization rate. In this way, it confirms the commonality of population growth in China's urbanization and also reflects the problem that a large number of people have not been incorporated into urban social security system, which needs to be addressed.

If consensus can be reached over these problems, another question is whether this rapid progress of urbanization can continue. We believe that, according to the urbanization law and stage characteristic of China's development, such progress is unlikely to continue during the 13th Five-Year Plan period. It is advisable to slow down the speed of urbanization and raise the quality of it, with the reasons as follows.

Firstly, as for world urbanization history and experience, if we take the industrial revolution as the starting point, world urbanization history can be divided into three stages based on world urbanization levels and progress of major developed countries. Each stage has its unique development speed. China is no exception.

The years from 1760 to 1850 were the initial stage of world urbanization.

During this stage, the United Kingdom was the first country to reach the urbanization rate of 50%, while urbanization rate of the whole world was still low. In 1760, the First Industrial Revolution broke out in the United Kingdom. Enclosure movement and establishment of large-scale industry prompted a great part of rural population to flow into the city. Scale of traditional cities expanded and many new cities emerged. The proportion of urban population in the United Kingdom increased from about 25% in 1750 to 33.8% in 1801, and later reached 50.2% in 1851. It took the United Kingdom over 100 years to basically achieve the urbanization. However, except for the United Kingdom, urbanization of the whole world was still very slow. World urbanization rate was 3% in 1800 and on a rise to 6.4% in 1850.

The years from 1851 to 1950 were the publicity stage of urbanization in developed countries, including Europe and America.

During this stage, France, Germany, the United States of America, and other developed countries were the main pushers for urbanization. These countries had already gone through the phase of the industrial revolution and a substantial increase in the proportion of urban population. In 1950, the proportion of urban population in developed countries reached 51.8%, symbolizing the basic realization of urbanization, which took a hundred years by estimation. The world urbanization rate increased from 13.6% in 1900 to 28.2% in 1950, and the whole world stood at the starting line of accelerated urbanization.

The years from 1951 until now are the stage of publicity and developing of urbanization in the world.

During this stage, along with accelerated urbanization in developing countries, the urbanization rate increased from 16.2% in 1950 to 30.5% in 1980, becoming the main drive of world urbanization in the period. Steadily led by the developed countries, the whole world has reached a high height of urbanization. In 1999, the urbanization rate of the whole world was 46%, with the rate of about 50% in 2010, which achieved the basic level of urbanization. According to the law of development for world urbanization, the speed of a country's urbanization in each development stage tends to show as "peaks at both sides and low in the middle". In urbanization, the initial stage is featured with the urbanization rate below 20%, the accelerated stage with speed increase is marked by the urbanization rate from 20% to 50%, the basic realization stage with a slowing pace is characterized by the urbanization rate from 50% to 60%, and the advanced stage with very little annual growth is distinguished by the urbanization rate from 60% to 80%. In this way, the urbanization shows an S-shaped evolution pattern.

This is a general rule with different performances of different countries in different historical periods. Relatively speaking, the scale and the speed of rural population moving to cities in the early industrialized countries are relatively smaller and slower than those countries in the later stage of industrialization. Britain, France, Germany, the United States of America, Japan, and other countries have successively realized urbanization based on the time of beginning industrialization. It took Britain 90 years to increase its urbanization rate from 26% to 70%. It took USA 130 years to increase its urbanization rate from 10% in 1840, beginning of the growth period, to 73% in 1970, with an average annual growth of 0.5%. In the fastest growth time from 1940 to 1960, its average annual growth for urbanization rate was by 0.65%. In contrast, it took France 130 years to increase its urbanization rate from 24% in 1846 to 73% in 1975, with an average annual growth of 0.38%. While for the later industrialized countries, their urbanization speed greatly accelerated with annual growth from 0.8 to 1.2%. For example, it took Japan only 50 years to increase its urbanization rate from 18% in 1920 to 72% in 1970, with an average annual growth of 1.08%, same as the average annual growth of the early developed countries.

According to our prediction in 2004, China's urbanization rate will reach 60% by 2020. It means that China spent about 40 years to realize its preliminary urbanization. Although the overall time is much shorter than that of the great powers in the last century, it still needs to follow the general rules of world urbanization. However, the pace of development will slow down when the urbanization rate reaches 50%.

Secondly, based on the rules of surplus rural labor transfer in industrial structure transformation, the development of urbanization is also affected by industrial structure changes in accordance with the characteristics of industrialization, urbanization, and evolution of relations between them. It is true of China's urbanization too.

Concerning the basic rules of industrial transformation and labor transfer in industrialized countries, the change from fast to slow growth of urbanization in industrialized countries is consistent with industrialization stage. Leading industries generally experienced the course of "textile industry (labor-intensive)—heavy chemical industry (capital-intensive)—heavy processing industry (technology-intensive)—information industry". In terms of the characteristics of non-agricultural transformation of agricultural labor, it was industry that mainly absorbed labor in the initial period, centered by labor-intensive consumer goods industry. In this period, on the one hand, the low requirement for quality of rural labor made it easy to convert agricultural surplus labor to non-agricultural industries. On the other hand, the labor absorption in industry was greater than that in service industry, and employment growth rate in industry was above 0.4% and that of service industry below 0.4%. After entering the period of growth, the feature of interaction between industrialization and urbanization became particularly obvious. Industrialization promoted urbanization, and the latter, in turn, advanced the former. In this period, economy developed in a rapid and stable manner, with non-agricultural rate and urbanization rate on a quick rise. The dominant position of labor-intensive consumer goods industry was gradually replaced by the capital-intensive and technology-intensive capital goods industries. It was reflected in the gradual decrease in average annual growth rate of industrial labor and the expanding gap between the former and that of urban population, roughly starting from the time when urbanization rate reached about 50%. Just from this period, service industry and the tertiary industry accelerated their development, which was embodied in the average annual growth rate of employment in those two industries which exceeded that of urban population. Meanwhile, the demand for labor quality increased. This feature was relatively typical in Japan and the United States of America.

As a later industrialized country, the average annual growth rate of industrial employment in Japan was slightly higher than that of the United States of America. During its initial stage of industrialization in 1910, the average annual growth rate basically maintained at 1% or above. From 1910 to 1930, Japan's industrial employment growth rate ranged from 0.4% to 0.6%, while that of USA ranged from 0.4% to 0.5% in the same period. From 1860 to 1870, the urbanization rate of both countries was about 25%. When the urbanization rate reached 70% and above, the average annual growth rate of industrial employment in Japan was around 0.2%, while that of the United States of America in the same period was about 0.1%. The overall growth rate of industrial employment in Japan was higher than that in the United States of America, and the time Japan took to achieve industrialization and urbanization is also shorter than that the United States of America took. When the annual growth rate of manufacturing or industrial employment fell to 0.1% or below, the average annual growth of urbaniza-tion rate decreased to 0.1–0.2%, with economic development entering the post-industrial society that based on information industry.

China's economy entered the stage of transformation and upgrading since the 12th Five-Year Plan period. The slump of economic growth and adjust-ment of economic and industrial structure will definitely affect and restrict the speed of urbanization.

Thirdly, in view of the upcoming "Lewis turning point", the number of rural migrant workers has been on a rise since 2010, but with a gradual slowdown in growth rate. China has stepped into the section of the "Lewis turning point".

In recent years, as the income growth in central and western regions has been significantly faster than that in eastern regions, the willingness for rural residents to transfer to urban areas has weakened, resulting in the obvious labor shortage. Meanwhile, the basic wages of ordinary workers through-out the country have increased about 20%. Despite the dispute on whether China has arrived at the so-called "Lewis turning point", in my point, the answer depends on China's national conditions. It is recommended to de-scribe and summarize the essence of the above-mentioned tensions in rural labor supply via the concept of "Lewis turning point", namely, by means of replacing the number of time points with the number of periods. All the signs indicate that China has entered the period of the so-called "Lewis turning point". It means the large-scale rural labor transfer in the past will evolve into a pattern of gradual increase based on large inventory. In the case that these rural migrant workers mainly contribute to urban popula-tion increase, urbanization in China will go at a slower pace.

Fourthly, concerning the upcoming society with aging population, the demographic dividend enjoyed by China for 30 years will gradually come to the end in recent years with the advent of "Lewis turning point". A concrete prediction indicates that it will gradually decrease after reaching the peak in 2015, which will affect China's rural population supply for urbanization.

Although the details of "demographic dividend" and "Lewis turning point" are different, their impacts on and direction of urbanization are con-sistent. It can be estimated from the sixth census data that China's future population will change to a pattern featured with relatively stability in juve-nile children population, declination in working-age population, and rapid expansion of aging population. Taking into account that the rural migrant workers are mainly young adults, with the decrease of working-age pop-ulation in the total population structure, the labor force of young adults coming from rural cities will inevitably decrease and result in the slowdown of urbanization.

Fifthly, the social problems and contradictions caused by land-centered urbanization in the past also require for a slowdown in urbanization.

According to the survey, 70% to 80% of the social problems and contra-dictions in recent two years are the results of land requisition and demolition in urban areas. Moreover, rapid urbanization leads to some outstanding problems and contradictions, including those between total migration population and the overall structure, those between landless farmers and rural construction, and in migrant workers identity and in social public resource allocation. Meanwhile, the tolerance of social moral system has reached its limit, which objectively requires for the slowdown of urbanization to facilitate an overall solution to these problems and contradictions.

The above-mentioned points indicate that drastic urbanization in the past ought to come to an end and China's urbanization will step into a new stage. As for development speed, it is rational to decrease it from the average annual growth of 1.08% in the past 30 year, or from the average annual growth rate of 1.38% in the recent ten years, to that of 1% in the next ten years or so.

III Relations between China's Urbanization and Balanced Urban-Rural Growth during the 13th Five-Year Plan Period

Since the reform and opening-up, China has started its rapid urbanization. In the recent ten years, the average annual growth rate has reached 1.4%. Urbanization has a positive effect on economic development, which created the miracle of maintaining an annual growth rate of 9.8% for China's GDP for consecutive 33 years. However, the development speeds in urban areas and rural areas are different. Specifically, the average annual growth rate of gross output in rural areas is 2.11% lower than that in urban areas, while the growth rate of output per capita in rural areas is 2.16% lower than that in urban areas. Such development difference has led to imbalance in development between urban and rural areas as well as to many social problems. It arouses the attention of scholars to the relations between urbanization and urban-rural development. They doubted whether the city, as a regional economic growth pole, will inevitably lead to the imbalance in urban and rural development. According to Kuznets's law, the relation between economic development and social inequality shows in the inverted U shape. In view of high correlation between urbanization and economic development, urbanization and urban-rural imbalance will also show in inverted U shape. However, as the growth pole, the city will have the effects of both polarization and diffusion on it. When urbanization develops to a certain stage, the diffusion effect will be stronger than the polarization one, and development between urban and rural areas will come into balanced growth from unbalanced growth.

Our research indicates that the urbanization in China in recent years has entered the phase in which the diffusion effect will exceed the polarization effect. Development between urban and rural areas has come in the stage of balanced growth from unbalanced growth. It is the result of comparison between China's urbanization and that of developed countries on the turning point from the unbalanced growth to balanced growth in urban rural areas, as well as the economic actual situation of narrowing income gap between urban and rural areas. However, the actual effect of balanced growth in urban and rural areas is not obvious.

Theoretical study affirmed that urbanization can promote balanced growth in urban and rural areas and, upon investigation of government behaviors, concluded that the government's price intervention and investment preference exacerbated unbalanced growth in urban and rural areas. Empirical study in support of such conclusion also found that China's long-term price intervention and investment preference weakened and offset the positive effects of urbanization on urban-rural balanced growth, and provided an explanation to the difference between theory and practice on relations of China's urbanization and urban-rural development.[1]

According to the research results, the implementation of urbanization has a positive effect on balanced growth of urban and rural areas, though it is affected by many factors. In order to better promote urbanization and play an active role in balanced development in urban and rural areas, the following policies are recommended:

1   To continue pushing forward urbanization and strengthen factor mobility between urban and rural areas. By promoting mobility of labor, capital, and technology in urban and rural areas, the urbanization narrows the development gap between urban and rural areas in production mode determined by industrial heterogeneity. Therefore, concerning the doubts on the current urbanization caused by urban-rural development problems, we should unswervingly continue to promote urbanization. Besides, for the purpose of intensifying the role of urbanization in promoting urban and rural balanced growth, we should vigorously strengthen the circulation of factors. On the one hand, we should promote the integration of factor markets in urban and rural areas, making urban and rural areas share the factor markets. On the other hand, we should promote the double flow of factors between urban and rural areas. At the beginning of reform and opening-up, it was in the pattern of "easy in and hard out" to transfer registered permanent residence from rural areas to urban areas, while in the new urbanization, it was in the pattern of "easy out and hard in". As these will hinder the flow of factors, we need to completely release the control over household registration.

2   To increase farmer-benefiting agricultural investment and reverse government investment preference. In the early stage of economic development, it was reasonable for the government to generally adopt the strategy of unbalanced growth and put resources in key areas and regions. However, when economy develops to a certain degree, we must pay attention to the balanced growth between industries and regions, otherwise it will lead to abnormal economic development. Furthermore, supportive investment should be in the weak industries and regions, the

cause of which was the long-term negligence. In view of the weak position of China's agricultural development and unbalanced growth in urban and rural areas, the government should increase investment in rural areas. First, the government should increase investment in productive infrastructure of rural water conservancy, electricity, and agricultural base. Second, the government should increase investment in living infrastructure of rural drinking water, gas, and roads. Third, the government should strengthen the construction in infrastructure for ecological environmental protection in countryside forest protection, water and soil maintenance, flood disaster defense, and garbage disposal. Fourth, the government should strengthen the construction in infrastructure for social development in rural compulsory education, culture, and local disease prevention and control.

3   To advance economic reforms and play the decisive role of the market. Because of dependence on the policy of "agriculture subsidizing industry", agricultural product prices have been relatively lower than those of industrial products for a long time with a slow growth, which further exacerbated unbalanced growth resulting from differences in production mode between urban and rural areas. To this end, we should propel economic reforms and play the decisive role of markets in determining product prices to advance balanced growth between urban and rural areas. "Market's determination of prices" means that the rise and fall of prices are in accordance with the demand and supply, and that finally prices remain unchanged when the markets clear. Once the price or output deviates from the equilibrium state, the price will be automatically adjusted to a new equilibrium state. At present, the agricultural products in China are generally at low price, which resulted in the rural surplus resource transfer to urban areas and reduced farmers' enthusiasm for farming. If we make market determine the agricultural product prices, the relative prices of industrial products are bound to go up as opposed to agricultural products. It will narrow the gap of output between urban and rural areas caused by price difference, thus promoting balanced growth between both areas.

Note

1 For the detailed analysis about this issue, see Chen Yongjun, Chen Yiguo, "Study on Relations between Urbanization and Urban-rural Balanced Growth in China", *Economics Perspectives*, 2014, Issue No. 12.

Bibliography

Chen Yiguo, Chen Yongjun. "China's Urbanization and Inclusive Growth of Urban and Rural Areas" *Journal of Jinan University (Philosophy & Social Science Edition)*, no. 10, vol 36, 2014:87–94, 162.

8 Research on China's Coordinated Regional Development and Development Path of Urban-Rural Integration during the 13th Five-Year Plan Period

I Overall Framework of China's Coordinated Regional Development in the 13th Five-Year Plan

From 18th CPC National Congress, the new central collective leaders put forward a lot of new ideas and thoughts on coordinated regional development. As for opening-up, the central government put forward the construction of the Silk Road Economic Belt and 21st Century Maritime Silk Road. In the case of domestic regional structure adjustment, it is required to narrow policy units, make policy target accurate, and vigorously foster trans-regional and sub-regional growth poles. In addition, the Third Plenary Session of the 18th CPC Central Committee of the CPC proposed to streamline the strategies of main functional areas to a new system, which displayed the resolve of China's central government to strengthen ecological protection and regulate land development order.

According to the new ideas and new requirements of the Central Committee on China's economic and social development and promotion of coordinated regional development, based on solving the main problems existing therein, we suggest creating the system of coordinated regional development in 13th Five-Year Plan. The system consists of the four parts of reconstruction of regional pattern, optimization of policy system, improvement of management structure, and solidification of legal foundation. Here we mainly explain the reconstruction of regional pattern, namely, the construction of the development areas of "two zones, three belts and several points".

A Connotation of "Two Zones, Three Belts and Several Points"

Here we put forward to build the regional pattern of "two zones, three belts and several points" to set up the spatial-patterned system with planes, lines, and points, and to take the system as the spatial structure for promotion of coordinated regional development.

The "two zones" is to divide the inland into "western policy-supported zone" and "eastern and central zone". The "western policy-supported zone" includes the 12 provinces, autonomous regions and cities in the west, as well as the contiguous destitute areas of Wuling mountainous area, southern foot mountainous area of the Greater Khingan, Yan-Taihang mountainous area, Lvliang mountainous area, Dabie mountainous area, and Luoxiao mountainous area. Though these contiguous destitute areas are located in the east and central parts of China, they share common development problems with that in the west part, and therefore enjoy preferential policies on the western policy-supported zone. The remaining 19 provinces, autonomous regions, and cities located in the geographical east and central parts are composed of the "eastern and central zone".

The "three belts" are the three economic zones constructed to link the east with the west based on the arterial traffic and rivers. From north to south, it includes the Continental Bridge Economic Belt, the Yangtze River Economic Belt, and the Pearl River–Xijiang River Economic Belt. The establishment of the "three belts" aims to strengthen economic ties between the east and the west, to promote the factor flow among the east, central, and west parts of China, and to narrow the development gap between the east and the west regions.

"Several points" refers to the cities or regions playing the role of significant demonstration and supporting in national scope for economic development. These points mainly include five types as follows: first, the innovative type, which mainly refers to the comprehensive reform demonstration areas approved by the government; second, the economic-growth-based type, including the central cities and the surrounding areas in good condition of comprehensive development of economy; third, the transformation type, which mainly refers to the resource-exhausted cities that need to extend regional vigor through transformation of industries; fourth, the opening and driving type, which mainly refers to the opening border cities; fifth, special functional type, including the main grain-producing areas and ecological functional areas, providing food and ecological security for economic and social development in China.

B Three Economic Belts Linking the Eastern, Central and Western Areas

The close economic relationship between Southern and Northern China makes the production factors freely flow nationwide through main lines of transportation, though there are structural differences between the south and north. Meanwhile, the eastern, central, and western regions showed a larger gap in development. The innate natural conditions make the interaction between the western and eastern coastal areas reduce, factor flow focus on resource and labor eastward in a one-way manner, and the two-way flow of industry, technology, capital, and talents relatively lag behind. These three aspects restrict the development of the western region.

In view of the poor communication between the east and west parts, it is a necessity in the future to strengthen economic ties between the eastern and western regions and to promote the bilateral flow of production factors. On the one hand, it can bring more investment and technology to meet the requirement of development in the western region. On the other hand, it can also adapt to the will of the eastern region, making industrial transfer westward in the context of the Belt and Road Initiative, as well as play the role of promoting the development of the western region and narrowing the development gap between the eastern, central, and western regions. Therefore, it is imperative to build a strategic channel to link the east and west and promote the interaction between both areas.

From our existing space pattern, the channels connecting the eastern, central, and western regions are mostly the main lines of transportation. The road traffic lines include LonghaiLanxin railway, Lianhuo expressway, Zhengxi high-speed rail, Huhanrong high-speed rail, Hurong expressway, Guiguang high-speed rail, and Nanguang high-speed rail; the water road traffic lines include the Yangtze River waterway, the Pearl River–Xijiang waterway, and the Yellow River waterway. As the important corridor to promote factor flow and strengthen economic ties, these traffic lines link the important economic areas in the eastern, central, and western regions. They can be incorporated into the Continental Bridge Economic Belt, the Yangtze River Economic Zone, and the Pearl River–Xijiang River Economic Belt.

From the northern, central, and southern lines, these three channels connect the western inland and eastern coastal areas and radiate to most of the western region, linking the economic developed areas of the Yangtze River Delta and the Pearl River Delta, as well as Hubei, Henan, and other central transportation hubs. These channels bring the eastern, central, and western parts into more close connection, and the advantage transmission mechanism of the eastern region smoother. Therefore, the Continental Bridge Economic Belt, the Yangtze River Economic Belt, and the Pearl River–Xijiang River Economic Belt will be the strategic channels connecting the eastern and the western regions of China.

C *"Several Points" for Main Support*

The spatial pattern of the "two zones" and "three belts" stressed the layout and orientation of the planes and lines, which need "several points" to assume the development strategy implementation and intensify the strategic arrangement of the planes and lines. Based on the difference of regional responsibilities, here we propose five types of "several points", including innovation demonstration, economic growth, transformation and development, opening-up drive, and special functions.

The innovation demonstration district undertakes the task of reform of national economy and society. It has implemented the spirit of the reform proposed at the third Plenary Session of the 18th Central Committee of the CPC, established the special initial pilot area and made exploration and innovation in institutional mechanism in certain geographical ranges, and accumulated experience for implementation of the comprehensive reform nationwide. Shanghai FTA negative list system has made bold innovation on the foreign investment management, broke through the bottleneck of the existing policies, provided institutional innovation experience for the opening, and promoted the current reforms with significant demonstration effects. In the future, such areas require special instruction and greater policy space to further enhance the enthusiasm of institutional innovation.

The regional growth pole is an important engine of regional economic development, for it can gather production factors and drive the development of the surrounding. Chongqing and Chengdu are important growth areas in Southwest China, with the industrial cluster focusing on electronics and information industries. The industrial cluster has become the highlight of industrial transformation and upgrading, which has promoted the development of related industries through diffusion effects. Therefore, more regional growth poles need to be cultivated to develop spatial structure of network and multilevel urban system, so that the region's economic ties will become smoother, which will enhance the growth poles' role in leading the development of the surrounding backward areas.

The transformation and development areas refer to those resource-exhausted cities, with overdraft in sources, deterioration of ecological environment in mineral districts, continuous poor industrial development, a huge population of laid-off workers, and enormous rundown urban areas that require transformation. According to the definition of the "planning for sustainable development of resource-typed cities (2013–2022)", there are a total of 262 resource-based cities, including 67 declined cities. In addition to difficulties in industrial development, these regions are also confronted with employment, relocation, and living security, involving about 2.4 million people. The proper solution to these problems has a bearing on social stability and sustainable development. Therefore, it is necessary to separate it as a single kind of area that requires addressing its industrial development and social livelihood.

The opening border cities are mainly concentrated in minority nationality areas. Expanding the opening-up can promote the economic development, develop borderland economy, increase residents' income, and promote border stability. Meanwhile, with the construction of the Silk Road Economic Belt, these border cities will have more space for development, including enhancement of traffic infrastructure construction, establishment of border economic cooperation zones, and implementation of cross-border RMB settlement. It is imperative to strengthen the instruction to enhance development of such kind of areas, so as to meet the new requirements of opening-up and development of borderlands.

The special functional areas mainly include grain-producing areas and ecological functional areas, both of which play an important role in ensuring national food safety and ecological security. Grain and other agricultural products belong to quasi-public goods, while the grain planting is a weak industry with low efficiency. Many counties with great output of grains are facing the predicament of economic development,[1] which made them lack enthusiasm in grain-growing. Although the ecological function area provides the society with the public goods of ecological environment, the imperfect compensation mechanism has made the area unable to get corresponding economic compensation and resulted in the lag of regional development. Therefore, in order to better safeguard the national food safety and ecological security, we need to focus on the area, improve its compensation mechanism, and strengthen support and investment efforts in it.

II Regional Policies for Management Innovation during the 13th Five-Year Plan Period

According to the analysis on the pattern of regional development, we believe that the regional policies during the 13th Five-Year Plan period need the targeted implementation of policy-making, improvement of regional management structure and solidification of legal basis, and coordinated regional development in the key areas. The key areas here mainly refer to the western backward regions, main grain-producing areas and ecological functional areas.

A Intensify Support to Western Backward Regions

The poor traffic conditions in the western region is a serious problem to be solved, and a thorough transportation infrastructure is an important prerequisite for the development of western regions. Scholars have demonstrated and measured the positive effect of transportation infrastructure investment to economic growth, but the financial strength of the regions is limited. As the capital is the main bottleneck of the infrastructure construction, the central government is supposed to increase special investment and attract the participation of social capital, set up investment platform like railway industry investment fund, issue special bonds of western infrastructure, and widely raise construction fund.

The general gap of economic development between the western and the eastern regions is impossible to be leveled in the short term. However, the equalization of basic public services can be taken as the focus of narrowing the development gap between regions.[2] It requires the central government to increase support to the western backward areas in redistribution of resource, enhance general transfer payment to balance regional differences, and reduce or cancel the counterpart funds of local earmarks. Meanwhile, given the tax return has the effect of expanding regional development gap,[3] the existing tax refund method is supposed to be adjusted. Moreover, it is necessary to speed up the release of the Law of Fiscal Transfer Payment,[4] establish a long-term mechanism to support the western backward areas, and provide financial guarantee for equalization of basic public services.

B Increase Compensation on Main Grain-Producing Areas

The researchers found that GDP per capita and net income of farmers per capita in the main grain-producing areas are lower than those in the main grain sales areas, with the gap between them widening.[5] In view of it, it is advisable to further improve the interest compensation mechanism and alleviate financial pressure on main grain-producing areas by increasing the proportion of grain risk fund by the central government. In addition, it is commendable to establish the compensation fund in the main grain-producing areas, which can be withdrawn from the main grain sales areas according to grain amount, with a view to make up for the loss to the interest in these areas. In terms of grain allowance, the "inclusive" agricultural subsidies are difficult to motivate farmers to plant grain, with the prominent problems of land abandonment in rural areas, "rice field from double cropping to single cropping", "change food crops to non-food cash crops" and "the contractors receive subsidies but the grain planters burden risks". Now, it is suggested to encourage grain experts and rural cooperatives to take charge of more cultivated land in compliance with the principle of "providing subsidies for those who plant grain with the amount on the basis of the planting volume", so as to improve professional management of grain-growing.

C Enhance Compensation on Ecological Functional Areas

For national key ecological functional areas, the existing vertical transfer payment is faced with limitation of central financial resource and difficulty in mobilizing the enthusiasm of local government to develop ecological functional areas.[6,7] Besides, it is also difficult to reflect the symmetry of the benefit to the cost of some public goods with externalities.[8] Carrying out horizontal ecological compensation can make the available information more comprehensive and the direction of funds clearer, thus improving the efficiency of resources in use. However, at present, as China's horizontal ecological compensation system is still imperfect and in the exploratory stage, problems still, exist especially in compensation standards and negotiation methods. The transfer payment system of "focusing on vertical one with supplementary horizontal one" shall be gradually set up during the 13th Five-Year Plan period. In such system, national ecological products are undertaken by the central government and the regional ones by the beneficiary areas, with the central government's role of supervision and coordination in negotiations with local governments. In the calculation of transfer payment amount, we not only consider the standard imbalance between financial revenues and expenditures, but also take the ecological environment factors as the main indicators for measurements. Meanwhile, we can innovate the ways of payment by taking as reference Beijing's experience in providing assistance in the construction of Zhongguancun Industrial Park at Nanyang, the headwork of South-to-North Water Diversion Project, and make up for the ecological functional areas by means of financial aid and enclave economy.

D Improve Regional Management Structure for Coordinated Regional Development

The management functions for China's coordinated regional development are dispersed. Each department has certain administration privilege but lacks a unified and authorized coordination mechanism. During the 13th Five-Year Plan period, China was supposed to improve management mechanism by learning from the experience of "land planning and regional action committee" in France, integrate the administration functions of regional development at central level, and establish the "national regional development committee" to ensure the smooth implementation of regional policies.

As far as the formulation of regional policies is concerned, the central government is in the dominant position, and the mechanism for relevant regions to participate in decision-making is not comprehensive. China can learn from the approach of the regional committee affiliated to European Union Commission of listening to the interest appeals of member states[9] and try to set up the "regional committee of discussing official business" comprising of representatives of the provincial and municipal governments. In policy-making, the "national regional development committee" is supposed to listen to the opinions of the "regional committee of discussing official business".

In this way, the two committees will be able to play important roles, which will not only integrate regional management functions but also coordinate the interest between the central and local governments, enhance the scientific nature and standardization in formulating regional policies, and ensure the authority of implementation of regional policies.

E Solidify Legal Basis for Coordinated Regional Development

A sound and thorough legal system is essential for coordinated regional development. European Union, Britain, Japan, Germany, France, and the United States of America have issued relevant legal documents to implement the regional development strategies.[10,11] Compared with the sound legal system of foreign countries, the basic law for instruction of regional coordinated development of China has not yet published. There is no legal basis for the development and governance behaviors in many regions, which is not conducive to the formation of long-term mechanism of coordinated regional development. Therefore, during the 13th Five-Year Plan period, we were supposed to learn from the experience of European Union and the United States of America, solidify the legal basis for coordinated regional development, as well as promulgate the "administrative regulations on promotion of coordinated regional development" and "management measures of regional planning"[12] at national level. Concerning some special areas, legal provisions at regional level can be published to form a combination of national and local legal systems to ensure the advancement of coordinated regional development.

III   China's Current Urban-Rural Integration: Lack of Impetus and Full of Contradictions

It was proposed in the outline of 12th Five-Year Plan that, by 2015, China's urbanization rate should increase from 47.5% to 51.5%, which put up a high target for urbanization of the 12th Five-Year Plan period. According to the analysis by Ma Jiantang, Director General of National Bureau of Statistics of China's operation characteristics in 2013, China's GDP in 2013 grew by 7.7% over the previous year, and urbanization rate increased by more than 1.16% over the previous year. These facts showed that China had realized in advance the objectives of urbanization rate of the 12th Five-Year Plan, with 2.23% higher than expected. Meanwhile, we need to realize the lack of drive for China's current urban-rural integration.

A   *Problems in New Urban-Rural Integration in China*

The ratio of rural residents' net income per capita versus urban residents' disposable income in 2013 was 1:3.03, which means the disposable income of urban residents is 3.03 times the rural residents' net income per capita. Such ratio arrived at its peak value in 2009, which is 3.33 times more. However, the unbalanced, uncoordinated, and unsustainable development problems are prominent, among which the uncoordinated development between urban and rural areas was the most obvious reason. Wei Houkai, Deputy Director of Institute of Urban Development and Environment of Chinese Academy of Social Sciences, held the view that the discoordination of development between urban and rural areas mainly appears in the following four aspects.

First, the growth of economy and income of urban and rural residents is in disharmony. From 2001 to 2010, China's fiscal revenue grew at an average annual rate 20%, GDP at an average annual rate of 10.5%, urban residents' disposable income per capita at an average annual rate of 9.7%, and farmers' income per capita at an average annual rate of 7%.

Second, the ratio of residents' income of urban areas versus that of rural areas in China has been fluctuating at high value for a long time. In the past ten years, such ratio has been higher than three. It was up to 3.33 in 2009 and 3.23 in 2010, with the growth rate of rural residents' average net income per capita higher than that of urban residents' average net income per capita and the ratio of residents' income of urban areas versus that of rural areas slightly down. Meanwhile, the less developed the areas are, the greater the ratio of residents' income of urban areas versus that of rural areas will be. Such ratio in Guizhou, Yunnan, Gansu, and other provinces are higher than four. Such ratio is less than 2.5 in coastal developed areas.

Third, there is inequality in occupation of resources in urban and rural areas and development opportunity. In 2010, the urban population was less than 50% of the total but shared about 87% of the total fixed asset investment. The urban investment also had the tendency to focus on large cities, with more than 50% of the rural population to share only about 13% of the total investment. As for development opportunities, about 220 million domestic migrant workers moved from the countryside to the urban areas. They did not receive the same treatment as urban residents in terms of employment, children's education, social security, affordable housing purchase, and other aspects.

Fourth, the segmentation between urban and rural systems is serious. Until now, China is still highly fragmented in urban and rural employment, construction land, housing markets, social security, public services, and welfare policies.

In recent years, real estate industry has been vigorously developing in China and has become the local pillar industry. However, the rapid development of real estate industry cannot promote sustainable and healthy economic development in rural areas. Meanwhile, in recent years, real estate industry has been facing double challenges from changes in external environment and macro-control policies. On the one hand, the low hierarchy of industry is particularly prominent in rural areas; on the other hand, the industrial development of rural areas is the fundamental force to support rural development, and industrial hierarchy directly affects the scale of rural economic output. Although the tertiary industry has become the leading industry with the urban-rural integration in some developed regions in China, the proportion of tertiary industry accounting for the rural economy is far less than the performance of the entire economy. This is an important reason for why China's rural economy has not made enough contribution to the whole economy.

B   Short of Impetus for Urban-Rural Integration in China

1   Take Chaoyang District as Example for Analysis on Drive of Urban-Rural Integration

In order to seek the new growth points for China's rural areas involving urban-rural integration, the author took Beijing villages of Chaoyang District as samples and established the panel vector auto-regression (PVAR) model of GDP of the villages and industrial output. PVAR model, combining the advantages of vector auto-regression (VAR) model and panel data model, can control unobservable individual heterogeneity and analyze dynamic response of GDP when other variables exert impact, and thus can more accurately analyze dynamic correlation between GDP and other variables. Because of the lack of other indicators of township data, a model was introduced to the data for the total revenue of real estate (RE) industry and the output of service industry (SI), with the removal of Jinzhan Village that had insufficient data, with the established third- order hysteresis PVAR mode expressed as follows:

$$y_{it} = \alpha_i + \beta_t + Ay_{it-1} + By_{it-2} + Cy_{it-3} + \varepsilon_{it} \qquad i = 1, \dots, 19; \ t = 1, \dots, 5 \quad (1)$$

$y_{it} = (GDP, RE, SI)$ is a vector containing three dependent variables, and A, B, and C are coefficient matrixes. Compared with VAR, PVAR imports the individual effect, which depends on regional characteristics. As the correlation between technology and output of various regions might be different, the model is assumed to have regional heterogeneity to make the results more explanatory. Upon estimation of formula (1), we can get the results for two-phase hysteresis GMM regression, as shown in Table 8.1.

From the results shown in Table 8.1, we can see that the one-phase hysteresis of township economic output has a weak negative impact on its own, and the two-phase hysteresis of township economic output has an impact even weak enough to ignore. It shows that since 2008, the total output of township economy presented unsustainable growth and the growth of previous period cannot drive rapid economic growth again, which is consistent with the declination of current economic growth rate year by year. It once again proves that the economy is in transition. To achieve the rapid development of economy again, we need to seize new opportunities in economic adjustment. While the one-phase hysteresis of real estate industry has a great negative effect on the economic output, the two-phase hysteresis of real estate industry has a positive effect, with far less impact than the former. Therefore, generally speaking, the development of real estate industry will reduce the growth rate of township economy. In this regard, the adjustment and optimization of industrial structure for gradual weakening the pillar position of real estate industry in tertiary industry is an important task at this moment. As the current representative major industry to be

Table 8.1 Estimated results of GMM under PVAR model

Explanatory variables	h_GDP total economic ouput		h_RE real estate output value		h_SI service industry output value	
	b_GMM	t_GMM	b_GMM	t_GMM	b_GMM	t_GMM
L.h_GDP	−0.199	−0.822	−0.340	−1.016	−0.043	−0.542
L.h_RE	−0.662	−0.664	−0.295	−0.562	−0.263	−1.672
L.h_SI	2.152	1.820	0.865	0.822	0.681	2.479
L2.h_GDP	0.001	0.005	−0.001	−0.011	−0.006	−0.239
L2.h_RE	0.132	0.177	−0.304	−0.612	−0.037	−0.218
L2.h_SI	−0.694	−2.93	−0.248	−0.720	−0.049	−0.611

Note: h_• represents that the variable has been implemented Helmert conversion. Li.h_• represents the i-order hysteresis of the corresponding variables.

focused on, the service industry's pulling role in economy development in the first phase is 2.15, namely, one unit of growth of service industry output will lead to 2.15 units of growth of total output. It indicates that the service industry has a strong development potential and gradual improvement of this sector will bring new opportunities for development of the overall economy. In recent years, the real estate industry has been gradually shrinking, and the proportion of added value in modern service industry decreased from 21.7% in 2010 to 19.3% in 2012. In contrast, the modern service industry as a whole showed rapid growth and greatly increased regional fiscal revenue. In 2012, the prime operating revenue of modern service industry was RMB846.2 billion, with annual growth rate up to 11.7%; the regional fiscal revenue was RMB18.87 billion, accounting for 56.5% of annual regional fiscal revenue, expected to reach at the end of the 12th Five-Year Plan Period the target of "realizing the regional fiscal revenue of modern service industry up to RMB22 billion, accounting for 60% of annual regional fiscal revenue". It appears from the aforementioned data that modern service industry is in rapid development, with increasingly obvious pulling effect on economy and finance, and will become the main force to support urban-rural integration; in the meanwhile, the dominant position of real estate industry has been rocked to some extent, with the potential for economic development focusing on leasing and business services, financial industries, cultural creative industries, and other service industries.

On the other hand, from the variance results shown in Table 8.2, from Phase 10 to 30, the proportion of the change in GDP, output value of industries of real estate, and service accounting for that the total output value remain 0.814:0.049:0.137. In other words, among all factors that contribute to GDP growth, about 5% are real estate industry and about 14% service industry. It shows that in current stage, the pulling effect of real estate industry on economy has been very limited, while the growth of service industry will contribute more to the total output value of villages and towns. To stick to the development of the four major industries is conducive to the stimulation of the economic growth potential in rural areas. It is imperative to optimize industrial structure.

Table 8.2 Results of variance decomposition of PVAR model

	Phase	GDP	RE	SI
GDP	10	0.8137	0.0493	0.1370
RE	10	0.1112	0.8208	0.0680
SI	10	0.1738	0.2821	0.5441
GDP	20	0.8137	0.0493	0.1370
RE	20	0.1112	0.8208	0.0680
SI	20	0.1738	0.2821	0.5441
GDP	30	0.8137	0.0493	0.1370
RE	30	0.1112	0.8208	0.0680
SI	30	0.1738	0.2821	0.5441

2 Analysis of Impetus Mechanism for Urban-Rural Integration

Based on the data of Chaoyang District, it is not difficult to find that the real estate industry is not strong enough to fuel economy to maintain rapid growth, while the development of the tertiary industry dominated by modern service industry plays an increasingly important role in driving urban-rural integration. As China's economy is now in a general adjustment period, economic growth cannot be self-driven and rapid for a long time. It is necessary to develop new pillar industries to lead healthy and rapid economic development.

To further determine the position of modern service industry (MS) in horizontal industry comparison and the role of other industries in economic operation, this chapter introduces the other two key industries, high-technology industry (HT) and cultural creative industries (CI), establishes the VAR model between GDP of Chaoyang District and various industrial venue from 2006 to 2012, as well as makes analysis of the dynamic correlation between economic variables. The estimated result of the VAR model is shown as follows:

$$
\begin{pmatrix} \ln(gdp_t) \\ \ln(ht_t) \\ \ln(ms_t) \\ \ln(ci_t) \end{pmatrix} = \begin{pmatrix} 4.08 \\ -4.66 \\ 5.08 \\ 2.80 \end{pmatrix} + \begin{pmatrix} -0.79 & -0.15 & 0.21 & 1.26 \\ 2.67 & 0.42 & -0.74 & -0.90 \\ -0.83 & -0.72 & 0.03 & 1.93 \\ -0.95 & -0.12 & 0.47 & 1.20 \end{pmatrix} \begin{pmatrix} \ln(gdp_{t-1}) \\ \ln(ht_{t-1}) \\ \ln(ms_{t-1}) \\ \ln(ci_{t-1}) \end{pmatrix} + \varepsilon_t
$$

The estimated result shows the following.

Firstly, the influence coefficient on the one-phase hysteresis of ln(GDP) itself is −0.79, that is, the economic growth at 1% in the last phase will reduce the current economic growth by 0.79%. It demonstrates the conclusion again that the present economic growth in Chaoyang District is in stagnation.

Second, the high-tech industry growth at 1% in the last phase will reduce the current economic growth by 0.15%, that is to say, the pulling effect of high-tech industrial growth on economy has not appeared. It is mainly due to the fact that the development of high-tech industry is low in the current urban-rural integration and the added value of industry occupies a small proportion of GDP. Therefore, we should seize the opportunities in new urban-rural integration during the 13th Five-Year Plan period and develop the innovation-driven urban-rural integrated industrial development, thus displaying the role of high-tech industry in promoting urban-rural integration.

Third, the modern service industry growth at 1% in the last phase will increase the current economic growth by 0.21%, that is to say, the pulling effect of modern service industrial growth on economy continues. The accelerated development of modern service industry is still the essential impetus for regional economic growth. In this regard, we should seize the opportunities of eastward moving of global economic center, make relevant transformation and structural upgrade, and further strengthen the leading position of modern service industry, in order to promote urban-rural integration by optimizing and upgrading modern service industry.

Fourth, the cultural creative industry growth at 1% in the last phase will pull the current economic growth by 1.26%, that is to say, cultural creative industrial has the greatest potential in regional economic development. In contrast with the mature service industry and bourgeoning high-tech industry, the cultural and creative industry is flourishing in China. From this perspective, the cultural creative industry undoubtedly has the greatest development potential. During the 11th Five-Year Plan period, some areas in China began to attach great importance to cultural construction, consider cultural creative industry as one of the four high-end industries that were the focus of regional development, and incorporate it into the overall planning of national economic and social development. During the 13th Five-Year Plan period, China is supposed to integrate the development of cultural creative industry with the accelerated development of urban-rural integration to advance the structure adjustment and development mode transformation of urban and rural economy. The detailed measures include the implementation of strategies of industrial high-end orientation and echelon development in line with development of industry scales, with a view to constantly optimize industrial structure, stimulate its potential to promote urban-rural integration, and enhance the sustainable development of urban and rural economy.

IV Thought of Advancing China's New Urban-Rural Integration during the 13th Five-Year Plan Period

A Urbanization in Humanity Context

Fundamentally, new urbanization concerns mostly about people. In terms of humanity urbanization, whether in metropolitans or small towns, the overall planning of urban and rural areas is of vital importance. The urbanization and rural development should be placed in "one game of chess" to avoid the urbanization to strike rural development or deviate from it. It is important to speed up the "integration" paces in urban and rural planning, industrial layout, infrastructure, public services, social security for employment, and social management, with a view to promote balanced allocation of public resources between urban and rural areas and equal exchange of development factors between urban and rural areas, as well as to achieve the benign interaction and common prosperity between the urban and rural areas.

Urban and rural areas are not opposite to each other in themselves. Rural population is neither necessarily to enter the cities nor to keep in line with the urban development, but to follow-up the industrial development. Because there are industries in the cities, this part of the population was taken into the cities. China's industrialization has gone through 20 years and now faces with great structural changes and adjustment. With the advent of such adjustment, the demand for land and population, especially for involved industrial workers, is also changing.

B Urban-Rural Integration: Industrial Integration between Urban and Rural Areas

In the past 20 years, the rural population has become smaller, but not all the farmers have entered the urban areas. Among those who have stayed in rural areas, a large number of them have transferred from primary to tertiary industry and have engaged in service industry in rural areas or for small and medium-sized cities. A part of the industries went from the city into the countryside, narrowing the distance between rural and urban areas, but this is only a part of the market. The government should invest more in rural areas to support their development. In the future, most of the industries might be considerably based in rural areas or small towns. Farmers not only do the jobs of primary industry but also engage in the jobs of tertiary industry in rural areas and small cities. Considering that the problems of dual structure in urban-rural economy have not been resolved, farmers have spontaneously adopted such way. If urbanization can solve the needs of human development, namely, people in rural areas can also develop something that really supports urban industrial system, it is verified to be the right orientation.

It is imperative to accelerate the transformation of agricultural production, to encourage large-scale operation, as well as to further improve the efficiency of agricultural production and farmers' income through scaled production ways of family farm and cooperatives plus peasant households. It is necessary to explore and promote the reform of property rights system of rural collective economic organizations, to encourage and instruct the collective assets to focus on the street-town first-level platform, and to improve revenue distribution mechanism through clarifying rights and shares, thus having farmers become aware of the benefits of the collective "cake". It is important to improve the supporting policies and measures for land transfer, to guarantee the employment of transforming rural labor, and to establish a mechanism for farmers' income to go on a long-term and stable rise by means of multi-pronged approaches.

C Fostering Rural Market and Establishing Specialized Rural Market System

The urbanization has stimulated the vitality of the rural market and resulted in the unprecedented prosperity of it. Under the influence of urbanization, the traditional concept for famers to value production but ignore marketing has been changed, and their enthusiasm and conscientiousness of caring and supporting the establishment and cultivation of the market is inspiring. Traditional farmers have become the new market players in rural market and have started to envisage the market, learn more about it, and actively participate in it. In addition, the development of agriculture prospers the rural market, which synchronizes the development of characteristic agriculture and rural economy. In this way, a rural system with "combination of small, medium and large markets, combination of wholesale and retail markets and combination of comprehensive and specialized markets" is established. In other words, the rural market system involves both the open big markets—with high standards, large scales, wide ranges, and full functions—and the small market places—with small scales and availability for local practice. Besides, the development of agricultural leading enterprises also promotes the prosperity of rural markets. The agricultural products processing enterprises and the rural markets supplement each other for mutual development, namely, there are active rural markets in the radiation range of each leading enterprise, and agricultural products processing enterprises around each rural market. Through such mode of "enterprise + market + farmer", both enterprises and markets grow, thus increasing the income of farmers.

We should give full play to the decisive role of the market in resource allocation. In the future new urbanization, we should pay more attention to the role of market, fully apply the laws of market, and make decisions on the new urbanization on such basis.

D Constructing Moderate Concentrated Rural Infrastructure Network with Joint of Lines and Dots

1 Scientific Planning and Rational Layout of Rural Communities

It is an important prerequisite to improve new rural construction and achieve urban-rural integration. During the 12th Five-Year Plan period, along with the rapid development of modern agriculture, the new rural planning in rural areas was developing from simple to zero to sophisticated, from pushing and dominating of the government to continuous participation of farmers and communities, thus increasingly rationalizing the planning and layout of rural.

Upon close combination of tourism and cultural industry, on the basis of the development of modern agriculture, rural communities were proposed higher requirements for their functions, thus accordingly demanding more scientific nature and reasonability of planning of villages and towns.

2 Increase Construction of Rural Transportation Network

The development of characteristic agriculture leads to higher requirements for the rapid turnover and circulation of agricultural products and processed finished products. The countryside tourism driven by characteristic agriculture also demands more convenient transportation for rural areas. During the 13th Five-Year Plan period, the improvement of rural road network was an important part for characteristic agriculture development and rural urbanization, as convenient communication and transportation conditions propel agriculture development and rural urbanization.

3 Build Comprehensive Rural Infrastructure System

The degree of completion of rural infrastructure determines the degree of sustainable development of rural industries and urbanization of rural areas. Only by seizing the key link of rural infrastructure can we provide the solid material foundation for the development of characteristic agriculture and s to ensure the stable construction of new socialist countryside. The local governments of Beijing, Hangzhou, and other cities attach great importance to both the development of characteristic agriculture and the enhancement of infrastructure construction in rural areas. In these cities, fiscal and credit funds are comprehensively utilized in construction of convenient rural transportation system, public transportation system, and electric power communication facilities.

Our tasks in the future shall include to intensify the "five projects of infrastructure for the new rural areas" and the initiatives of "to make rural areas light up, farmers warm up and agricultural resources cycle up"; to promote the use of clean energy, renewable energy, and energy-saving products; to gradually improve the construction of rural public service information system by establishing mechanism of managing and protecting expenditure collection and investment in infrastructure construction.

4 Promote Modernization of Farmers' Production and Lifestyle

The urban-rural integration has made the countryside burst into vigor by bringing benefits to agriculture and increasing income of farmers.

Notes

1 Wei Houkai, Wang Yeqiang, On Theoretical Basis and Policy Guidance for Development of Major Agricultural Production Areas Supported by Central Government of China. *Economic Perspectives*, 2012 (11): 49–55.
2 Chi Fulin, "On Accelerating Equalization of Basic Public Services". *Review of Economic Research*, 2008 (3): 19–25.
3 Xu Bo, "On Tax Returns under Tax Distribution System". *Public Finance Research, 2010* (4): 69–71.
4 Zhang Daoqing, "On Legal Regulation on Relation between Central and Local Fiscal Transfer Payments", *Modern Law Science*, 2007 (11): 56–68.
5 Wei Houkai, Wang Yeqiang, On Theoretical Basis and Policy Guidance for Development of Major Agricultural Production Areas Supported by Central Government of China. *Economic Perspectives*, 2012 (11): 49–55.

6 Zhong Daneng, "Research on Plight of Financial Transfer Payment System Developed in National Key Ecological Function Areas", *Edition of Humanities and Social Sciences of Journal of Southwest University for Nationalities*, 2014 (4): 122–126.

7 Zhang Hongyan, Dai Xinxin, "Exploration and Analysis of Horizontal Transfer Payment System for Ecological Compensation in China's Key Function Areas", *Ecological Economy*, 2011 (2): 154–157.

8 Yang Xiaomeng, "On Establishment of Ecological Compensation and Horizontal Transfer Payment System in China", *Public Finance Research*, 2013 (2): 19–23.

9 Wang Yamei, "Study on Regional Policies of European Union" [D], Chengdu: Sichuan University, 2005.

10 Zhang Guangcui, "Study on EU Regional Policies" [D], Changchun: Jilin University, 2006.

11 Zhou Yezhong, Zhang Biao, "To Promote Analysis of System Theory on Legal Mechanism for Coordinated Regional Development" [J], *Hubei Social Sciences*, 2012 (5): 142–147.

12 Department of Regional Economy of National Development and Reform Commission, "On In-depth Implementation of Overall Strategies for Regional Development and Active Promotion of Coordinated Regional Development" [J], *China Economic & Trade Herald*, 2014 (2): 9–11.

Bibliography

Cao Kehai, Wang Haixia, Lang Xuehong. "Ecological Construction: Strategic Choice of Sustainable Development of Western China", *Environmental Forum*, no. 12, 2000, pp. 1–3.

Chen Yao. "Acting Point of China's Coordinated Regional Development in New Era", *China National Conditions and Strength*, no, 2, 2013, pp. 12–14.

Chen Yao. "Study on Major Issues of China's Regional Economy", *Regional Economic Review*, no. 1, 2013, pp. 24–28.

Chi Fulin. "On Accelerating Equalization of Basic Public Services", *Review of Economic Research*, no. 3, 2008, pp. 19–25.

Department of Regional Economy of National Development and Reform Commission. "On In-depth Implementation of Overall Strategies for Regional Development and Active Promotion of Coordinated Regional Development", *China Economic & Trade Herald*, no. 2, 2014, pp. 9–11.

Du Ying. "Comprehensive View on Regional Economic Development for Continuous Momentum of Coordinated Development", *China Economic & Trade Herald*, no. 2, 2014, pp. 4–8.

Fan Hengshan. "Challenges and Solutions to Coordinated Regional Development", *China Reform Daily*, 2011–07–29.

Fan Hengshan. "The Momentum to Write a New Chapter in Coordinated Regional Development", *China Energy News*, 2011-01-03.

Fan Hengshan. "Theory and Practice of Promoting China's Coordinated Regional Development", *Comparative Economic & Social Systems*, no. 6, 2011, pp. 1–9.

Fan Hengshan. "Basic Direction and Key Tasks to Promote Coordinated Regional Development", *Review of Economic Research*, no. 13, 2014, pp. 62–68.

Fan Hengshan. "China's Basic Experience in Promoting Coordinated Regional Development", *People's Daily*, 2014-04-01.

Fan Hengshan. *Five Major Breakthrough in Coordinated Regional Development*, www.lwgcw.com. Accessed 2014-03-31.

Fan Hengshan. "The Fan Hengshan. "Challenges and Guan Yongbin. "Construction and Empirical Analysis of China's Evaluation Indicator System for Interregional Gap of Basic Public Services", *Reform of Economic System*, no. 5, 2011, pp. 13–17.

Hu Shaowei. "Thoughts of Promoting Regional Coordinated Development", *China Opening Journal*, no. 10, 2013, pp. 40–43.

Huang Yanfang. "Exploration and Analysis on Partner Assistance Operation Mechanism", *Economic Vision*, no. 6, 2011, pp. 180–181.

Lin Quanzhen, Yao Huajun. "On Enlightenment of Development Experience in Southern Italy to Development of Western China", *Geology in China*, no. 7, 2000, pp. 15–17.

Liu Huajun, Zhang Quan, Yang Sai, Yang Baoli. "Spatial Disequilibrium of China's Basic Public Services and Its Relation with Regional Economic Disparities", *Research on Economics and Management*, no. 2, 2014, pp. 53–59.

Liu Shenglong, Hu Angang. "Transportation Infrastructure and Economic Growth: A Perspective of Regional Gap in China", *China Industrial Economics*, no. 4, 2010, pp. 14–23.

Liu Zhibiao. "Basic Path and Long-term Mechanism of China's Coordinated Development of Regional Economy", *Journal of China University of Geosciences (Social Sciences Edition)*, no. 1, 2013, pp. 4–10.

Lu Dadao. "Economic Belt Construction Is the Best Choice of Economic Development Layout: The Enormous Potential for the Changjiang River Economic Belt", *Scientia Geographica Sinica*, no. 7, 2014, pp. 769–772.

Meng Quansheng. "Study on Formation Mechanism and Countermeasures for Rural Poverty in Western China", *Agricultural Research in the Arid Areas*, no. 1, 2007, pp. 53–57.

Qin Chenglin. "Research on Coordinated Regional Development Mechanism", *Economist*, no. 4, 2011, pp. 63–70.

Qin Chenglin, Jiang Wenxian. "Connotation, Motivation and Mechanism of Coordinated Regional Development", *Research on Development*, no. 1, 2011, pp. 14–18.

Wang Jiaxu. "Analysis of Momentum and Cause of Disparity of Economic Development between Regions of China", *Research on Development*, no. 5, 2013, pp. 18–22.

Wang Yamei. "Study on Regional Policies of European Union", Doctoral Dissertation, Chengdu: Sichuan University, 2005.

Wang Yongcai. "Problem of Counterpart Support in Ethnic Areas and Reflection on Rule of Law", *Ethno-National Problem Studies*, no. 2, 2014, pp. 16–21.

Wang Yongfu. "Exploration and Analysis on Status of Basic Law of Coordinated Regional Development", *Journal of Hubei University of Economics (Humanities & Social Edition)*, no. 2, 2014, pp. 90–91, 94.

Wei Houkai. "Differences in Development between Regional Infrastructure and Manufacturing in China", *Management World*, no. 6, 2001, pp. 72–81.

Wei Houkai, Gao Chunliang. "Connotation and Mechanism of Coordinated Regional Development in New Era", *Fujian Tribune (The Humanities & Social Sciences Bimonthly)*, no. 10, 2011, pp. 147–152.

Wei Houkai, Gao Chunliang. "China's Situation of Coordinated Regional Development and Policy Adjustment Ideas", *Henan Social Sciences*, no. 1, 2012, pp. 73–81, 107–108.

Wei Houkai, Wang Yeqiang. "On Theoretical Basis and Policy Guidance for Development of Major Agricultural Production Areas Supported by Central Government of China", *Economic Perspectives*, no. 11, 2012, pp. 49–55.

Wu Jinglian. "On Migration of Rural Surplus Labor and "Three Rural Issues", *Macroeconomics*, no. 6, 2002, pp. 6–9.

Xu Bo. "On Tax Returns under Tax Distribution System", *Public Finance Research*, no. 4, 2010, pp. 69–71.

Xuan Xiaowei. "Inclined Framework of China's Regional Economic Policy Adjustment", *Reform*, no. 8, 2012, pp. 59–67.

Yang Xiaomeng. "On Establishment of Ecological Compensation and Horizontal Transfer Payment System in China", *Public Finance Research*, no. 2, 2013, pp. 19–23.

Yang Mengkai. "Fostering Transregional Growth Poles to Become Focus of Regional Development", *China Business Journal*, 2013-11-11.

Yang Mengkai. "Five Highlights to Promote Strategic Deployment of Coordinated Regional Development", *China Investment*, no. 1, 2014, pp. 96–97.

Yang Mengkai. "Understanding of Relevant Content in Government Work Report for Accurate Recognition of New Requirements of Promoting Coordinated Regional Development", *Macroeconomic Management*, no. 4, 2014, pp. 26–27.

Zhou Yiren. "Improvement of Zhang Daoqing. "On Legal Regulation on Relation between Central and Local Fiscal Transfer Payment", *Modern Law Science*, no. 11, 2007, pp. 56–68.

Zhang Guangcui, Jing Yuejun. "On Enlightenment of Development Experience in Underdeveloped Areas in USA and Japan to Development of Western China", *Northeast Asia Forum*, no. 1, 2003, pp. 31–34.

Zhang Guangcui. "Study on EU Regional Policies", Doctoral Dissertation, Changchun: Jilin University, 2006.

Zhang Hongyan, Dai Xinxin. "Exploration and Analysis of Horizontal Transfer Payment System for Ecological Compensation in China's Key Functional Areas", *Ecological Economy*, no. 2, 2011, pp. 154–157.

Zhang Lijun, Tao Tiantian, Zheng Yingchao. "On Evaluation and Thought of Implementation Effect of Opening Up Policies in China Border Areas", *Ethno-National Studies*, no. 2, 2011, pp. 10–20, 107.

Zhang Xingmei. "On 'Three Rural Issues' (Agriculture, Rural Areas and Farmers) in Rise of Central China", *Economic Geography*, no. 1, 2008, pp. 128–130.

Zhang Xueliang. "Regional Comparative Analysis of Transportation Infrastructure and Economic Growth", *Journal of Finance and Economics*, no. 8, 2007, pp. 51–63.

Zhong Daneng. "Research on Plight of Financial Transfer Payment System Developed in National Key Ecological Functional Areas", *Edition of Humanities and Social Sciences of Journal of Southwest University for Nationalities*, no. 4, 2014, pp. 122–126.

Zhou Yezhong, Zhang Biao. "To Promote Analysis of System Theory on Legal Mechanism for Coordinated Regional Development", *Hubei Social Sciences*, no. 5, 2012, pp. 142–147.

Zhou Yiren. "Improvement of Macroeconomic Management for Coordinated Regional Development", *Macroeconomic Management*, no. 1, 2014, pp. 26–27.

9 Foreign Investment Environment, Foreign Investment, Transition of Industrial Structure, and Outlook for Economic Growth during the 13th Five-Year Plan Period

I Relations between China's Foreign Investment Environment, Foreign Investment, and Economic Growth

A Relation between China's Foreign Investment Environment and Foreign Investment

Investment environment refers to the summation of all the surrounding circumstances and conditions during the entire investment activities. In summary, it includes natural factors, social factors, economic factors, political factors, and regulation policy factors that impact investment activities. The economic factors, natural factors, and regulation policy factor are three core ones that constitute foreign investment environment. The relation between these three core factors and foreign investment are described as follows.

1 Relation between Economic Factors and Foreign Investment

Economic factors mainly include the market and the infrastructure, with the relation with foreign investment mostly presented in the following aspects.

First, the larger the scale of market development, the higher the market demand will be and greater the amount of foreign investment will be. In terms of market, the developing scale and demand of the market have significant impact on the foreign investment. With a population of more than a billion, China is a huge market with the highest potential in the world. Besides, with the constant rapid growth of China's economy, its marketing economic system has improved, with its potential as a huge market being gradually exploited. In other words, China has become the enormous market of raw material, talents, sales, and capital for worldwide transnational corporations. Such geographic conveniences are beneficial for transnational corporations to display their monopolistic advantages. According to a study by Chinese Academy of International Trade and Economic Cooperation (CAITEC), the huge market in China is exactly the main reason why China attracts foreign investors. Additionally, the increasing improvement of living standard of Chinese people, gradual rise of disposable income of Chinese residents, and the constant expansion of effective demand of the market are also the causes. Moreover, the continuous increase of consumption ability, consumer's confidence, and consumption amount of Chinese residents promotes the diversification in demand. It makes the investment profit of foreign investors higher and more stable. For example, within the China's inland areas, the eastern provinces and cities with higher consumption, like Guangdong, Jiangsu, Shandong, Zhejiang, Fujian, and Shanghai, have greater attraction for foreign direct investment (FDI) than the western areas. Therefore, we can say that the larger the market development scale, the higher the market demand will be, and larger the amount of foreign investment will be.

Second, solid infrastructure and industries are beneficial to attract foreign investment. The basic industries and infrastructure mainly include the industries of agriculture, forestry, husbandry and fishery, raw material, transportation, post service and telecommunication, water conservancy management, energy industry, and urban public service. Although solid infrastructure construction is not the key point for direct input of foreign investment, it can accelerate the flow and accumulation of factors and guarantee smooth and efficient utilization of foreign investment. For example, China's eastern coastal areas have advantages in geographical location based on plain territory, crisscrossing network of railways and highways, convenient transportation, centralized trunk lines of telecommunication network, speedy and smooth information communication, and advanced production equipment. In contrast, most of the central and the western regions are highland, with restricted transportation, unsmooth information communication, low efficiency, and outdated equipment. In this case, foreign investment will naturally favor the eastern areas and keep away from the central and the western regions. In view of information exchange, the smooth, timely, and effective communication will be helpful for reduction of searching acquisition cost for markets, convenient for enterprises to adjust products design as soon as possible according to market feedback at any time, and easy for rapid localization of products, thus achieving competitive advantage. Therefore, solid basic industries and facilities are beneficial to draw in foreign investment.

2 Relation between Natural Factors and Foreign Investment

Natural factors include natural resource and human capital factors. Its relation with foreign investment is presented in the following two aspects.

First, abundant and high-quality natural endowment is advantageous to attract foreign investment. In term of natural resource, total amount and the distribution of natural resource have vital impact on attraction of foreign investment. For example, China signed contracts for joint exploitation of oil with many transnational corporations from the United States of America in early 1980s. Most of the direct investment from the United States of America flew into the energy exploitation, where the American enterprises made significant benefits. Some enterprises in need of rare metal resources for production relied on their choice of production address. If these enterprises can produce in the region with abundant resource reserve, they can significantly reduce production cost. Therefore, the natural resource is an important factor for this type of foreign enterprises to consider for addressing choice for their investment. In addition, China's natural resource totals in huge amount but is unevenly distributed, which, to some extent, intensifies the regional imbalance of foreign investment. It is obvious that it is easy for those countries with abundant natural resources and good natural resource endowment to attract the inflow of FDI.

Second, low-cost and high-quality human capital draws foreign investment. In theory, the labor cost shows negative correlation with the amount of FDI. In the case that the prices of other factors are constant, namely, the higher the price of labor force is, the lower the enterprise's operating profits will be. In this connection, the capital will choose the investment with higher profits under the essence of capital in pursuit of profits. That is, for one region, the lower the labor cost is, the higher the inflow of foreign investment will be. On the contrary, the attraction of this region to FDI will reduce. Therefore, in terms of cost factor, the cost of human capital affects the flow direction of FDI. For example, many foreign investment enterprises realized the low-cost labor from China and set up their manufacturing sector in China before they exported completed products to other countries and regions. However, the advantage of cheaper labor cost of China has been weakening. On the one hand, this type of FDI is influenced much by the foreign exchange rate. With the appreciation of RMB to USD exceeding by 28% from 2004 to 2011, the competitiveness of "made in China" products was weakened, export capacity was sluggish, and utilization of foreign investment in manufacturing industry was curbed. On the other hand, with the development of China's economy and society, the average salary of employees in urban units increased from RMB2,140 in 1990 to RMB41,799 in 2011. In addition, from the point of human capital quality, sufficient highly competent talents can promote technology transfer and production expansion of transnational corporations, reduce training costs, and accelerate localization of products. Even though the cost for highly competent labor is higher than the cost for low-quality labor, the former has a stronger attraction to foreign investment than the latter because highly competent labor creates higher profits. The actual competition in the 21st century is that of talents. As human capital becomes increasingly more important in enterprise development—the higher the human capital quality is, the lower the cost for searching efficient workers will be. In normal circumstances, the region or industry the FDI is focused on is either the one with low labor cost or the one with intensive talents.

B Relation between China's Foreign Investment and Economic Growth

1 Quantitative Analysis Based on Industrial Perspective

Based on industrial perspective, by virtue of the amount of actual utilization of FDI in the three industries, contribution to GDP, and pulling effect on GDP, we will examine the relation between foreign investment and China's economic growth.

(1) FOREIGN INVESTMENT IN PRIMARY INDUSTRY REMAINS LOW AND
    STABLE WITH SMALL CONTRIBUTION TO ECONOMIC GROWTH

Primary industry: The amount of actual utilization of FDI attracted by the primary industry continuously went on a steady rise from 1997 to 2004, significantly dropped from 2005 to 2006, and rose again from 2006 to 2011, so did the proportion of it, which was rising from 2008 to 2011, but no more than 2%. As shown in Figure 9.1, the contribution rate of primary industry to GDP exhibited a stable fluctuation momentum from 2000 to 2011, except that it dropped to 3.4% in 2003 and 3% in 2007, and then suddenly rose to more than 7.8% in 2004; the contribution rate in other years remained from 4% to 6%. Moreover, as shown in Figure 9.2, the pulling rate of primary industry to GDP was below 1% from 2000 to 2011, with the shape of fluctuation in accordance with that of its contribution rate to GDP. In general, compared with the secondary and tertiary industries, the foreign investment amount as well as the contribution rate and pulling effect on GDP of the primary industry was relatively stable in recent ten years, still at a low level. That is, the total amount of foreign investment in the primary industry was small, with narrow amplification and low contribution and pulling effect on economic growth.

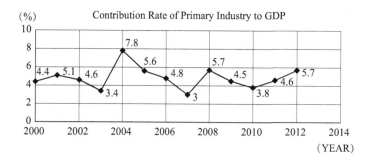

Figure 9.1 Contribution rate of primary industry to China's GDP from 2000 to 2011.
Data source: China Statistics Yearbook (2001–2012).

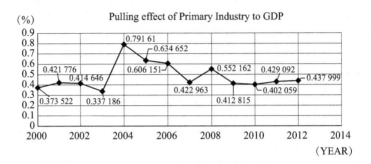

Figure 9.2 Pulling effect of primary industry on China's GDP growth from 2000 to 2011.

Data source: China Statistics Yearbook (2001–2012).

(2) FOREIGN INVESTMENT PREFERS SECONDARY INDUSTRY, WHICH
ENORMOUSLY CONTRIBUTES TO ECONOMIC GROWTH

Secondary industry: Except an apparent decrease in 1998, the total amount of FDI in secondary industry maintained a stable growth in other years. From 1990 to 1993, the proportion of total amount of FDI slightly decreased. From 1994 to 2004, the proportion of secondary industry quickly increased, with huge gap with the tertiary industry. Moreover, the FDI was highly concentrated, which was objectively beneficial to China's industrialization. From 2005 to 2011, the proportion of FDI in manufacturing industry remarkably declined, which was mainly caused by the rise of China's labor cost. However, from the data from 2008 to 2011, even though the proportion of the amount of actual utilization of FDI attracted by the secondary industry declined, the total amount was above USD50 billion, which indicated that the secondary industry was still the key industry for foreign investment, wherein manufacturing industry still ranked top in the list of FDI—far ahead from other industries. According to Figure 9.3, in recent ten years, the contribution rate of such industry to GDP was basically above 50% and reached its peak of 60.8% in 2000, which fully reflected the attraction of China's cheap labor to foreign investment. It dropped to below 50% in 2001, 2002, and 2008, and headed downward from 2010 to 2011. Furthermore, as shown in Figure 9.4, in terms of the pulling rate of secondary industry to GDP growth from 2000 to 2011, it dropped to 3.9% only in 2001, reached its peak of 7.2% in 2007, fluctuated within the range of 4% to 6.5% in other years, with the shape of fluctuation generally in line with that of the contribution rate of secondary industry to GDP, except in 2007. In general, in recent ten years, the secondary industry has become the key industry for foreign investment, which contributed enormously to China's economic growth and greatly pulled its economic growth, which was objectively beneficial to its industrialization. Besides, it should be noted that the amount

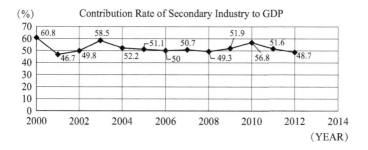

Figure 9.3 Contribution rate of secondary industry to China's GDP from 2000 to 2011.
Data source: China Statistics Yearbook (2001–2012).

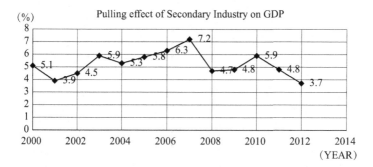

Figure 9.4 Pulling effect of secondary industry on GDP growth from 2000 to 2011.
Data source: China Statistics Yearbook (2001–2012).

of foreign investment contribution rate to GDP and pulling effect of the secondary industry declined in the last two years.

(3) FOREIGN INVESTMENT IN TERTIARY INDUSTRY STEADILY ARISES WITH REMARKABLE CONTRIBUTION TO ECONOMIC GROWTH

Tertiary industry: The total amount of foreign investment in the tertiary industry was basically steady with a small rise from 1999 to 2006 and a significant growth from 2006 to 2011. The proportion of the tertiary industry rapidly increased from 1990 to 1993, and its proportion in the total amount of FDI increased to 49%, basically equivalent to the proportion of the secondary industry. This is mainly due to the increase of investment in real estate industry. In 1993, the amount of FDI contracts in real estate, public utilities, and service industry was USD 43,770 billion, 2.4 times as that in 1992. The FDI in the tertiary industry distinctly decreased in 1994 and fell behind secondary industry by nearly 40% in 1995. Because of China's macro-control over real estate industry and relevant policies concerning FDI, the gap between the two industries never narrowed until 2004. In the second half year of 1993, Chinese government cleaned up and rectified the real estate market. In 1997, Chinese government released the *Catalog for Guidance of Foreign Investment Industries* and proposed that high-end hotels, villas, high-end office buildings, international convention centers, and tracts of land will not be allowed to develop by wholly foreign-owned companies. However, the new *Catalog for the Guidance of Foreign Investment Industries* issued in 2002 encouraged foreign investors to invest in development and construction of residential housing. From 2004 to 2007, FDI in real estate industry rapidly arose. The amount of actual utilization of foreign investment increased nearly three times, and the proportion of FDI total amount in real estate industry increased to 22.9% in 2007, up by 13%. From 2005 to 2011, the tertiary industry became the key point of FDI, which is objectively beneficial to promote the optimization and upgrading of industrial structure. In addition, since 2004, China's opening-up in service industry constantly increased and attracted a great deal of FDI, which promoted the proportion of FDI in the tertiary industry to keep on a rise. From Figure 9.5, it can be seen that, from 2000 to 2011, except that China's contribution rates of the tertiary to China's GDP were below 40% in 2000, 2003, 2004, and 2010, the rates were more than 40% in all other years, reaching its peak of 48.2% in 2001 and showing another growth momentum since 2011. Besides, as shown in Figure 9.6, in recent ten years, the pulling effect of the tertiary industry on GDP was significant, reaching its peak of 6.6% in 2007. Except that it fell to below 4% in 2000 and 2003, the pulling rates in other years fluctuated between 4% and 6%. In general, in recent ten years, the attraction of the tertiary industry to foreign investment gradually increased, showing a momentum to catch up with the secondary industry as the attraction of the latter declined, with its contribution to and pulling effect on GDP exhibiting the momentum of steady growth.

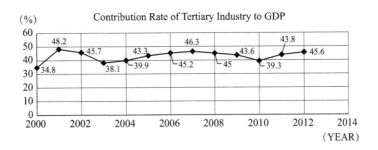

Figure 9.5 Contribution rate of tertiary industry to China's GDP from 2000 to 2011.
Data source: China Statistics Yearbook (2001–2012).

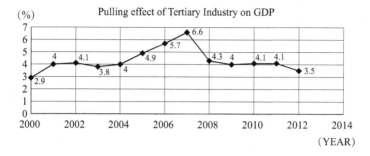

Figure 9.6 Pulling effect of tertiary industry on China's GDP growth from 2000 to 2011.
Data source: China Statistics Yearbook (2001–2012).

According to the above analysis on relation between foreign investment and China's economic growth based on industrial perspective, we can find that the key industries that foreign investment focuses on in different period are different, and the industry with an increasing amount of foreign investment in certain periods has a great contribution to and pulling effect on GDP. In the meantime, the development of relevant industry, the increase of profit margin, and the good news about relative policies will further attract the inflow of foreign investment. Therefore, the influence of foreign investment on China's different industries is obviously different. The investment amount flowed into the primary industry is lower than that in the secondary and tertiary industries, while the inflow amount of the secondary and tertiary industries is greater than that in the primary industry, with a momentum of reduced inflow amount of the secondary industry and increased inflow amount of the tertiary industry. With the transfer of key industries utilizing foreign investment, the industrial contribution to economic growth also changes in response. Objectively, it is beneficial to the optimization and upgrading of China's industrial structure. In other words, from industrial perspective, foreign investment and China's economic growth show a positive correlation.

2 *Quantitative Analysis Based on Regional Perspective*

The relation between China's foreign investment and economic growth in different regions can be analyzed from dynamic and static aspects as follows:

(1) DYNAMIC ASPECT

As shown in Table 9.1, the investment share of FDI in the eastern regions was more than 85% from 1996 to 2004, gradually decreased since 2005, and declined to 74.61% in 2011. The investment share of FDI in the central

Table 9.1 FDI share and GDP share in different regions of China from 1996 to 2011 (%)

Time (year)	FDI share by region			GDP share by region		
	Eastern regions	Central regions	Western regions	Eastern regions	Central regions	Western regions
1996	85.34	8.48	6.17	57.81	25.53	16.66
1997	86.56	8.75	4.68	57.53	25.84	16.63
1998	84.88	9.86	5.26	57.78	25.78	16.45
1999	86.24	8.96	4.80	58.12	25.51	16.36
2000	86.05	9.48	4.47	58.68	25.09	16.22
2001	86.14	9.16	4.70	59.32	24.80	15.88
2002	87.05	8.89	4.06	59.65	24.58	15.78
2003	86.70	9.41	3.88	60.11	24.22	15.67
2004	87.04	9.43	33.53	60.65	23.82	15.52
2005	83.97	11.45	4.58	59.43	25.16	15.41
2006	82.13	12.87	5.00	60.64	23.84	15.52
2007	82.33	12.26	5.41	60.65	23.62	15.73
2008	79.11	15.15	5.75	60.25	23.75	16.01
2009	77.73	15.48	6.79	59.38	24.22	16.40
2010	76.62	15.97	7.41	59.13	24.12	16.74
2011	74.61	16.83	8.56	58.44	24.53	17.03
Average	83.28	11.40	5.32	59.22	24.65	16.13

Data source: collated on the basis of data of CSMAR database.

regions was below 10% from 1996 to 2004, gradually increased since 2005, and reached to 16.83% in 2011. The investment share of FDI in the central regions was below 5% from 1996 to 2004, gradually increased since 2005, and reached to 8.56% in 2011. In general, the average investment share of FDI was 83.28% in the eastern region, 11.40% in the central region, and 5.32% in the western region. It indicates that the distribution of FDI in the eastern, central, and western regions was extremely uneven. Although such imbalance had a slight change since 2005, the investment share of FDI in the eastern regions far exceeded that in the central and western regions. Such an uneven distribution resulted from the relatively superior investment environment of the eastern regions, including advantageous location, technical foundation, and preferential policies. With the constant advancement of China's opening-up from coastal areas to inland since 2005, the gap between the central and western regions and the eastern regions has been gradually narrowing in investment environment and opening up.

Also, on the basis of the contribution rates of the eastern, central, and western regions to GDP shown in Table 9.1, we can find that contributions of these regions to economic growth were stable, respectively, undulating around 59.22%, 24.65%, and 16.13%, with small range of fluctuation. Moreover, it can be seen that the change of investment share of foreign investment between the three regions from 2005 to 2011 had little impact on each economic growth.

(2) STATIC ASPECT

As shown in Figure 9.7, in 2010, the growth rate of actual utilization of foreign investment in the eastern regions was 20% and GDP growth rate nearly 25%; the growth rate of actual utilization of foreign investment in the central regions was about 32% and GDP growth rate approximately 30%; the growth rate of actual utilization of foreign investment in the western regions was nearly −15% and GDP growth rate nearly 22%. It is evident that, in term of the growth rate of actual utilization of foreign investment, the western was not as good as the eastern region and the utilization rate of the central region that year was the highest; regarding the GDP growth rate, in the western regions it is not as good as that in the eastern regions and is the highest that in the central regions. Compared with the sufficient foreign investment in the eastern regions, the growth rate of actual utilization of foreign investment in the eastern regions is not optimistic; in the western regions, the amount of foreign investment is low, and the utilization of foreign investment is poor as well. In contrast, although the total amount of foreign investment in the central regions is small, the growth rate of both actual utilization of foreign investment and GDP are better.

As shown in Figure 9.8, in 2010, the relative GDP proportion of national economic and technical development zones in the eastern regions was 71%, in the central regions 18%, and in the western regions 11%. Firstly, as for the number of national economic and technical development zones, that in the eastern regions was even higher than the summation of that in the central and western regions, while these economic and technological development zones were precisely the major forces to attract foreign investment. Secondly, the contribution of these economic development zones to GDP was

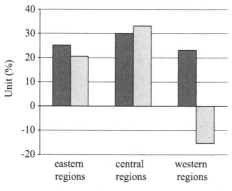

■ growth rate of GDP (%)
□ growth rate of actual utilization of foreign investment (%)

Figure 9.7 Growth rate of GDP and actual utilization of foreign investment in eastern, central, and western China in 2010.
Data source: China Statistics Yearbook (2011).

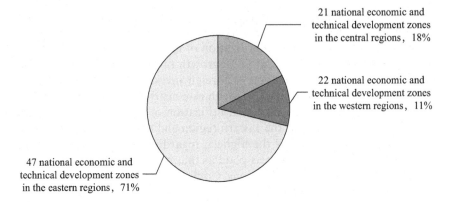

Figure 9.8 GDP's relative ratio of national economic and technical development zones in eastern, central, and western China in 2010.
Data source: China Statistics Yearbook (2011).

significant. The contribution to GDP in the eastern regions was higher than the summation of that in the central and western regions. The number of national economic and technical development zones in the central regions was one less than that in the western regions, while the GDP of the former was higher than the latter by 7%.

As shown in Figure 9.9, in 2010, the relative proportion of actual utilization of foreign investment by national economic and technical development zones in the eastern regions was 80%, in the central regions 15%, and in the western regions 5%. The amount actual utilization of foreign investment by national economic and technical development zones in the central regions was four times as much as the summation of that in the central and western regions. The number of national economic and technical development zones in the central regions was one less than that in the western regions, while the amount of actual utilization of foreign investment by national economic and technical development zones in the eastern regions was four times as much as that in the western regions.

Through this analysis on the relation between China's foreign investment and economic growth in dynamic and static aspects based on regional perspective, we find that China's foreign investment presents a great regional disparity with gradient declination in sequence from the eastern to the western regions, and the contribution to GDP also shows a similar momentum. An important reason for causing the extreme unevenness of China's regional distribution of FDI is the opening-up strategy gradually advanced from the eastern coastal regions to the central and western regions. Benefiting from national and local preferential policies and superior geographical locations, the eastern regions are the earliest beneficiary of reform and opening-up. FDI was initially utilized in the coastal special economic zones

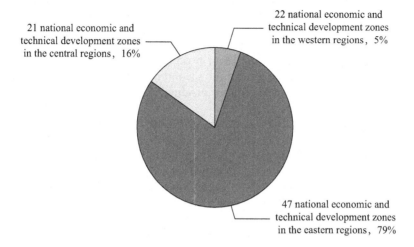

21 national economic and
technical development zones
in the central regions, 16%

22 national economic and
technical development zones
in the western regions, 5%

47 national economic and
technical development zones
in the eastern regions, 79%

Figure 9.9 Relative ratio of actual utilization of foreign investment in eastern, central, and western China in 2010 (USD 100,000,000).
Data source: China Statistics Yearbook (2011).

and development zones, which vigorously promoted the development of local economy and provided advantageous conditions for later attraction of FDI in the eastern regions. In other words, the reason for FDI mainly invested in the eastern regions at early time mainly depends on policies and geographical locations. The main reasons for the continuous utilization of FDI in the eastern regions lie in that the solid infrastructure benefited from the earlier economic development, labor force, and other production factors flowing into the eastern regions, as well as industrial clusters and other economic development environment.

II Literature Review

China's economy has been growing at high speed since reform and opening-up. From 1978 to 2013, its average economic growth rate was 9.85%, with its GDP leaping to the second place in 2010 from the tenth in 1978 in the world. However, since 2007, China's economy growth has been undergoing remarkable changes, with the economic growth rate significantly falling. China's average economic rate was 11.23% from 2002 to 2007 and 8.98% from 2008 to 2013, far lower than that from 2002 to 2007 and the long-term average value from 1978 to 2013. This continuous decelerated economic growth has posed challenges during the 13th Five-Year Plan period (2015–2020).

Researchers commonly believe that this decelerated economic growth is probably driven by the long-term structural factors, among which the most outstanding one is the concept of structural slowdown. According to Yuan Fuhua (2012), the so-called structural slowdown refers to

> during the evolution of the service-orientation of industrial structure of developed countries, the labor productivity of the tertiary industry is generally lower than that of the second industry, which results in the reduction in growth rate of labor productivity in the whole society.

But "the national incomes in those countries where the growth rate of labor productivity slows down will meet with decelerated growth rate". In other words, international experience shows that the economic growth will be on a long-term declining trend when the proportion of the tertiary industry increases, while China is now progressing in this phase. The reason why this viewpoint attracts great attention is other causes for the standing decelerated economic growth put forward by researchers, such as the aging population, low efficiency of SOE, obsolete advantage of low labor costs, declining growth rate of export and investment, and excessive country controlling, which are all the problems the government has been striving to address. It means that solving these problems does not contradict with the government's policy objectives. Only the structural slowdown goes against the government's policy objectives, due to its set purpose to upgrade the industrial structure by enhancing the proportion of the tertiary industry. In case that the proportion of the tertiary industry boosts and causes structural slowdown, the government's objectives of "stabilizing growth" and "upgrading industrial structure" will be in a contradictive dilemma.

The viewpoint "structural slowdown" seems to fit in for China's realistic situations, as the proportion of the value added and the employment of China's tertiary industry has been on a rise since reform and opening-up. However, it is noteworthy that China also experienced continuous decelerated economic growth from 1987 to 1990 and from 1993 to 1999, which subsequently proved to be periodic economic slowdown. However, during these two periods of economic slowdown, the proportion of the value added and employment of the tertiary industry still increased. For what reason do we mention that the above-mentioned deceleration in economic growth is periodic while the one starting from 2008 is structural? There is no clear answer from researchers for it. We deem that it is imperative to discriminate the reasons for decelerated economic growth. Currently, this decelerated economic growth has not exceeded the above-mentioned two in terms of range and time of deceleration. Therefore, it is necessary to figure out whether this decelerated economic growth is structural on a logical basis, which helps us actually predict the economic growth during the 13th Five-Year Plan period. Provided that the decelerated economic growth genuinely appears structural, the decision-making section has to regulate the economic growth objective downward during the 13th Five-Year Plan period.

The research literature about the slowdown in China's economic growth can be categorized into two kinds. One is to study the reasons for decelerated economic growth through economic growth accounting methods, and the other is to discuss whether the decelerated economic growth is structural with quantitative methods.

There are many research literatures studying China's economic growth through growth accounting methods, such as Chow (1993) and Young (2003). However, all these cover the phase of China's high-speed economic growth, without analyzing the problem of China's deceleration in economic growth. Research literature regarding this has emerged in recent years. Wang et al. (2007) analyzed the relation between GDP and such factors as capital, labor, marketization, urbanization, and foreign trade through quantitative methods, and factored the TFP into the explainable and the unexplainable parts with growth accounting methods. It concluded that China's economic growth was not the input-type growth without productivity progress as Paul Krugman predicted, while the governmental administrative costs and final consumption structure distortions led to the reduction of TFP and probably reduced the future economic growth. Zheng et al. (2009) considered that China's economic growth depended much upon the capital accumulation, of which the utility and efficiency were overwhelmingly twisted by SOEs and the intervention by the government, thus leading to China's decelerated economic growth. Eichengreen et al. (2012) set the measurement framework for economies' slowdown and researched the experience from success and failure of world economies through economic growth accounting methods. They found that the economic slowdown possibly occurred when the GDP per capita reached USD16,740, and predicted that China's economic slowdown would happen from 2015 to 2017. Lee et al. (2012) analyzed the growth experience of 12 Asian developing countries through economic growth accounting methods and discovered that the growth of these countries conform to the rule of "conditional convergence". They forecasted that China's economy would reduce to 6.09% and 4.98% in the next two decades, while proper reform policies would postpone the economic growth slowdown, maintaining them at 7% and 6.23%. Chen Yanbin and Yao Yimin (2012) probed into the economic growth slowdown since 2008 through economic growth accounting methods. They anticipated that the economic growth rate during the 12th and 13th Five-Year Plan periods would decrease by 2.3% and 4%, respectively, compared with that from 2000 to 2010, with the reasons for the slow growth rate including the decelerated growth in export and investment, gradual loss of low cost advantage, and downward growth rate of TFP.

Research literature on structural slowdown emerged in recent one or two years. Yuan Fuhua (2012) factored the output per capita into labor productivity, labor participation rate, and working-age population ratio with the definition formula of labor productivity and measured the influence of transition of industrial structure on labor productivity in developed countries, and found that the primary reason for economic growth in developed countries after 1970 was the rise of proportion of the tertiary industry. Lv Jian (2012) delved into the phenomenon of China's structural slowdown via the spatial panel data model and found that its economic growth was of spatial autocorrelation, as the eastern regions were experiencing structural slowdown and the central and western regions were experiencing structural acceleration. The Cutting-edge Research Group of China's Economic Growth (2012) deemed that the three forces dominating China's economic growth are demographic transition, reversion of elastic parameter of the factors, and the development of service-oriented economic structure, and predicated that GDP per capita was expected to be ranked in the list of developed countries, though China was expected to enter the stable growth phase. Zhang Ping (2012) rendered that China's economic growth was structural and not periodic, and it would never work for it to adopt the conventional macro-policy stimulated by the volume of money, and the economic system demanded structural reform to adapt to the challenges due to structural slowdown. Besides, Zhang Xiaojing (2012), Shen Kunrong, Teng Yongle (2013) and Wang Qing et al. (2011) expounded the "structural slowdown" by means of statistical analysis, comparisons between China and foreign countries, and qualitative analysis. The research literature discussed the effect of structural factors with the indicator like the proportion of the tertiary industry to represent the transition of industrial structure. However, such indicator cannot completely embody the relation between labor transfer in different directions of industries and economic growth, especially neglecting the impact of industrialization and urbanization of labor force on economic growth.

Different from the existing literature, this chapter infers one economic growth accounting framework that can be segmented at industrial level.[1] This framework can divide China's economic growth rate into the contribution to labor productivity of the primary, secondary, and tertiary industrial sectors, contributions of production factors within the three industries, and the contributions of the total reallocation effects (TRE) of resources within the three industries, thus completely reflecting the influence on economic growth of the labor force transfer in different directions of industries. It enables us to realize whether the decelerated growth since 2008 is of structural nature. In this case, we can reach reliable conclusion on the reasons for decelerated growth and give correct policy suggestions.

III Analytical Framework

In this section, we will deduce one accounting analysis framework for economic growth, which can be subdivided at industrial level. We will factor the GDP growth rate through three steps. First, factor the GDP growth rate into the growth rates of labor productivity and labor force; second, factor the growth rate of labor productivity into that of labor productivity of the three industries and the TRE of resources; finally, factor the productivity growth rates of labor in each industry into the productivity growth rates of material capital, human capital, land, and total factors. The result of each step is the source of proving in the next step. Through these three steps, we can factor the economic growth rates at industrial level.

Step 1: Factor the GDP growth rate into the growth rates of labor productivity and labor force. The output, labor force, and output per capita are expressed by Y, L, and y, and GDP equals to the product of labor productivity and labor force, that is,, $Y = yL$. $\dot{Y}_i$ refers to the increment of total output, dY or ΔY, $\dot{y}_i$ refers to the increment of output per capita (i.e. labor productivity), dy or Δy.

Then we get the following formula:

$$\dot{Y}_i = \frac{dY}{dt} = \frac{dy}{dt}L + \frac{dL}{dt}y \tag{1}$$

$$\frac{\dot{Y}}{Y} = \frac{\dot{y}L}{Y} + \frac{\dot{L}y}{Y} = \frac{\dot{y}}{y} + \frac{\dot{L}}{L} \tag{2}$$

Therefore, it is practicable to factor the GDP growth rate into the ones of output per capita (labor productivity) and labor force. Now, we refactor the labor productivity growth rate as follows.

Step 2: Factor the growth rate of labor productivity into that of labor productivity of the three industries and the TRE of resources. Suppose there are i categories of industries and i=1, 2, 3. $wi = Li/L$, the output per capita is:

$$y = \frac{Y}{L} = \sum_i \frac{Y_i}{L} = \sum_i \frac{Y_i L_i}{L_i L} = \sum_i w_i y_i \tag{3}$$

Therefore, it is feasible to denote the labor productivity as the sum of the weighted output per capita of various industries. Then we factor the growth rate of labor productivity:

$$\dot{y} = \frac{dy}{dt} = \sum_i \left(\frac{dy_i}{dt} w_i + \frac{dw_i}{dt} y_i \right) = \sum_i (w_i \dot{y}_i + \dot{w}_i y_i) \tag{4}$$

$$\frac{\dot{y}}{y} = \sum_i \left(\frac{\dot{y}_i}{y} w_i + \frac{y_i}{y} \dot{w}_i \right) = \sum_i \left(\frac{\dot{y}_i}{y} \frac{L_i}{L} \frac{y_i}{y_i} + \dot{w}_i \frac{y_i}{y} \right) = \sum_i \left(\frac{\dot{y}_i}{y_i} \frac{Y_i}{Y} + \dot{w}_i \frac{y_i}{y} \right) \tag{5}$$

Therefore, the growth rate of labor productivity can be factored into the one of the labor productivities of the three industries and the TRE of resources. The growth rate of labor productivity refers to the efficiency improvement when the labor force transfers from low productivity industries to high productivity industries. Wherein the growth rate of labor productivity is

$\sum_i \dfrac{\dot{y}_i}{y_i}\dfrac{Y_i}{Y}$, representing the weighted sum of the changes in growth rate of

output per capita in each industry and aiming to measure the changes in growth rate of the labor productivity in each industry, without involving the factor mobility within industries; TRE of resources is $\sum_i \dot{w}_i \dfrac{y_i}{y}$, representing

the weighted average of increments of the labor factors in all industries. It is called TRE of resources on account that this item means the reallocation of factors within industries, without involving the changes in labor productivity in each industry as time goes by.

Formula (5) can only estimate the TRE of resources in a general sense and is unable to perceive the efficiency improvement when the labor force flows from one specific industry to another. Therefore, it is necessary to further subdivide the TRE of resources. Suppose there are two sectors of the agriculture: A and the non-agriculture B. They are the source and destination of labor mobility, with their labor share, respectively, expressed as

$w_A = \dfrac{L_A}{L}, w_B = \dfrac{L_B}{L}$, then we get the following formula:

$$w_A + w_B = 1 \tag{6}$$

$$\dot{w}_A + \dot{w}_B = 0 \tag{7}$$

$$\dot{w}_A = -\dot{w}_B \tag{8}$$

Combining formulas (5) and (8), the growth rate of labor productivity can be further factored as:

$$
\begin{aligned}
\dfrac{\dot{y}}{y} &= \dfrac{\dot{y}_A}{y_A}\dfrac{Y_A}{Y} + \dfrac{\dot{y}_B}{y_B}\dfrac{Y_B}{Y} + \dot{w}_A\dfrac{y_A}{y} + \dot{w}_B\dfrac{y_B}{y} = \dfrac{\dot{y}_A}{y_A}\dfrac{Y_A}{Y} + \dfrac{\dot{y}_B}{y_B}\dfrac{Y_B}{Y} - \dot{w}_B\dfrac{y_A}{y} + \dot{w}_B\dfrac{y_B}{y} \\
&= \dfrac{\dot{y}_A}{y_A}\dfrac{Y_A}{Y} + \dfrac{\dot{y}_B}{y_B}\dfrac{Y_B}{Y} + \dfrac{y_B - y_A}{y}\dot{w}_B
\end{aligned}
\tag{9}
$$

Now the factorization result of the TRE of resources from agricultural sector to the non-agricultural sector can be recorded as "Effect 1". Similarly, provided there are two subdivisions of the secondary and tertiary industries in non-agricultural sector B, that is, $Y_B = Y_2 + Y_3$, we can further factor the labor reallocation situation of the sector B as follows:

$$
\begin{aligned}
\dfrac{\dot{y}_B}{y_B} &= \dfrac{\dot{y}_2}{y_2}\dfrac{Y_2}{Y_B} + \dfrac{\dot{y}_3}{y_3}\dfrac{Y_3}{Y_B} + \dot{w}_2\dfrac{y_2}{y_B} + \dot{w}_3\dfrac{y_3}{y_B} = \dfrac{\dot{y}_2}{y_2}\dfrac{Y_2}{Y_B} + \dfrac{\dot{y}_3}{y_3}\dfrac{Y_3}{Y_B} - \dot{w}_3\dfrac{y_2}{y_B} + \dot{w}_3\dfrac{y_3}{y_B} \\
&= \dfrac{\dot{y}_2}{y_2}\dfrac{Y_2}{Y_B} + \dfrac{\dot{y}_3}{y_3}\dfrac{Y_3}{Y_B} + \dfrac{y_3 - y_2}{y_B}\dot{w}_3
\end{aligned}
\tag{10}
$$

Under the categories of the third industrial sectors and according to the characteristics of China's labor mobility direction within the three industries, we can factor China's TRE of resources into two types of effects: "Effect 1" refers to the contribution to economic growth when the labor force flows from the primary industry to the secondary and tertiary industries; "Effect 2" indicates the contribution to economic growth when the labor force flows between the secondary and tertiary industries. In this case, we can analyze the impact on economy growth rate of the specific aspects of labor mobility and then obtain more accurate policy implication.

Step 3: Factor the productivity growth rates of labor in each industry into the productivity growth rates of material capital, human capital, land, and total factors. Suppose the production function is CD production function:

$$Y = AK^{\alpha}(LH)^{\beta} S^{1-\alpha-\beta} \tag{10}$$

Wherein A, K, H, S, α, and α, respectively, represent TFP, material capital stock, human capital stock, land capital, share of material capital, and share of human capital. Take the logarithm of both sides of the equation and derivate and we get:

$$\ln(y_i) = \ln(\frac{Y_i}{L_i}) = \ln(A_i) + \alpha_i \ln(\frac{K_i}{L_i}) + \beta_i \ln(\frac{H_i}{L_i}) + (1-\alpha_i-\beta_i)\ln(\frac{S_i}{L_i}) \tag{11}$$

$$\frac{y}{y} = \frac{d\ln(y_i)}{dt} = \frac{d\ln(A_i)}{dt} + \alpha_i \frac{d\ln(k_i)}{dt} + \beta_i \frac{d\ln(h_i)}{dt} + (1-\alpha_i-\beta_i)\frac{d\ln(s_i)}{dt}$$
$$= \alpha_i k_i + \beta_i h_i + (1-\alpha_i-\beta_i)s_i + A_i \tag{12}$$

In formula (8), the growth rate of labor productivity is factored into the contributions of per capita material capital growth $\dot{k_i}$, per capita human capital growth $\dot{h_i}$, per capita land growth $\dot{s_i}$, and TFP growth rate $\dot{A_i}$ in each industry. From this we can subdivide the growth rate of labor productivity in each industry into the contributions of various production factors, thus factoring the GDP growth rate into the contributions of various factors in the three industries.

IV Data Description

The growth accounting in this chapter requires the data from 1978 to 2012 on GDP, labor force, material capital stock, land, and human capital. Without special instructions, all data come from China Statistical Yearbook.

The path of China's transition of industrial structure can be seen through the data description.

A Growth Rate of GDP and Labor, Labor Productivity in the Three Industries

China Statistical Yearbook provides us with the time series of GDP and the added value of the three industries. We deflate the time series data with the GDP deflator between the gross and the three industries. The "Number of Staff and Workers at the Year-end" in Statistical Yearbook offers the labor data on the basis of nation and the three industries. The added value divided by the labor data will produce the time series data of labor productivity in the three industries. Figure 9.13 describes the time path of the growth rates of total labor productivity and labor productivity in the three industries. As shown in Figure 9.10, from 1978 to 2012, the annual average growth rate (AAGR) of total labor productivity reached 7.76%; per capita growth in primary industry increased from 362 Yuan to RMB1,819, with the AAGR being 4.86%; per capita growth in the second industry increased from RMB2,512 to RMB28,626, with the AAGR being 7.42%; per capita growth in the tertiary industry increased from RMB1,784 to RMB10,316, with the AAGR being 5.3%. It is easy to find that the labor productivity of the second industry is far higher than those of the primary and tertiary industries.

These labor productivities of the three industries times their respective employment shares equal the weighted productivity. Then we can discover that the weighted labor productivities of the three industries total up to 6.17%, with a gap of 1.59% toward the total labor productivity of 7.76%. Such gap is called "TRE of resources", which can be rendered as the productivity growth resulting from the optimization of distribution of resources

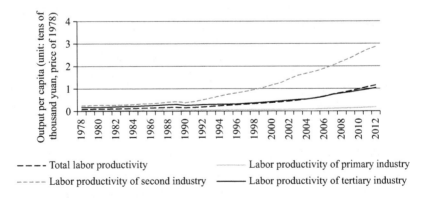

Figure 9.10 Comparisons of labor productivity of the three industries.

after the labor flows from low productivity sectors to high productivity ones (Bosworth and Collins, 2008; Peneder, 2003)

B Material Capital and Land

The author adopts the conventional perpetual inventory method for the calculation of material capital stork, with the formula of $K_t = K_{t-1}(1-\delta) + I_t$, where K represents the material capital stock. It is difficult to gain the base-period capital stock on the basis of nation and various industries without official data. Taking Young (2003) for reference; base-period fixed capital divided by 10% equals the base-period capital stock where the total material capital stock in 1978 is calculated as RMB 738.87 billion, with the material capital stock of the three industries, respectively, being RMB73.89 billion, RMB 464.9 billion, and RMB 236.09 billion.

I_t refers to the indicator of various annual investment flows, which is selected in this chapter to be the item of "fixed capital formation" in Statistical Yearbook. It should be deflated to eliminate the influence of price factor. Since 1991, the statistical bureau announced that the "price index of investment in fixed assets" was the most suitable deflator, which was substituted by "producer price index" before 1991. With the above-mentioned methods, this chapter systemizes the investment flow indicator as the fixed capital formation at constant price.

δ is depreciation, the rate of which is supposed to be 0.05. As for base-period initial stock, we take the material capital stock proposed by Young (2003) in 1978 for reference. We substitute various annual indexes into the formula of perpetual inventory and obtain the data of material capital stock for each year.

Considering the role of land factor in primary industry, the land as production factor is only recorded into the primary industry, instead of the secondary and tertiary industries. The land indicator can be expressed by the index of "Total Seeded Area of Crops" in the Statistical Yearbook.

C Human Capital

We take the examples by Bosworth and Collins (2003) for reference to calculate human capital. Suppose the annual rate of return to education is 7%, and the calculation formula for human capital is $H = (1.07)^S$, with H and S, respectively, representing human capital and education years. The data of education years per capita from 1978 to 2005 are from the average education years of Chinese labor force provided by young (2003). The data from 2006 to 2012 are calculated according to the related data formed by the population educational levels in *China Population and Employment Statistics Yearbook*. In this case, the education levels include the levels of never-going-to-school, primary school, junior high school, senior high school, junior college, university, and postgraduate study, with the education years for each level being 0, 6, 9, 12, 15, 16 and 19, respectively, weighted by the proportion of the population in each education level accounting for the total population, thus obtaining the annual average population education years in that year.

D Output Share

In the calculation by Bosworth and Collins (2008), α is directly given the constant value 0.4, supposed on the basis of the following two aspects. First, α has little influence on the conclusion when it is given a constant value upon the verification of Bosworth and Collins; second, adopting a small share is because adding education years to human capital can make its share relatively grow, thus making the physical capital share correspondingly decline Therefore, this chapter applies the assumption of α=0.4.

V Factorization Results of Economic Growth Accounting

Taking advantage of the aforementioned analysis framework and data, we can factor the economic growth rate from 1978 to 2012. According to the curve of total output growth rate shown in Figure 9.11, we factor 35 years into three periods in which the economic growth rate increases, and four time periods in which the economic growth rate decreases.[2]

As per the above-mentioned classification standard, we divide the factorization results of economic growth rate from 1978 to 2012 into seven time periods, with the results presented in Table 9.2 as follows.

A Overall Factorization Results

First, if we analyze the factorization results of total labor production labor rate, we can get the total output growth rate, labor growth rate, and per capita output growth rate as presented by the data in lines two to four in Table 9.2. Over the 35 years, the average growth rates of total output growth rate and labor productivity growth rate are, respectively, 9.83% and 7.76%.

Through comparisons of these seven time periods, it is not difficult to discover that China's economic growth rates show obvious fluctuations. There

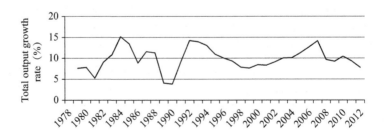

Figure 9.11 Curve of growth rate of total output.

Table 9.2 Factorization results of economic growth rate from 1978 to 2012 (growth rate %)

Time period	1978– 1981	1982– 1984	1985– 1990	1991– 1992	1993– 1999	2000– 2007	2008– 2012
Total output	6.88	12.99	7.87	14.24	9.78	10.79	9.17
Labor	2.88	3.15	5.36	1.01	1.11	0.63	0.38
Labor productivity	3.89	9.54	2.38	13.10	8.57	10.10	8.77
Labor productivity in primary industry	0.63	3.48	−0.10	1.34	0.92	0.83	0.85
Material capital	1.28	0.80	0.16	0.38	0.42	0.30	0.48
Human capital	−0.03	0.07	0.15	0.07	0.08	0.05	0.04
Land	−0.21	−0.02	−0.25	0.04	0.09	0.07	0.13
TFP	−0.38	2.55	−0.15	0.83	0.32	0.41	0.18
Labor productivity in the secondary industry	1.32	2.14	1.23	7.79	4.77	3.86	3.16
Material capital	0.56	0.49	0.50	1.01	1.19	1.59	1.86
Human capital	−0.05	0.12	0.28	0.16	0.24	0.20	0.22
TFP	0.81	1.51	0.44	6.44	3.24	1.99	1.02
Labor productivity in the tertiary industry	0.28	0.92	0.53	2.14	1.50	3.47	2.84
——Material capital	0.39	0.20	0.31	0.76	1.19	1.64	2.00
Human capital	−0.02	0.06	0.20	0.13	0.18	0.17	0.21
TFP	−0.09	0.65	0.02	1.22	0.12	1.58	0.59
Reallocation effects	1.65	3.00	0.72	1.83	1.38	1.93	1.93
Effect 1[3]	1.78	3.27	0.78	1.44	1.51	1.92	1.75
Effect 2[4]	−0.13	−0.27	−0.06	0.39	−0.13	0.01	0.18

were four times of economic growth slowdown over the 35 years that occurred in the four phases of 1978–1981, 1985–1990, 1993–1999, and 2008–2013.[5] The third slowdown period was as long as seven years, longer than that since 2008. Only from the perspective of economic growth rate, we cannot find the difference between the fourth period and the previous three ones. To explore the nature of this time of economic growth slowdown, we need to further factor the growth rate of the total output and labor productivity and discuss which part has led to the economic growth slowdown.

From lines 5 to 20 in Table 9.2, we factor the total labor productivity growth rate into the labor productivity growth rate of the three industries and the TRE of resources. Through comparing the contributions to economic growth rate of the labor in these seven time periods and the labor productivity growth rate of the three industries since the reform, we can find the following characteristics.

1   Labor growth serves as the contribution to economic growth rate, which started to continuously decrease from 1991 to 1992, and only contributed 0.38 percentage points to economic growth rate, with the contribution rate lower than 5%. It indicates that the current economic growth can only depend on the rise of labor productivity instead of the rise of labor input, due to the decrease of China's surplus labor and demographic dividend. Moreover, the contribution of labor growth started to decline from 1991 to 1992, so it is improper to explain the economic growth slowdown since 2008 with this factor.

2   From the average results over 35 years, we can see that the average economic growth rate contributed by the labor productivity of the second industry is 3.38%, the highest within the three industries; however, the economic growth rate contributed by the labor productivity of the tertiary industry shows a tendency of increase, with a gap of 0.32 percentage points with that of the secondary industry from 2003 to 2007. The economic growth rate contributed by the labor productivity of the primary industry remains low. These phenomena demonstrate that China's economic growth increasingly relies on the rise of labor productivity of the tertiary industry. However, we have not found any sign that the labor productivity of the tertiary industry has put a drag on economic growth. The economic growth rate contributed by labor productivity of the tertiary industry from 2008 to 2012 was still as high as 2.84%, though being lower than that from 2000 to 2007, and higher than that in the boom period from 1991 to 1992. This fact explains that the labor productivity of the tertiary industry is promoting instead of encumbering the economic growth, which seems to disaccord with the features of structural slowdown. Furthermore, the contribution of labor productivity of the secondary and tertiary industries to economic growth from 2008 to 2012 dropped compared with that from 2000 to 2007; this same case occurred to the economic growth slowdown from 1985 to 1990 and from 1993 to 1999, which is known to be periodic economic growth slowdown instead of structural one. From the factorization results in Table 9.1, we are unable to reach to the conclusion that the contribution to economic growth from labor productivity of the secondary and tertiary industries from 2008 to 2012 is long-term, while the identical situations in other phases are short-term.

3   From the TRE of resources, we can see that the labor transferred from the secondary industry to the tertiary industry from 2008 to 2012, namely, the "service-oriented industrial structure", did not encumber economic growth but contributed 0.18 percentage points to the economic growth. Though the contribution is small, it is noticeable that

the contribution to economic growth of the service orientation of industrial structure from 2008 to 2012 was even higher than that in the high-speed growth phase. In other words, the contribution to economic growth of the service orientation of industrial structure was still on a rise. This outcome is out of step with the prediction of Yuan Fuhua (2012), who claimed that the service orientation of industrial structure would cause the slowdown of national income. Besides, the labor transfer among different industries has always been the factor to promote economic growth over 35 years as presented in Table 9.2, which showed no sign of weakening from 2008 to 2012. Thus, the labor transfer from primary industry to the secondary and tertiary industries played a vital role in promoting economic growth. This again implies that the structural deceleration is lack of evidence, because even if the contribution of industrial structure service to economic growth is negative, the effect may be offset by the positive contribution of rural-urban migration of labor to economic growth, let alone the positive contribution of industrial structure service to economic growth.

In short, from the perspective of labor productivity and resource reallocation of the three major industries, it is in insufficient in evidence to say Chinese economy is in structural deceleration. However, we still need to figure out the reasons for China's economic slowdown since 2008, which requires further factorization of these factors forming the labor productivity of the three industries.

B Specific Factorization Results of the Labor Productivity of the Three Industries

On the basis of the economic growth accounting model in the third part, we factor the growth rate of labor productivity of the three industries into the growth rates of material capital, land, human capital, and TFP. The results are shown from lines 6 to 17 in Table 9.2. This table provides us with the change tendency of the contributions to economic growth rate of each production factor. Figures 9.12–9.14 present the change tendency of the contributions to economic growth rate of each production factor in the three industries over the 35 years.

From the angle of material capital input, from 2008 to 2012, the economic growth rate contributed by the material capital input of the primary, secondary, and tertiary industries declined. However, even after the fallback, they still maintained the balance with those from 2000 to 2007. Overall, the average economic growth rates contributed by the material capital input of the primary, secondary and tertiary industries from 2008 to 2012 were, respectively, 0.48%, 1.86%, and 2.00%, higher than that up to 0.20%, 1.59%, and 1.64% from 2000 to 2007. Therefore, this time of decelerated economic growth did not result from the slowdown of material capital input.

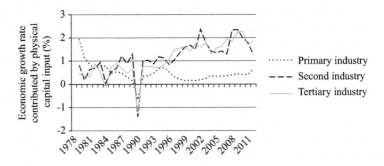

Figure 9.12 Economic growth rate contributed by material capital input.

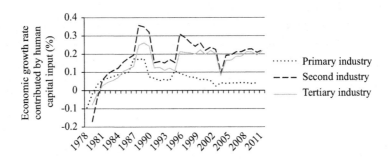

Figure 9.13 Economic growth rate contributed by human capital input.

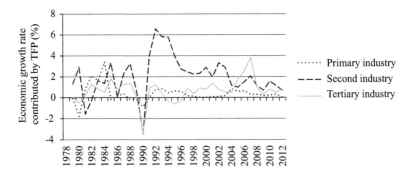

Figure 9.14 Economic growth rate contributed by TFP.

From the increase of human capital input, we can see that the economic growth rate contributed by human capital input of the primary industry fluctuates downward, while that of the secondary and tertiary industries fluctuates upward. In the decelerated economic growth from 2008 to 2012, the average economic growth rate contributed by human capital input of the secondary and tertiary industries were, respectively, 0.22% and 0.21%, higher than that up to 0.20% and 0.17 in the boom period from 2000 to 2007, with only that of the primary industry reducing slightly from 0.05% to 0.04%. Therefore, this time of economic growth slowdown did not result from the slowdown of human capital input either.

As TFP includes other aspects unexplained with the factor growth, the measurement of TFP indicates the technology progress to a certain extent, thus becoming an important standard for evaluating economic development quality. From Figure 9.4, the economic growth rate contributed by TFP growth of the three industries from 2008 to 2012 remained sluggish, respectively, reducing from 0.41%, 1.99%, and 1.58% in the period from 2000 to 2007, to 0.18%, 1.02%, and 0.59% in the period from 2008 to 2012. From Table 9.1, it is clear that the economic growth rate contributed by total labor productivity declined from 10.10% from 2000 to 2007, to 8.77% from 2008 to 2012, which was the main cause for the decelerated economic growth. However, among all factors influencing the contribution of total labor productivity, the material capital and human capital in the tertiary industry and the land factor in the primary industry all contributed greater (except the slight declination of the contribution of human capital in primary industry) percentage points to economic growth. Only the TFP of the three industries contributed overwhelmingly less to the percentage points of economic growth. It means that the slowdown of growth rate of TFP of the three industries may be the "real culprit" of this time of slowdown of economic growth.

However, we still cannot come to the conclusion of structural slowdown from the performance of TFP of the three industries. There are two reasons for it. First, the contribution to economic growth of TFP of the three industries all declined without structural difference. In case only the contribution of TFP of the tertiary industry decreases and that of the secondary industry increases, it can be claimed that there is a sign of structural slowdown. However, this was not the case. Second, the previous literature demonstrates that China's TFP was both pro-cyclical and strongly explainable to the fluctuation of economic growth rate (Heetal, 2009), which agrees with the factorization results in Table 9.1. From Table 9.1, we note that the percentage points of contribution to economic growth of TFP of the three industries also decreased in the economic growth slowdown during the periods from 1985 to 1990 and from 1993 to 1999. It is doubtful whether the downturn of TFP of the three industries is periodic in this time of growth slowdown. Of course, we cannot make this conclusion because this growth slowdown is still on the way. However, at least now, it is still lack of evidence to define this economic slowdown as a structural one.

VI Conclusions

Since 2008, a slowdown has occurred to China's economic growth. There have not been any convictive researches at home and abroad on such slowdown. This chapter sets up the analysis framework for economic growth accounting that can be factored at industrial level. The framework factors the economic growth rate into the contributions of the growth rate of labor productivity of the three industries, various production factors within the three industries, and labor reallocation within industries, thus enabling us to probe into the reasons for economic growth slowdown at industrial level. With this method, we have measured the contributions of structural factors and production factors in China's economic growth slowdown from 2008 to 2012, and tried to make reliable judgment of the reasons and the nature of this economic growth slowdown through comparison between the results and the previous economic growth slowdown. Thus, we concluded that:

1   Starting from the early 1990s, the contributions of labor growth to China's economic growth rate have been gradually declining. On the one hand, this indicates that China's economic growth cannot rely on the increase in labor input, but more on the increase in labor productivity. On the other hand, it is improper to illustrate the economic growth slowdown from 2008 to 2012 with the factor of slower labor growth.

2   The labor transfer between industries has always been the promoting factor of economic growth over the 35 years, which did not recede from 2008 to 2012. In addition, the labor transfer from the secondary industry to the tertiary from 2008 to 2012 brought greater contribution to the economic growth rate than that from 2000 to 2007. Meanwhile, the economic growth rate, still as high as 2.84%, contributed by labor productivity of the tertiary industry, turned lower than that from 2000 to 2007, greater than that in the boom period from 1991 to 1992. These results state that it is lack of evidence to define China's economic slowdown as a structural one. To say the least, the reasons for this economic growth slowdown cannot be the so-called structural slowdown, even though it is long-lasting.

3   From 2008 to 2012, the contribution to overall economic growth rate of the TFP of the three industries and the labor productivity of the secondary and tertiary industries turned lower than those in boom period from 2000 to 2007. However, the above-mentioned situation came about in the economic growth slowdown from 1985 to 1990 and from 1993 to 1999 while these two periods were both periodic, but not structural. Therefore, it is inadequate to deny that this economic growth slowdown is periodic only with the current evidence.

4   The lower contribution to economic growth of the TFP of the three industries is inevitably the main reason for this economic growth slowdown, whatever the nature it has.

According to the conclusion in this chapter, it is lack of evidence to define China's economic growth slowdown as a structural one which poses challenges to us on how to judge the future direction of economic growth. In light with the research results in this chapter, there has not been any sign of structural slowdown so far. Therefore, we cannot deny whether this economic growth slowdown is the same as those from 1985 to 1990 and from 1993 to 1999, which is possibly periodic. The previous part points out that the slow increase of TFP of the three industries is the "real culprit" for this economic growth slowdown, despite of the high pro-cyclicality of TFP. It means that, if China can boost the growth rates of TFP during the 13th Five-Year Plan period, there still remains possibility for China's economy to return to the track of high growth. However, if the growth rates of TFP of the three industries remain downturn, China's economic growth rate will further go down. Moreover, this problem cannot be resolved through structural adjustment as all the growth rates of TFP of the three industries appear lower.

The conclusion thus demonstrates that it is difficult for us to make the accurate prediction in economic growth rate during the 13th Five-Year Plan period because of the coexistence of the two possibilities. However, one major conclusion reached in this chapter is the industrial structure upgrading or increase of the proportion of the tertiary industry cannot lead to the economic growth slowdown during the 13th Five-Year Plan period, as this factor was not in itself the reason for economic growth slowdown from 2008 to 2012. This helps to avoid the dilemma where government policies shall be caught between "stabilizing growth" and "upgrading industrial structure". It is advisable for Chinese government to strive to enable China's economy to get back to the track of high growth by means of "stabilizing growth". Meanwhile, the government should also lay emphasis on the increase of TFP of the three industries and promote the labor transfer between industries.

Notes

1 Bosworth and Collins (2008) also factored the economic growth rate into labor growth rate and the growth rate of labor productivity in each industry. The major difference between the economic growth accounting framework and this chapter is that our growth accounting model can respectively estimate the contribution to economic growth of labor transfer between the agricultural and the non-agricultural sectors, the agricultural and the industrial sectors, the service and non-service industries, while Bosworth and Collins (2008) were unable to make it, thus failing to apply their method to judge the existence of "structural slowdown".

2 The upward phases for economic growth rates in the phases of 1986–1987 and 2009–2010 were short with limited range of rise, so we deem these two phases as the temporary rebounds between the two declining phases of 1985–1990 and 2008–2012.

3 "Effect 1" is the contribution to economic growth of the labor transfer from primary industry to the secondary and tertiary industries.

4 "Effect 2" is the contribution to economic growth of the labor transfer between the second and tertiary industries.
5 The State Statistics Bureau has not published the data of the three industries in 2013 when the author finished writing, so the deadline in Table 9.1 is in 2012.

Bibliography

Alwyn Young. "Gold Into Base Metals: Productivity Growth in China during the Reform", *Journal of Political Economy*, no. 111, 2003, pp. 1220–1261.

B. Bosworth, S. Collins. "The Empirics of Growth: An Update", *Brookings Papers on Economic Activity*, no. 2, 2003, pp. 113–179.

B. Bosworth, S. Collins. "Accounting for Growth: Comparing China and India", *Journal of Economic Perspectives*, no. 22, 2008, pp. 45–66.

B. Eichengreen, D. Park, K. Shin. "When Fast Growing Economies Slow Down: International Evidence and Implications for China", *Asian Economic Papers*, no. 11, 2012, pp. 42–87.

Chen Yanbin, Yao Yimin, "Reasons, Challenges and Count-measures for China's Economic Growth Slowdown", *Journal of Renmin University of China*, no. 5, 2012, pp. 76–87.

Chinese Academy of Social Sciences. *Blue Book of Macro-economy: Report on China's Economic Growth (2012–2013)*, Beijing: Social Sciences Academic Press, 2013.

Cutting-edge Research Group of China's Economic Growth. "Long-term Path, Efficiency and Potential Growth of China's Economy", *Economy Research Journal*, no. 11, 2012. pp. 4–17, 75.

G. C. Chow. "Capital Formation and Economic Growth in China", *Quarterly Journal of Economics*, no. 108, 1993, pp. 809–842.

Ding Cuicui. "Dynamic Effects and Regional Differences of Impacts of Foreign Direct Investment to China's Economic Growth", *Statistics and Decision*, no. 16, 2013, pp. 116–119.

EichengreenHe Canfei. *Location of Foreign Direct Investment: Theoretical Analysis and Empirical Study*, Beijing: China Economic Publishing House, 2005.

He Hongbo, Tu Xinnuan, "Empirical Test of Relation between FDI and China's Economic Growth", *Statistics and Decision*, vol. 21, no. 3, 2005, pp. 62–63.

HeJ. Lee, K. Hong. "Determinants and Prospects for Asia's Economic Growth", *Japan and World Economy*, no. 24, 2012, pp. 101–113.

J. Zheng, A. Bigsten, A. Hu. "Can China's Growth be Sustained? A Productivity Perspective", *World Development*, no. 37, 2009, pp. 878–888.

Li Fan, Li Jie. "Comparative Study on Policies about FDI Utilization between China and Indian", *Journal of Shijiazhuang University of Economics*, no. 8, 2009, pp. 56–60.

Liu Shengjun, Zheng Xue. "Analysis on FDI and Investment Environment Optimization in China", *Economic Research Guide*, no. 5, 2012, pp. 192–193.

Lv Jian. "Differentiation between Industrial Structural Adjustment, Structural Slowdown and Economic Growth", *China Industrial Economy*, no. 9, 2012, pp. 31–43.

M. Peneder. "Industrial Structure and Aggregate Growth", *Structural Change and Economic Dynamics*, no. 4, 2003, pp. 427–448.

Q. He, T. Chong, K. Shi. "What Accounts for China's Business Cycle?" *China Economic Review*, no. 20, 2009, pp. 650–661.

Ren Xiaojie. "Analysis on Determinant Factors of Foreign Direct Investment in China", *Economic Research Guide*, no. 9, 2014, pp. 249–250.

Shen Kunrong, Teng Yongle. "China's Economic Growth under Structural Slowdown", *Economist*, no. 8, 2013, pp. 29–38.

Wang Jingjing, Huang Fanhua. "Whether Structural Transformation of FDI Promotes Economic Growth", *Southern Economic Journal*, no. 12, 2013, pp. 1–12.

Wang Qing, Zhang Jun, Ernest Ho. "China's Economy before 2020: It Is Not about Whether Growth Slowdown Will Occur, But How", *Financial Development Review*, no. 3, 2011, pp. 26–36.

Xiaolu Wang, G. Fan, P. Liu. "Pattern and Sustainability of China Towards 2020", ACESA 2007 Conference: China's Conformity to the WTO: Progress and Challenges, 2007.

Yang Zheng, Jiang Ying. "Empirical Survey and Industrial Comparison of Foreign Direct Investment, Industrial Features and Economic Growth", *On Economic Problems*, no. 4, 2014, pp. 23–28.

Yuan Fuhua. "One Explanation to 'Structural Acceleration' and 'Structural Slowdown' in Long-term Growth", *Economic Research Journal*, no. 3, 2012, pp. 127–140.

Zhang Ping. "China's Option for Macro Policy and Institutional Mechanism under Structural Slowdown", *Economics Information*, no. 10, 2012, pp. 3–9.

Zhang Xiaojing. "China's Future Growth Prospect: Growth Slowdown Is Not "the Wolf Is Coming", *International Economic Review*, no. 4, 2012, pp. 51–62, 6.

Zheng Xianyong, Hu Chun. "Evaluation on China's FDI Policy under System Stability and Transition", *Special Zone Economy*, no. 8, 2010, pp. 240–241.

10 SOE Reforms during the 13th Five-Year Plan Period

Mixed Ownership under Fair Competition Orientation[1]

The reform and opening-up, as a profound social change, has unleashed immense dividends for the rapid development and growth of China's economy and SOEs (state-owned enterprises). During the 13th Five-Year Plan period, in the context of China's fundamental realities, China shall adhere to and improve its basic economic system of socialism for better implementation of SOE reforms, which means to stick to the Two "Never Wavers", to unswervingly take the market-oriented reform as the deepening direction, to continuously seek for effective realization from and of new path for intensifying the in-depth combination of socialist public ownership and market economy, as well as to enhance the vitality and international competitiveness of SOEs,

I Domestic and Foreign Challenges for China's SOE Reforms during the 13th Five-Year Plan Period

A New Situation of SOE Reforms

The new wave of SOE reforms will meet with more complicated environment at home and abroad. From international level, SOEs have unprecedentedly started to become the new issue for China-US dialogues since the 2012 Fourth Round of the China-US Strategic and Economic Dialogues, covering such fields as the well-known anti-dumping, anti-subsidy, financial reform, and intellectual property. Moreover, such position as "China will steadily increase the delivery ratio of SOE dividends" is firstly included in the outcome of China-US Strategic and Economic Dialogues. Particularly, in recent years, the United States of America and other countries have more positively dominated and boosted the new TPP Agreement different from the WTO rules and vigorously set a higher threshold in the rules and standards for such aspects as intellectual property and financial reform. Moreover, it has incorporated the "SOE" in TPP by borrowing the "competitive neutrality" policy, aiming to dominate the Asia-Pacific Economic Cooperation System across the Pacific Ocean and collapse the "East Asian Community" to strategically restrain China's rise and development on an objective basis. In this regard, at least we can see that the SOE term highlights the foresights of China-US Strategic and Economic Dialogues and the TPP negotiations dominated by the United States of America. The United States of America has fully realized that SOEs serve as one of China's major competitiveness sources, and the aspects it will genuinely compete with China in the future not only include political system and military power but China's increasingly powerful SOE. Therefore, it naturally turns the American strategic priorities to construct the new game rules in favor of American competitiveness, limit and curb China's SOE, and rapidly escalate these constraint means into international rules, to

> fill the gap that the existing international economic rules is unable to ensure fair competition between SOE and private enterprise, and requires the fair competition of SOE in international market and the acceding states to further open up the domestic market and implement equal treatment to the enterprises at home and abroad.

Jose W. Fernandez, the Assistant Secretary of State in charge of economic and business affairs in the United States of America Department of State, explicitly expressed the intent to "make China's SOE more like commercial enterprises", which is all too similar with the competitive neutrality policy required to adopt by TPP. The Prime Minister of Singapore Lee Hsien Loong also believed that "there still exist many problems in China and SOE reform remains the top priority". Facing with such strategic challenges as TPP and TTIP, China needs to constantly change its unfavorable position in global governance system and economic trade frame. Whether China has participated into such international negotiations as TPP, these challenges will surely exert profound influence on China's domestic economic system reform. What is unavoidable is that China's SOEs will inevitably be affected by the related terms in TPP dominated by the United States of America, and such new competitive neutrality rules in international sphere as TPP will pose new challenges to China's SOE reform. Therefore, China, the developing world's second largest economy, has become the important participant in global governance and the important facilitator in governance mechanism reform. China increasingly needs to adjust her international behaviors dependent upon the value judgment of global vision and global governance, and China's SOE reform direction under the opening system requires more rational reflections and firm choices.

B New Situation of SOE Internal Power

From the domestic aspect, in the recent years since the outbreak of international financial crisis, with the constant rise of the proportion of government investment accounting for the total investment in fixed assets due to the government's response to crisis, the constant rise of the share of national financial revenue in national income, as well as the growing encumbrance from the transformation due to the progressive decrease of competitiveness of the enterprises relying on the traditional comparative advantage in the context of international financial crisis, private small and medium-sized enterprises are facing increasingly prominent plight of financing and problems of transformation and upgrading. "The state advances as the private retreats" has thus become a hot topic of social concern. Therefore, the voice of proposing the SOEs or state-owned economy to withdraw from competition fields for de-nationalization was heard without end. Meanwhile, the concern that the privatization of SOEs might cause such systematic problems as more corruption, erosion of state assets, and wider gap in distribution of social welfare fueled the disputes over SOE reform. Moreover, internal governance and external supervision of SOEs did not reach the standard. In this regard, there will be no turning back for the new round of SOE reform, which is all ready for startup. For this reason, at the Third Plenary Session of the 18th Central Committee of the CPC, Chinese government proposed to propel the perfection and development of the socialist system with Chinese characteristics as well as the advancement of the national governance system and modernization of governance capability as the overall objective for deepening reform in all aspects. It was also put forward that "China will remain in primary stage of socialism for a long time" should be the foothold for deepening the reform in all aspects, and "to make the market play a decisive role in the allocation of resources and better play key governmental functions" should be the focal point for deepening the reform in all aspects. It was also brought forward that China should adhere to and improve the basic economic system of common development of diversified forms of ownership based on the main body of public ownership, which serves as the pillar and institutional foundation supporting the socialist system with Chinese characteristics and the socialist market economic system. Therefore, it is necessary to constantly perfect the property rights protective system, actively develop the mixed ownership economy, push ahead SOEs to improve modern enterprise system, and advance China's economic development in a more effective, fair, and sustainable manner for the purpose of displaying the leading role of state-owned economy and supporting and guiding non-public economic development. However, as for how to realize the important form of the basic economic system with diversified mixed ownership, some scholars believed that to develop mixed ownership economy meant to reduce the proportion of state-owned economy and finally to realize "de-nationalization" and "divestment of public ownership". Some even put forward that the state-owned economy was only systematically suitable for providing public service and supposed to withdraw from competitive sectors. These propositions and opinions went against both the tenor of the Third Plenary Session of the 18th Central Committee of the CPC and China's practical and international development experience, and thus turning out to be completely wrong.

The challenge of deepening the SOE reform has always been a much concerned and controversial problem related to the Party and the country. It requires us to use our mind and seek for the proper solutions to Chinese problems according to China's national situations in the context of historical evolution and international experience.

II Researches and Enlightenments of State-Owned Enterprise Reforms Both at Home and Abroad

State-owned enterprises are prevalent in almost every country of the world.

However, their sizes, distributions, locations, and functions differ from each other due to different economic development stages, social systems, and historical cultures of each country, and so do their directions and approaches of reforms and development due to different social natures and development conditions. The analysis of overseas SOE reforms experience and its latest research progress play a significant reference meaning in guiding China's SOE reforms.

A International View: State-Owned Enterprise Reforms under Comparative Horizon

After the breakout of capitalist economic crisis in 1930s and following World War II, capitalist countries began to make comprehensive intervention into economy, and the state-owned economy rapidly grew. After World War II, both the number and size of state-owned enterprises reached the peak. New changes took place to each country's economic development and the global economic situations, with a decline of Keynesianism and prevalence of neoliberalism. Since 1970s, a large-scale privatization movement spread out across the whole world, which led to a significant decrease for both the number of state-owned enterprises and distribution of state-owned economy. However, state-owned enterprises still played an important role in many economic entities and competed with private enterprises in competitive markets. Judging from the privatization and effects of OECD countries, state-owned enterprises did not retreat from competitive sectors after privatization reforms. As they often had to undertake certain social goals in many countries, it was necessary for them to exist and develop. As a result, the effects of privatization reform aiming at improving operation efficiency of state-owned enterprises vary from country to country.

From the global perspective, state-owned enterprises are prevalent in almost all market economy countries. They are still holding 20% investment share and 5% employment share in general; in some countries, the output share is even up to 40%. Among the high-income economy group OECD countries, there are 2085 state-owned enterprises at central level, with a total shareholder value of USD14,168 and 4.33 million employees. Supposing we regard all OECD countries as a whole, its population in total is slightly less than that of China and the GDP is more than six times that of China, with a per capita equity of USD1557 in the central-level state-owned enterprises which is much higher than USD1100 of China's per capita net value in central enterprises.[2]

When looking at the European countries, the average SOEs' equity ratio to GDP exceeded 10%, which varied from one country to another before and after the financial crisis that broke out in 2008. The most outstanding pictures came from Nordic countries and some of the transitional countries in East Europe where their SOEs' equity ratio to GDP held the highest ground, with Norway, Finland, Sweden, Poland, and Czech Republic ranking top 5, each over 20%. Norway's central government owned 46 state-owned enterprises with over 230,000 employees in total, about 9.4% of the total employment in Norway and the highest of all the OECD countries, with an estimated aggregate corporation value (including three holding companies) of USD131 billion. In 2008, its SOEs' equity ratio to GDP came nearly 70%, a 10% increase compared with 2004. By 2009, the central governments of two transitional countries, Poland and Czech Republic, had, respectively, owned 586 (only including the listed and non-listed holding companies) and 124 SOEs. While the central government of France, with the largest number of SOE employees, owned 51 companies, holding the majority ownership with 838,000 employees. Its SOEs' equity ratio accounting for GDP is around 15%, ranking six among European countries.

According to statistics, Russia's fixed asset investment of state-owned enterprise accounts for 40%, the GDP controlled by state-owned economy is nearly 50%, and the employment in state-owned economy reaches 31%; moreover, the state-owned economy of the Republic of Belarus exceeds 70%. From the perspective of developed countries, the state-owned economy of Germany, France, and India is all above 20%. In fact, whether in Russia and India in the BRICS, Singapore in East Asia, or such developed countries as France and Germany, SOE has been playing a vital role in national economy to different degrees. Actually, many countries have not completely or absolutely privatized all the SOEs, and their governments hold the majority of shares of some partially privatized enterprises and most governments are reluctant to dispense with the supervision over SOE.

The outcome of global large-scale privatization indicates that privatization is not a cure-all medicine to resolve SOE challenges. Besides the disputes in academic circle on whether the privatization reform has improved the enterprise performance, it is an unquestioned fact that SOEs still exist and develop in many countries. The government maintaining the ownership and control rights of SOE mainly aims to realize the non-commercial goals (social objectives). As for Western countries, their governments hope SOEs can settle the market failure and external problems unsolvable by private enterprises. In some emerging economies, SOEs can also be endowed with the aims of protecting their own economic security, implementing industrial policies and cultivating the market environment. Specifically speaking, the motivation for the government to own SOEs mainly lies in the following four aspects. First is to provide public goods and services. The government provides public goods and services through the SOEs whose control rights they possess, and will accordingly give financial support on account that some SOEs provide products at rather low price. Second is to promote the economic development. The government usually provides support when SOEs access the emerging industries and participate in international market competition. Besides, to maintain the leading place of the SOEs in some industries and protect them from being acquired by foreign enterprises, the government will also support the SOEs. Third is to achieve other social objectives. The government can help increase the employment and laborers' income through SOEs. During economic crisis, the government can support the private enterprises depending on their owned SOEs. Fourth is to obtain financial revenue. Some SOEs serve as the main sources of financial revenue, such as energy exploitation and the monopolistic SOEs in processing industry. SOEs offering public goods mostly are monopolistic, and the motivations for the government' pursuing financial revenue probably lead the government to support these enterprises to participate in competitive activities by exploiting their monopoly. Moreover, political factor also explains why the government owns and controls SOEs.

With the development of modern enterprise system, more and more enterprises have developed into large groups or multinational corporations. How to handle the agent problem in modern enterprises has attracted worldwide attention. At the end of 20th century, the corporation governance started to prevail globally, with countries in the world setting foot on the corporation governance reform. Internationally, OECE issued the OECD Principles of Corporate Governance in 1999, to provide a reference to corporation governance for various countries. However, the then corporation governance only focused on private enterprises, while the governance problems of SOEs rarely received attention at home and abroad. As SOEs all over the world developed, an increasing number of SOEs conducted corporatization reform. The newly established SOEs were mostly modern enterprises founded according to the Corporation Law. A bunch of SOEs turned into corporations with diversity of equities after listing and took an active part into international competition. Therefore, the corporation governance of SOEs finally brought about the world attention and gradually promoted a series of reform practices. Some international organizations have already delved into the governance problems of SOEs, for instance, the OECD issued OECD Guidelines for Corporate Governance of SOE in 2005, which had a major impact on the construction and perfection of SOE governance mechanism of the 25 member states of OECD and other countries. The reform objectives centered on corporation governance demonstrate two aspects: firstly, to improve the efficiency of SOEs, secondly, to create a fair competitive environment between SOEs and private enterprises. Therefore, the reform priorities focus on two problems: firstly, how the government can avoid improper intervention on the business management activities of SOEs, when effectively performing the functions of owners; secondly, how to ensure the fair competition between SOEs and private enterprises and guarantee the government not to distort the trade rules when exercising market supervision functions.

Since 2009, OECD has probed into the competitive neutrality problem, further studied SOE reform from the perspective of regulating the relation between the government and SOEs, and put forward the framework of competitive neutrality policy, which has actually solved the problem of integration between SOE and market economy. The competitive neutrality policy is to illustrate that the fair competition between SOEs and private enterprises can be realized, so long as the execution of state ownership can be regulated, the social and economic objectives can be distinguished, and the special treatment enjoyed by SOEs during business activities can be removed. The point of SOE reforms is not to withdraw from competitive arena but to improve the supervision framework and corporations and enable SOEs to fairly compete against private enterprises as per market-oriented rules.

B Reasons for Developing and Expanding State-Owned Economy under Socialist Market Economy System from Historical Angle

Over the past 30 years, the mainstream of China's economic system reform has been the exploration, establishment, and perfection of the basic framework of socialist market economy system, so as to carry out the system reform from traditional planned economy to socialist market economy. In this great system reform, we have experienced the marketing process of operation rights reform of SOEs, market subject cultivating, reform of SOE ownership and corporate property rights, reform of SOE supervision system, as well as market mechanism perfecting. Such process has realized the separation between the government and enterprises, the government and state-owned asset management, as well as the ownership and operation rights, and the evolution of reforms of related supportive system and legal system. The main task of SOE reforms as the key point of economic system reform is to transform the governmental appendage under the planned economy to microeconomic subjects in the context of socialistic market-driven economy.

Throughout the 30 years of SOE development, with tireless explorations and reform innovations in theory and practice, SOEs have made great achievements and accumulated valuable experience. Theoretically, SOE reforms have been continuously conducting theoretical exploration and innovation in such aspects as "commodity economy", "separation between ownership and operation rights", "the primary stage of socialism", "socialist market economy", "modern enterprise system", "basic economic system of socialism", "major realization forms of shareholding system and public ownership" and "the system of SASAC", and have made a breakthrough in understanding the functional localization, layout, and realization forms of SOEs.

From practice perspective, the development of SOE reforms has always been revolving around three aspects. First is to make the separation between the government and enterprise, between the government and the state-owned asset management to handle the relation between the government and SOEs. Second, to construct scientifically rational internal and external governance structure, build up modern enterprise system, and handle the relation between enterprise and market economy. Third is to carry out reform to properly deal with the relation between SOEs and the external environment. The socialist market economy system is internally required to form independent subject of market economy and fair competitive environment; therefore, China needs to push the development of her market mechanism from activating and shaping microeconomic unit. The 30 years of exploration on SOE reforms have made us realize that to settle the challenges against SOE reforms, it is imperative to develop and expand, but not shrink, the state-owned economy, so as to play its leading role. We should be keenly aware that although SOE reforms have made important progress and phased achievements, there is still a long way to go. Some deep-seated contradictions and problems still need in-depth reform for effective solutions at the root.

1 To Develop and Expand SOEs: Intrinsic Need of Economic Development in Primary Stage of Socialism

With the development of productivity, the social division of labor is increasingly refined, the industrial chain also gets more and more complicated, and the capital accumulation and concentration endow the production with more social characters. The growing refined and complex socialized production and constantly developing productivity objectively demand the means of production to be distributed and uniformly managed in the whole society for common ownership of the social public, only by which can the real needs of further economic development be met. As a developing country in the primary stage of socialism, China has to firmly rely on, develop, and expand the state-owned economy, so as to realize great-leap-forward development. Because under the market economy environment where state-owned economy and the economy with different types of ownership have been racing to develop in the primary stage of socialism, SOEs function as the effective carrier to accelerate new industrialized construction, the leading power to realize great-leap-forward development to surpass and construct innovative country, the important dependable force to keep national economy security, and also the most active force to promote China's economy development and social progress. SOEs can be deemed as the means of realization for effective macroeconomic regulation and control and the embodiment of the superiority of socialist system, which is to "concentrate resources for great events".

With the rapid development of economic globalization, China, the developing country, has to develop and expand SOEs, so as to handle the increasingly fierce international competition. Under the circumstance of economic globalization, the international monopoly capital is centered on such aspects as resources, technologies, markets, and talent, and cements the control on global economy through intellectual property, capital, technology, and trade. The multinational companies keep pushing competitive pressure on national economy. As for developing countries with backward productive forces, to remain invincible in the fierce international competition and maintain national economic security, it is the inevitable trend of economy development to cultivate internationally competitive SOEs, with the aid of national power, to accelerate capital centralization and accumulation. Chinese SOEs need to enhance the resources allocation levels in China, and more the resources allocation ability worldwide, and make full use of "two kinds of resources, two markets" to enable the country to keep control on key fields concerning national economy security and to boost international competitive force of SOEs and the country. Therefore, to develop and expand SOEs reflects our real demand in this certain economy development stage.

The reports of 16th CPC National Congress stressed that "to develop and expand state-owned economy which controls the national economic lifeline plays a crucial role in giving play to the superiority of the socialist system and cementing China's economic power, national defense strength and national cohesion". Comrade Hu Jintao warned us in "his speech to celebrate 90th Anniversary of the Founding of CPC, China", that

> though we have made remarkable achievements, the basic national condition keeps unchanged that we are still and will remain in the primary stage of socialism, the major social contradiction keeps unchanged that the principal contradiction in China's society is still the one between the ever-growing material and cultural needs of the people and the backwardness of social production, and the international status keeps unchanged that China is the world largest developing country.

The basic national condition, the major social contradiction, and the international status determine that it is imperative to develop and expand state-owned economy to promote competitive and controlling forces of SOEs, but neither gradually desiccate state-owned economy nor privatize SOEs.

2 To Develop and Expand SOEs: General Requirement for Normal Operation of Socialist Market Economy

Socialist market economy is also a market economy with the operating characteristics of the common market economy. As for the common market economy, the presence of SOEs is of great significance and a natural need for normal operation of market mechanism, mainly remedying the market failure. The market, "the invisible hand", is not almighty. Owing to such market malfunctions as the public goods, natural monopolies, externalities, and incomplete and asymmetric information, as well as such insuperable defects as spontaneity, blindness, and backwardness, SOEs are required to enter the domain of "market malfunction", which the private enterprises are reluctant to operate or the market mechanism cannot adjust, to cover the shortage of the private enterprises and market mechanism, safeguard the conditions for social reproduction and push the continuous, stable, and healthy development of national economy.

In fact, the state-owned economies worldwide all assume the duty that the country or the government will intervene and adjust the economy to ensure the normal operation of market economy. The general functions of SOEs in market economy operation specifically include the following fouraspects. First is to provide public goods or public services—to provide "Free Ride" whose costs are greater than benefits due to the market's non-excludability and non-competitiveness, which requires SOEs to provide the society with needed public goods. Second, faced with such functions as international competition and developing strategic industries, SOEs are required to act as the carrier, participate in international competition, and undertake the strategic industries concerning national development and economic security that the private sectors are reluctant to undertake because of uncertain risks and costs. Third, the safeguarding and rescuing functions on private enterprises are to ensure stable operation of the economy. To safeguard and rescue the private enterprises in crisis, state-owned economy, as a tool to control economy, can serve the function of "stabilizer". Fourth, such comprehensive functions as to promote the economic and social development are to be promoted—to promote and stabilize economic growth, to narrow regional gap, and to establish SOEs in backward areas to realize redistribution of wealth and incomes and advance the equal development of society and shorten the regional disparity. It is also one of the functions of SOE development to fulfill such social political targets as creating employment chances and supporting medium and small-sized enterprises to boost and stabilize the economic growth. In this regard, SOEs, as the prevalent phenomenon in market economy countries, are not exclusive to capitalist countries, and their functions are determined by the defects of market economy and government's requirement for intervention in economic affairs.

Therefore, SOEs do not solely aim to pursue the profits as the extension of the government's economic and social functions and the policy instrument for fulfilling the intention, which distinguishes them from the common private enterprises. SOEs not only pursue the profits to realize the economic aim of common enterprises but take other non-profit social goals into account as well. Different from SOEs in capitalist society, those under socialist market economy condition are linked to basic socialist economic system. In a capitalist society, an SOE is naturally closely related to capitalist system, and its presence is mainly to keep the normal reproduction of the capitalist society and create favorable conditions for the reproduction of monopoly capital, ensuring the capitalist classes to gain continuous high profits. The SOE in the capitalist society is the appendage of capitalist system, as it serves the personal economy and capitalist classes. However, SOEs in the socialist society aim to serve the people and finally achieve common prosperity among the whole nation.

From the perspective of SOEs realizing the general functions of market economy operation, SOEs in either socialist society or capitalist society are primarily to remedy market malfunctions and mostly located in the basic and strategic industrial and public utility field, financial field, military industry and special franchise fields, and emerging industry field. Such industries as water service and electric power, characterized by natural monopoly, require immense fixed capital input and are important basic industries vital to national well-being and the people's livelihood. In this case, SOEs are needed to provide the public services under the national macrocontrol. They assume the social responsibility by not solely focusing on profits, by avoiding pursuing high monopoly profit, and by satisfying the needs of the normal social production and the daily life of the public. In another example, some private capital enterprise cannot operate well or is unwilling to operate the strategic and pillar industries often because they refuse to, or fail, to invest, facing high risks and high investment. However, such strategic industries as high-tech industry and strategic emerging industry play an irreplaceable role in the long run, so the government will guide and push these sectors through SOEs to support the participation and development of non-state-operated economy and increase the efficiency of national economy.

3   To Develop and Expand SOEs: Essential Request for Adherence to Socialism Basic Economic System

Though the market economy cannot normally operate without SOEs, the essential request of China's socialism basic economic system is to greatly develop and expand SOEs. As a socialist country, the national economy is directly related to socialism basic economic system. SOEs are the basic force for the country to guide and push economic and social development, which embodies the essential request of socialism and ensures the elimination of polarization and common prosperity for people.

The essence of socialism is liberation and development of the productive forces, elimination of exploitation and polarization, and the ultimate achievement of prosperity for all. Distribution is determined by production, distribution relation is by property relation, and different income distribution systems are by different ownerships. The occupation relation of the means of production determines people's positions and mutual relation during production, distribution, and exchange. Therefore, it is far from perfect to resolve the increasing and excessive income gaps emerging during the economic and social development only through distribution and redistribution.

It is necessary to uncover the problems of the increasing and excessive income gaps from the perspective of ownership structure and property relation. Strengthening the dominant position of public ownership can settle this problem at the root. The ownership of the means of production belongs to all the people, and not to any individual, which fundamentally removes the social contradiction between the capital and the labor. Thus, only by adhering to public ownership of the means of production can the income distribution system be formed in which "multiple patterns of distribution coexist, with the distribution according to labor as principal parts", and can ultimately curb the widening income gap, prevent polarization, and realize common prosperity.

SOEs belong to the whole nation and the profits created come from people and naturally for the people, which manifests the property of bringing benefits to people of the state-owned economy. SOEs promote the maintenance and appreciation of state-owned assets and enhance the rights and interests of all people as the owners of SOE through raising labor productivity, to create a solid economic foundation for better developing the productivity and satisfying the people's growing material and cultural needs. To develop and expand SOE and make it stronger and better helps to deal with the contradictions between the production socialization and the private ownership of the means of production, so as to achieve organic combination between the whole social benefits and partial interests, long-term benefits and current benefits, and public benefits and personal benefits, creating economic foundation for constructing harmonious society. The *Decisions of the CPC Central Committee on Several Important Problems for the Reforms and Development of SOE* passed in the Fourth Plenary Session of the 15th Central Committee of the CPC indicated that "the public ownership economy, including state-owned economy, is the economic foundation of China's socialist system, the basic strength for China to guide, push, and regulate the economic and social development, and the important guarantee to realize the fundamental interest of most people in China and common prosperity". Comrade Deng Xiaoping stressed that "only when the public ownership dominates in China's economy can the polarization be avoided", which is a profound conclusion.

Therefore, the relation between "the state" and "the private" must be fully understood in "the state monopolies and competes with the private for profits", "the state advances as the private retreats", or the adverse opinion. Actually, the so-called "the state" refers to the "state-owned economy", while "the private" refers to the "private economy". However, the "private economy" is not a legal concept, which is generally defined as "non-public sector of economy" and actually refers to the "private enterprise" or "private economy". However, some media and scholars in favor of the theories of "the state advances as the private retreats" and "the state monopolies and competes with the private for profits" deliberately exaggerated the so-called conflicts between "the state" and "the private". They whitewashed the enterprises "private economy" as the enterprises representative of "the public" and the SOEs owned by the whole nation as the "bureaucratic capital" of "national monopoly". In this way, they intentionally changed the concept, hyped the conflict between "the state" and "the private", and surreptitiously supersede the normal competition between the market subjects of SOEs and private enterprises with the false concept of "the state competes with the private for profits". As a matter of fact, the actual purpose for such censure is to require SOEs not to contend with private enterprises and capital for profits. Thus, SOEs will be forced to withdraw from all competitive industries and finally from the vital sectors concerning national interest, people's livelihood, and national security. Such move is nothing but an attempt to deceive everybody, confuse the public attention, and realize the absolute privatization. Under the circumstance of socialist market economy, all kinds of ownership economy, including state-owned economy and non-public sectors of the economy, are supposed to conform to the operation rules of market-oriented economy. We ought to make both of them fairly compete with each other and display respective advantage for mutual promotion and common development, instead of proposing one against the other.

III Suggestions on Policies about Mixed Ownership Reform under Orientation of Fair Competition during the 13th Five-Year Plan Period

The SOE reform in the new era is ultimately to adapt to marketization and push the international development, and further promote the combination between SOEs and market economy to enable the SOE to be the real market subject. From the international experiential analysis, SOEs not necessarily withdraw from the competitive arena. In particularly, under China's current economic development level, SOEs still need to exert leading influence on the state-owned economy in the competitive arena. The main reform challenge is not whether SOEs should withdraw or not, but to realize the advance and retreat of state capital on the basis of comprehensively analyzing the function and position of SOEs. However, the fair competition and competition neutrality demonstrate that if SOEs and market economy fuse, they have to participate in market competition according to market discipline, cancel the competitive edges enjoyed by SOEs because of state ownership, and play the decisive role of market mechanism in adjusting the allocation of state-owned capital. Moreover, SOEs should internally construct the modern enterprise system and corporation governance structure adaptable to the demand of marketization and operate according to market discipline. A new round of SOE reform is expected to enhance the operation efficiency and market competitiveness of SOEs through optimizing the configuration of state-owned capital and promote the fair competition between SOEs and private enterprises by adhering to the market-oriented reform. We need to formulate policy initiatives for SOE equity diversity reforms in the new era, combining such related measures as competitive neutrality policy while performing the mixed ownership reform.

A To Clarify Functions and Position of SOEs and Practice Classified Reforms

During deepening SOE reform, it is required to base on a single SOE and implement reform strategies according to the function and position. In the light with the aforementioned analyses about SOE functions, SOE can be broadly divided into such three types as public policy nature, special functional nature, and general competitive nature. As for the above three types SOEs, the reform manners should differ. Different types of enterprises have different operation objectives. In reality, each SOE usually assumes various social and economic objectives more or less, which requires to consider the specific situations of each enterprise so as to handle the shareholding proportion of state-owned capital and categorically promote the diversity of equities of SOE.

B To Optimize Ownership Structure of SOEs Based on Industry Characteristics

In line with the function and position of SOE and the competition extent of different industries, the ownership structure of SOEs can be further optimized, with the following four forms to be adopted. First, the wholly state-funded form is applied to the few SOEs and state-owned capital operation corporations concerning national security. Second, for important industries related to national interest and people's livelihood and SOE in key fields, the SOEs featured by public policy nature and special functional nature should maintain the majority shareholding and develop the ownership structure where several shareholders counterbalance one another by the shareholding of several state-owned capital operation corporations. In addition, the business of these enterprises should be further classified, allowing non-SOE to hold equity interest of competitive businesses. Third, for SOEs in pillar industries, high-tech industries, and other important industries, most SOEs are featured by special function type. They keep the relative state-owned holding and actively introduce the social capital to participate in the investment through marketization. Fourth, for industries not requiring the control of state-owned capital, namely, the SOE of general competitive nature, the state-controlled shareholding or all state-run withdrawing can be adopted. The shareholding proportion of state-run stock right should increase and decrease rationally in according with national development strategy, and the state-run stock right should withdraw through standardization for property market, in avoidance of the erosion of state assets.

C To Adapt to the Momentum of Diversified Equities of Mixed Ownership and Perfect Supervision System of State-owned Property

With the development trend of the diversity of equities, state-owned capital combines with social capital for mutual development in the enterprises with diversity of equities. It is not a single SOE under the supervision of SASAC, but the state-run stock right distributed in the mixed ownership enterprises. Therefore, the traditional supervision pattern oriented to enterprise management is not suitable for the diversified development of equities of SOEs, so it is imperative to cement the supervision on SOEs oriented to "capital management".

1 To Establish State-Owned Capital Operation Corporations and Implement Responsibilities of Sponsors

Through establishing state-owned capital operation corporations, SASAC, as the "ultimate sponsor representative", exercises uniform management in state-run stock right and diversifies the subjects fulfilling the sponsor responsibilities by entrusting the state-run stock right to multiple equity operation institutions, for example, the state-owned capital operates the corporation. Under the pattern of three-tier framework of SASAC, state-owned capital operation corporation and SOE (including the wholly state-funded, the state-owned holding, the state-controlled shareholding), SASAC, as the ultimate sponsor representative, is mainly responsible for stipulating development strategies of state-owned capital on the whole, compiling operation budget, assigning the person chiefly in charge in state-owned capital operation corporations and audit major events, as well as achieving uniform supervision on state-owned capital through managing state-owned capital operation corporations. The state-owned capital operation corporations, as the special subject of SASAC for fulfilling sponsor responsibilities, should adopt the wholly state-funded manner in principle and exclusively invest the state-controlled shareholding enterprises as a shareholder. The "strengthening and weakening" as well as the "maintenance and appreciation" of the state-owned capital can be realized through capital operation, without working on specific product operation; the third-tier SOE enjoys independent legal person property right and assumes the operation and management responsibility of state-owned property through independent operation, with profit maximization as the goal.

Under the pattern of three-tier framework, SASAC, as the uniform supervisor and the ultimate sponsor representative, conducts the capital operation of state-owned capital operation corporations after stipulating the overall development strategies. Besides, the state-owned capital operation corporations can balance the social and profit objectives of SOEs, dependent on the stock rights held in specific SOE and the power of shareholders, so as to provide SOEs engaging in some operations with clear objective orientation, in avoidance of low efficiency resulting from vague objectives.

2 To Enhance Supervision Oriented to "Capital Management" and Increase Operation Efficiency of State-Owned Property

The supervising pattern of state-owned property oriented to capital management stresses more on the operation capability of state-owned capital and the operation performance and earning power of SOEs. On the one hand, fortifying the investment of state-owned property needs to support the structural layout optimization of state-owned economy and then invest in important industries and fields, in avoidance of blind investment expansion. On the other hand, the state-owned stock assets in some overcapacity or well-established sectors withdraw through transforming into the capital form, which will not exert unfavorable influence on the real economy. In addition, it can optimize the configuration and raise the operation efficiency of state-owned property on the whole, through reinforcing the supervision on state-owned property oriented to capital management and checking the operation efficiency of state-owned capital with market-oriented standards.

D To Adapt to Market and Perfect Modern Enterprise System of SOEs

In the case that SOEs become the real market subject, it is necessary to establish the modern enterprise system suitable to market economy. Through perfecting corporation governance structure, the reform effects of the diversity of equities can better play the role. In the enterprises with diversity of equities, the counterbalance among shareholders can boost the operation efficiency and market competitive force of SOE. Therefore, to construct and complete modern enterprise system sets the precondition and base for the operation of SOEs according to market principles.

1 To Perfect Corporation Governance Structure of SOE

The essence of corporation governance structure is to handle the agent problem arising from the separation between ownership and operation rights, which specifically refer to the arrangement of rights and responsibilities among shareholder's meeting, board of directors, board of supervisors, and managers. Currently, to improve the corporation governance structure of SOE is to construct and complete the modern corporate governance structure adapted to the power balancing of China's SOEs, regulate the authority-responsibility relation between shareholder's meeting and board of directors, and between board of directors and managers, cement the supervision of board of supervisors over shareholder's meeting and managers, as well as perfect the system of external supervisors being assigned by the sponsors or employed from the outside.

2 To Perfect Incentive and Restraint Mechanism of SOE Entrepreneurs

The mechanism of scientific and rational incentive and restraint can help eliminate opportunistic behaviors and ethical risks of the operators, reduce the agent cost, and enhance corporation operation efficiency. All in all, the incentives of SOE entrepreneurs should link up with their operation performance. During actual operation, to design diverse incentives can promote the long-term standardization of entrepreneurs' behaviors. Generally speaking, the remuneration of SOE entrepreneurs consists of risk-free return and incentive payment. The stock ownership incentive can tie the interest of shareholders to that of the entrepreneurs and enable the entrepreneurs to pay attention to the long-term development of enterprise. Therefore, it can be adopted in SOEs with diversity of equities.

3 To Strengthen External Supervision of SOE

The restraints on SOE entrepreneurs are mainly from enterprises' internal and external supervision. Internal supervision is the one of shareholders meeting, board of directors, and board of supervisors, as well as the restraint by the article of association. External supervision chiefly refers to the supervision of such intermediate bodies as mechanism and audit. Owing to the complex principal-agent relation of SOEs, the responsibilities of shareholders meeting, board of directors, and board of supervisors are to be improved. Therefore, the external supervision on SOE entrepreneurs will be realized through improving stock market, professional manager market, and product market. Moreover, it is also the crucial way to supervise the entrepreneurs' behaviors to perfect the important role of intermediate bodies in SOE information disclosure.

Notes

1 This achievement was sponsored by the project of Study on the Reform of Primary Distribution System with Coordination of Efficiency and Fairness, a key project on the subject of philosophy and social science research launched by the Ministry of Education (project number: 08JZD0013), and by the project of Youth Funds of Institute of China's Economic Reform & Development of Renmin University of China.

2 It is converted on the basis of the exchange rates according to the provided total net assets 0.95 billion yuan of the central enterprises reported in *People's Daily*. Bai Tianliang: "Doubling main operational indicators of SOEs in five years with annual average value maintaining and increment of state-owned asset up to 115% – bolstering up Chinese spirit", *People's Daily*, January 25, 2011.

Bibliography

Bai Tianliang. "Doubling Main Operational Indicators of SOEs in Five Years with Annual Average Value Maintaining and Increment of State-owned Asset up to 115% – Bolstering up Chinese Spirit", *People's Daily*, 2011 January 25

Liu Guoguang."Public Ownership: Cornerstone of Basic Economic System in Primary Stage of Socialism", *China SOE*, no. 7, 2011, pp. 35–41.

"What Shall State-owned Enterprises Do?", *Guangming Daily*, Edition 16, 2012 April 18.

World Bank IFC. *Approach by World Bank on Improving Corporate Governance of State-owned Enterprises.* Doi: <http://www.ifc.org/ifcext/corporategovernance. nsf/AttachmentsByTitle/Improving_+CG_SOE/$FILE/Improving_CG_SOE. pdf>

Zhang Yu. "Correct Understanding of Status and Role of State-owned Economy in Socialist Market Economy", *Research on Mao Zedong's Thoughts & Deng Xiaoping's Theories*, no. 1, 2010, pp. 23–29, 85.

11 Judgment Standard on Rationality of China's Proportion of Residents' Income[1]

I Introduction

In recent years, against the backdrop of the widening gap in income and the continuous downturn of consumption, scholars cast their vision of study on the distribution pattern of national income, focus on the rise of proportion of capital income and the decline of proportion of residents' income, and probe into the real amplitude and reason for the reduction of the proportion of residents' income, so as to attempt to answer whether the control of capital or government's income over labor exists in the pattern of national income distribution and make scientific explanation. However, the scholars have not given a firm and clear answer as to whether the proportion of China's residents' income is too low, and whether it is necessary to timely reverse the current trend. Therefore, it is impossible to obtain the reasonable interval for proportion of China's current residents' income, which makes the policy for rise of the proportion of residents' income lack theoretical and practical basis. The main reason for it is that the academia has not constructed a scientific standard to judge the proportion of residents' income in China.

In the existing studies, the judgment on whether China's proportion of residents' income was too low was mainly based on the following considerations. First, China should reverse the trend out of concern about the negative impact of the decline in proportion of residents' income. For example, Cai Fang (2005, 2006) pointed out that from 1998 to 2003, the capital proportion of residents' income went on a year-on-year rise and inevitably led to the uneven distribution of income.[10][11] Kujis (2006) of the World Bank and Wang Tongsan (2007) believed that the reduction of labor proportion of residents' income and the proportion of residents' income influenced consumption growth. Chongen et a. (2009a) held that if the residents' income was too low, the investment rate would be too high, thus affecting the efficiency. Second, based on the comparison with other countries in terms of the proportion of residents' income, the proportion of labor remuneration in China was thought to be too low. For example, Luo Changyuan et al. (2009) pointed out that compared with the proportion of labor income of most countries in the world, namely, from 55% to 65%, China's share of residents' income in GDP was too low. Xiao Hongye et al. (2009) compared China's data with the transnational data adjusted by Gollin (2002) and indicated that the share of China's residents' income in GDP was not only significantly lower than that of developed countries but also lower than the average of developing countries. However, Chongen et al. (2009b) pointed out against such judgment that the comparability in the cross-national comparisons in factor distribution share should be addressed to question the conclusion by simply adopting international comparisons. In addition to the comparability of factor distribution shares, the comparability of development stages is more important. Third, attention should be paid to the conclusion of the relationship between labor proportion of residents' income and economic development based on theoretical and empirical analysis. As for the relationship between the proportion of residents' income and economic development, there are many different viewpoints in academia as follows. First, Kaldor, in his typical facts, believed that the proportion of factor income is stable. However, the fact that the proportion of national labor income declined before and after 1980s posed a challenge to the typical facts, forcing scholars to seek the theoretical explanation to the reality via the direction decided by labor remuneration proportion. Second, it was thought that labor share and economic development change in the same direction. It was basically consistent with the research findings of Li Daokui (2007). Li Daokui pointed out that the share of labor in the United States and the United Kingdom from 1935 to 1985 was on a slow rise, essentially between 65% and 80%. The UN data also showed that with the increase of per capita income, the share of labor in most countries would remain between 70% and 80%. On such basis, it was believed that China's share of labor was too low. Third, it was thought that the changes of labor share in economic development exhibited U-shaped pattern. Li Daokui et al. (2009) pointed out that in the development of economy, labor share firstly decreased and then increased, showing U-shaped fluctuation, with the turning point when GDP arrived at about USD6,000 per capita, which was the PPP in 2000, which affirmed the rationality of the previous reduction of China's labor share.

Obviously, owing to the lack of standards, contradictions or unclear expressions for opinion occurred to scholars in the judgment whether China's residents' income accounted for a reasonable proportion. Therefore, the policies and measures show lack of theoretical basis and quantity standards to increase the proportion of residents' income in national income distribution, narrow gap of income, and enhance residents' consumption.

In this paper, the study on distribution of national income was correlated with that on the stages of economic development, especially with that on industrialization. By the use of the experience of change in the proportion of residents' income in Japan, South Korea, and China Taiwan in their industrialization, this paper tries to summarize the general rules of change in residents' income in different stages of industrialization and judge the rationality for the existence of the change in the proportion of residents' income in China's industrialization, so as to provide the basis and space-time quantity standard for improvement of national income distribution pattern.

II Selection and Basis of Reference System and Data

Our basic idea to explore China's standard for the proportion of residents' income in industrialization is to choose the experience data of change in the proportion of residents' income in Japan, South Korea, and China Taiwan in their industrialization and summarize the general rules of change in residents' income in different stages of industrialization. Through the comparison with the equal stages of industrialization of these countries and regions, we can get the quantity interval for proportion of residents' income at different stages in China's industrialization.

Here what matters most is why we choose the data of change in proportion of residents' income of Japan, South Korea, and China Taiwan in their industrialization to get the assessment criteria for the proportion of residents' income in China's industrialization. In fact, our thoughts are mainly based on the following considerations:

1   Japan, South Korea, and China Taiwan are all later-developed countries and regions that have completed industrialization. As later-developed industrialized country and region, they have historical tasks of speeding up industrialization and realizing catch-up with other industrialized countries. Their industrialization shows different rules and paths from early-developed countries. In the process of catch-up, Japan, South Korea, and China Taiwan have successfully completed industrialization and have successively become developed economies. China is now in the later period of the middle stage of industrialization and will finish industrialization around 2020. As a later-developed country, China has similarity with Japan, South Korea, and China Taiwan in industrialization.

2   Japan, South Korea, and China Taiwan experienced economic transition in industrialization, when all of them were confronted with the pressure and demand for economic transition, with the main manifestations as follows. Firstly, these countries and regions showed obvious characteristics of investment dominance. They had high rates of investment and promoted rapid economic growth in industrialization, especially in heavy industrialization stage. They gradually turned to the economic growth mode mainly driven by consumption in the late stage of industrialization. For example, Japan's fixed-asset investment growth rate from the post-war recovery to the end of industrialization in 1973 was far higher than that in other periods. Japan implemented the national income-doubling plan to accelerate economic transition since early 1960s. Second, these countries and regions experienced changes in

the external environment in industrialization, like the rise of prices of energy and other raw materials. In the industrialization of these countries and regions, two "oil crisis" successively broke out in 1973 and 1978, which led to the sharp rise of oil price and the constant increase of production and labor costs, thus forcing the economy to gradually turn to innovation and knowledge-intensive one. Currently, China is also in economic transition for acceleration of the transformation of economic development mode, with many similarities in terms of path and external conditions of industrialization.

3   Japan, South Korea, and China Taiwan have gone on a rapid growth for 20 to 30 years in industrialization stage, whose industrialization was similar with that in the rapid economic growth period. From 1956 to 1973, Japan's average annual growth rate was over 9.2%; from 1963 to 1991, South Korea's average annual economic growth rate reached 9.6%; from 1961 to 1989, China Taiwan's actual economic growth rate reached 9% on average. Such period was precisely the stage of industrialization of these countries and regions. Since the reform and opening-up, China went on a rapid economic growth for more than 30 years. In addition, from the perspective of foundation and room of development, China's reform will possibly continue to maintain a relatively high growth before the completion of industrialization, which embodies the similar features of growth in Japan, South Korea, and China Taiwan.

4   Japan, Korea, and China Taiwan are Asian countries with cultural similarities. Culture, as an informal institution, has a binding role in economic development and lifestyle of a country. China, as well as Japan and South Korea, admires Confucian culture; China has even the same culture with China Taiwan areas. The oneness of culture determines the similarity of value judgment, thus leading to convergence of industrialization path and social habits.

As for the selection of data, we applied the relevant data of Japan from 1955 to 2000, of South Korea from 1972 to 2010, and of China Taiwan from 1965 to 2004. These data mainly come from the database of the World Bank, statistical yearbook of countries or regions, as well as bank data of countries or regions, with the time span covering their whole industrialization, most of the processes, and the later period of industrialization. Such interval can clearly describe the changing rule of the proportion of residents' income in different stages of industrialization in Japan, South Korea, and China Taiwan.

To enhance the comparability of the development stage of industrialization, we adopted the method of Chen Jiagui in the Report on China's Industrialization. By use of the five indicators of GDP per capita, proportions of three industries, proportion of manufacturing added value in the added value of total goods production sectors, urbanization rate, and employment proportion of the first industry, we estimated industrialization indicators and separate the development stages of industrialization. In the comparative study, we considered that the industrialization of Japan, South Korea, and China Taiwan was relatively early, with a great time span in comparison. For the convenience of comparison, we modified the average method of exchange rate-PPP in the calculation of China's GDP per capita into the conversion of exchange rate, and use the constant price denominated by US dollar in 2005.

III Features of Variation in Proportion of Residents' Income in Later-Developed Economies

A Features of Variation in Japan's Proportion of Residents' Income

After a brief post-war recovery, Japan resumed its industrialization around 1955, when the industrialization index was 41. In 1974, the industrialization index was 99, which symbolized the completion of industrialization. Later, Japan entered into its post-industrialization stage. Correspondingly, as shown in see Figure 11.1, the changes in the proportion of Japan's residents' income can be divided into the following four stages.

Stage I (1955–1961): When the industrialization index was from 41 to 69, the proportion of residents' income slowly decreased from 46.2% to 44.9%; when the industrialization index was over 50, the latter got on a rise for a while, but soon fell.

Stage II (1962–1970): When the industrialization index was from 71 to 92, the proportion of residents' income increased rapidly from 44.9% to 50.3%, up about five percentage points, stabilizing at about 50%.

Stage III (1971–1975): When the industrialization index was from 93 to 100, the industrialization was basically completed, and the proportion of

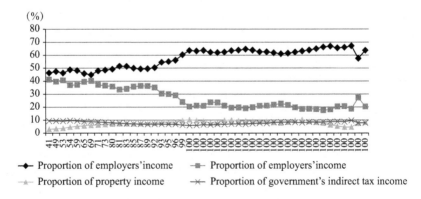

Figure 11.1 Changes of national income distribution pattern in Japan's industrialization and post-industrialization stages.

Data source: calculated according to the data from the website of Japan Statistical Office.

residents' income increased rapidly from 50.3% to 63.5%, up over ten percentage points.

Stage IV (after 1975): Since the post-industrialization period, the proportion of residents' income was once again stabilized at the interval from 60% to 65%; although it broke through 65% in some years, it basically remained around 65%.

The change in Japan's proportion of residents' income indicated that in the middle stage of industrialization, the proportion of residents' income slowly went down in its fluctuation, basically below 50%; in the late half of the middle stage of industrialization, the proportion of residents' income quickly went up about five percentage points and remained at around 50%; when the industrialization was basically completed and the industrialization index reached 93, the proportion of residents' income went on a substantial rise, by about ten percentage points; in the post-industrialization, the proportion of residents' income further increased by about five percentage points.

B Features of Variation in South Korea's Proportion of Residents' Income

South Korea began its industrialization around 1963. In 1972, Korea's industrialization index was 12. In 1998, Korea's industrialization index reached 99, which symbolized the completion of industrialization. Later, South Korea entered into its post-industrialization stage. As shown in see Figure 11.2, the changes in the proportion of South Korea's residents' income can be divided into the following five stages.

Stage I (1972–1980): When the industrialization index was from 12 to 49, the proportion of residents' income quickly went up from 32.9% to 39.9%, with the greatest amplitude over eight percentage points.

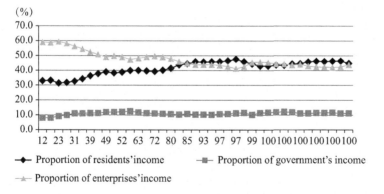

Figure 11.2 Changes in national income distribution pattern in Korea's industrialization and post-industrialization.

Data source: calculated according to the data from South Korea's banks.

Stage II (1981–1987): When the industrialization index was from 49 to 77, the proportion of residents' income fluctuated slightly and stabilized at about 40% with small fluctuation.

Stage III (1988–1991): When the industrialization index was from 80 to 88, the proportion of residents' income increased rapidly again, exceed through 40% and remained at about 46%, up about six percentage points.

Stage IV (1992–1996): When the industrialization index was from 93 to 97, the industrialization was nearly completed, with the proportion of residents' income on a slight rise from 45.8% to 47.6%, up less than two percentage points.

Stage V (since 1997): After entering the stage of post-industrialization, the proportion of residents' income was on a slight decline and stabilized at the interval from 42% to 47%.

Relatively speaking, the overall share of Korea's residents' income was lower than that of Japan. The fluctuation of South Korea's proportion of residents' income indicated that the initial level of Korea's proportion of residents' income was low. In the early stage of industrialization, South Korea's proportion of residents' income went on a rapid rise at around 40%. In the middle stage of industrialization, South Korea's proportion of residents' income remained at around 40%. In the late stage of industrialization, when industrialization index reached 80, South Korea's proportion of residents' income went on a rapid rise again and was stabilized at around 46%. In the stage of post-industrialization, Korea's proportion of residents' income remained at the interval from 42% to 47%.

C Features of Variation in China Taiwan's Proportion of Residents' Income

China Taiwan began its industrialization around 1961. In 1966, the industrialization index in China Taiwan was 12, which symbolized its initial stage of industrialization. In 1997, its industrialization index reached 97, which indicated its basic completion of industrialization.[2] As shown in Figure 11.3, the change in China Taiwan's proportion of residents' income can be mainly divided into the following five stages.

Stage I (1966–1972): When the industrialization index was from 12 to 39, the proportion of residents' income increased slowly from 37.4% to 42.1%, with the growth rate less than five percentage points.

Stage II (1972–1982): When the industrialization index was from 39 to 64, the proportion of residents' income went on a fast growth from 42.1% to 50.9%, up about nine percentage points.

Stage III (1983–1986): When the industrialization index was from 66 to 76, the proportion of residents' income remained stable with a slight decline, basically maintaining at around 50%, and dropped to 48.2% in 1986.

Stage IV (1987–1995): When the industrialization index was from 78 to 94, the proportion of residents' income increased rapidly from 48.2% in 1986 to 58.7% in 1995, up about ten percentage points.

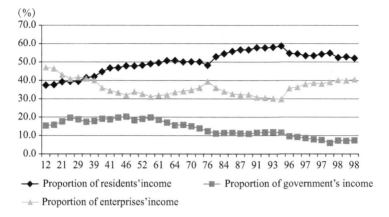

Figure 11.3 Changes in national income distribution pattern in industrialization in China Taiwan.

Data source: calculated according to the data from China Taiwan Economic Yearbook.

Stage V (1995–2004): When the industrialization index was from 94 to 99, the industrialization was basically completed, and the proportion of residents' income slightly declined from its peak value of 58.7% to 52.1% in 2004.

The changes in China Taiwan's proportion of residents' income indicated that as the initial proportion of residents' income was low in early stage of industrialization, China Taiwan's residents' income was on a rapid rise by around 50%, and it remained in the middle stage of industrialization. In the post-industrialization stage when the industrialization index reached 76, the proportion of residents' income went on a rapid rise by about ten percentage points.

IV General Rule of Changes in Proportion of Residents' Income in Industrialization

A General Rule of Proportion of Residents' Income in Industrialization

In industrialization, the initial proportions of residents' income of South Korea and China Taiwan were low, with a slow or rapid increase in the early stage of industrialization. Thanks to the availability of data, we have focused on the rule of changes in their proportions of residents' income since the middle stage of industrialization, when the changes in the proportions of residents' income of Japan, South Korea, and China Taiwan exhibit obvious rules as follows, as shown in Figure 11.4.

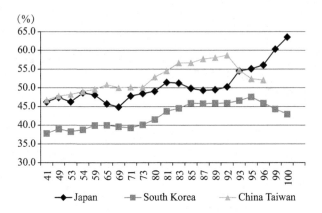

Figure 11.4 Changes in proportion of residents' income of Japan, South Korea, and China Taiwan since middle stage of industrialization.

Data source: calculated and compiled according to the data from the websites of Japan Statistics Bureau, Korea's banks and China Taiwan's Economic Yearbook.

First, in the middle stage of industrialization, their proportion of residents' income was less than 50%, and then went on a slow rise and then declined.

Second, in the late stage of industrialization when the industrialization index was from 70 to 80, the proportions of residents' income of these countries and regions rapidly increased by about five percentage points and remained at around 50%. When the industrial index was 71, Japan's proportion of residents' income rapidly rose from 45% to about 50% and remained at around 50% until the industrial index was 92. South Korea's proportion of residents' income speeded up its rise from 40% to 45% when the industrial index was 80 and remained at around 45% until the industrial index was 97. China Taiwan's proportion of residents' income went on an expedite growth when the industrialization index was 78, with a large amplitude from 48.2% to its peak value of 58.7%. However, compared with Japan and South Korea, since the late stage of industrialization, China Taiwan's industrialization was the slowest; after the industrialization index reached 94, China Taiwan's proportion of residents' income continuously declined to 52%, with a regression trend toward 50%. Overviewing the industrialization of the United States, its proportion of residents' income remained at around 50% from 1929 to 1951 and skyrocketed from 1951 to 1970, which showed the similar momentum to that of Japan, South Korea, and China Taiwan.

Third, since the end of industrialization when the industrialization index reached 90, their proportions of residents' income went on different trends. The proportion of Japan's residents' income went on a rise. The proportion of South Korea's residents' income slightly rose and dropped, with the maximum rate at 47.6%, up less than 3%.

B Reason for Change Rule of Proportion of Residents' Income during the in Industrialization

The proportion of the residents' income was shown low in the early and middle stage of industrialization, but higher upon a rapid rise in the late stage of industrialization, with the possible reasons as follows.

First, in the early and middle stages of industrialization, the accumulation of capital was the key issue of economic development. According to the dualistic economic theory proposed by Lewis, as in the early and middle stage of industrialization, the rural areas are affluent in surplus labor but in relative shortage of capital, the mode of distribution of income inclined to capital will be conducive to economic growth. However, if the salary income grows too fast, the industrialization will be influenced. The inclination of enterprises in the income distribution pattern in the early and middle stages of industrialization of economies is consistent with the theory. Meanwhile, China Taiwan wandered for a long time at the end of industrialization, possibly related to the too fast increase in the proportion of residents' income in the late stage of industrialization, thus forcing the proportion of residents' income to go down back to around 50%. With the constant rise of urbanization rate, the relative shortage of capital and labor is changed, and so is the pattern of income distribution.

Second is the impact of labor shortage. With the continuous advancement of industrialization, most of the economies faced shortage of labor, which led to the rapid growth of salary in the late stage of industrialization and the rapid rise in the proportion of residents' income. When the proportions of residents' income of Japan and South Korea went on a rapid rise, the urbanization rates of both countries were, respectively, 77% and 89%, which indicated the basic completion of urbanization. Compared with that of Japan and South Korea, the urbanization of China Taiwan was relatively slow. However, when its proportion of residents' income went on a rapid rise, its rate of urbanization reached 65%, with surplus labor completely exhausted, which was possibly the main reason for the increase of the proportion of residents' income in the late stage of industrialization.

Third, the impact of economic transition is another reason. Japan, South Korea, and China Taiwan all adopted foreign trade-oriented development strategy for industrialization. By relying on cheap labor to support rapid development of foreign trade, they had their economy in a rapid development mode. However, with the increase of trade frictions, labor and raw material costs continuously increased, which promoted economic transition in all the three economies. In 1960s, Japan proposed the "doubling plan for national income". In middle 1980s, South Korea put forward the overall goal of "adjusting industrial structure to realize technology-based national development". Meanwhile, China Taiwan launched economic transition by promoting industrial upgrade and supporting the development of small and medium-sized enterprises, which led to the rise of its proportion of residents' income.

Fourth, continuous improvement of human capital exerted certain impact. Japan adopted a series of measures to rapidly restore education development after World War II. By 1970, Japan's enrollment rate of higher education reached 18.7%. In 1980, high school enrollment was over 90%. South Korea also made rapid progress in education by increasing investment in education. By 1980, South Korea's enrollment rate of high schools reached 63.3%. From 1970 to 1990, the number of institutions of higher education increased by 6.4 times. Similarly, the education development in China Taiwan was also rapid. In 1984, the gross enrollment rate of higher education in China Taiwan was less than 15%, but was up to 32.4% in 1991 and was further increased to more than 50% in the middle of 1990s. The rapid development of education greatly improved human capital and labor productivity, making it possible for the rise of residents' income. According to the research result from UNESCO, labor productivity and workers' education degree are positively related. Compared with illiteracy, primary school graduates can increase labor productivity by 43%, junior high school graduates by 108%, and graduates from universities and colleges by 300%.

V China's Application of Rule of Proportion of Residents' Income in Industrialization

A Judgment on Rationality of Change of China's Proportion of Residents' Income

In industrialization, China's proportion of residents' income went through the following two stages,[3] as shown in Figure 11.5.

Stage I (1985–2007): When the industrialization index was from 16 to 45, the proportion of residents' income of residents continued to decline. Especially since 2004, when the industrialization index was 35, the residents'

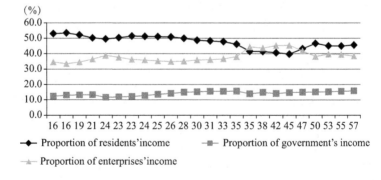

Figure 11.5 Changes in China's national income distribution pattern in industrialization.
Data source: calculated according to the data of China Statistical Yearbook.

income decreased greatly[4] from 53% in 1985 to 39.7% in 2007, down more than ten percentage points.

Stage II (from 2007 to the present): When the industrialization index was 45, the proportion of residents' income increased rapidly and stabilized at about 45%. When the industrialization index reached 58 in 2012, the proportion of residents' income was 45.6%.

The biggest difference between China's proportion of residents' income and that of Japan, South Korea, and China Taiwan was that China's initial proportion of residents' income was higher. For example, when China's industrialization index was 16, its proportion of residents' income was as high as from 53% to 53.4%; when the industrialization indices of South Korea and China Taiwan were, respectively, 20 and 17, their proportions of residents' income were, respectively, 33.2% and 37.7%, far below that of China. This determined that in industrialization, China's proportion of residents' income turned out to be at the reversal trend of that of Japan, South Korea, and China Taiwan. According to the above-mentioned concluded rule of changes in the residents' income in industrialization, China's proportion of residents' income was in a regular decline, which was back in the reasonable range. It was to a certain degree consistent with the capital tendency of income distribution in the early and middle stages of industrialization, with certain rationality.

However, as China's proportion of residents' income constantly went down, when the industrialization index was about 42 in 2006, China's proportion of residents' income was slightly higher than that of South Korea in equivalent industrialization but far lower than that of Japan and China Taiwan; when the industrialization index was 45, the former even went below to that of South Korea in equivalent industrialization, as shown in Table 11.1. Evidently, compared with other later-developed countries and regions, China's proportion of residents' income near the middle stage of industrialization was indeed too low, which required improving. Therefore, before the middle stage of industrialization, China's proportion of residents' income got on a great rise, which accorded with the rule of changes in the proportion of residents' income in industrialization.

B Time and Space Standards for Changes in China's Future Proportion of Residents' Income

In 2009, China's industrialization index reached 50 and it entered the middle stage of industrialization. In 2013, it increased up to 57, equivalent to the industrialization of Japan in 1959, with industrialization index at 59; South Korea in 1983, with industrialization index at 58; and China Taiwan in 1979, with industrialization index at 55; thus, China was in the late half of the middle stage of industrialization. At this point, China's proportion of residents' income was 45.6%, and Japan, Korea, and China Taiwan were, respectively, 48.1%, 39.9%, and 49%. China's proportion of residents' income was still relatively lower by three percentage points.

Table 11.1 Comparison of proportion of residents' income in industrialization between China, Japan, Korea, and China Taiwan

Japan		South Korea		China Taiwan		China	
Index of industrialization	*Proportion of residents' income*	*Index of industrialization*	*Proportion of residents' income*	*Index of industrialization*	*Proportion of residents' income*	*Index of industrialization*	*Proportion of residents' income*
41	46.2%	43	37.8%	41	46.7%	42	40.6%
49	47.4%	49	39.0%	42	46.9%	45	39.7%
53	46.3%	49	38.3%	46	47.9%	47	43.2%
54	48.7%	52	38.8%	48	47.8%	50	46.6%
59	48.1%	58	39.9%	52	48.2%	53	45.0%
65	45.7%	63	40.0%	55	49.0%	55	44.9%
69	44.9%	65	39.6%	61	49.6%	57	45.6%

Data source: calculated and compiled according to the data from the websites of Japan Statistics Bureau, Korea's banks, China Taiwan's Economic Yearbook, and China Statistical Yearbook.

From the development stages of industrialization until the industrialization index reached 80, the proportion of residents' income of Japan and China Taiwan remained at around 50%, with the peak value of Japan up to 49.1% and that of China Taiwan up to 52.9%. The proportion of residents' income of South Korea remained low, with its highest rate at 41.5%. According the momentum of China's current proportion of residents' income, it is more likely to be consistent with that of Japan and China Taiwan. According to the general rule of the changes in the proportion of residents' income in these countries and regions, when the industrial index reached 80, China's proportion of residents' income might be steadily on a rise to about 50%. Based on the estimation of the current industrialization, it will be in around 2020. The proportion will remain at 50%, with the upward possibility at about five percentage points.

Concerning the international environment regarding the rise of the current costs of raw materials, energy, environment, as well as the need of economic transition, as China's urbanization rate was only 53.7% in 2013, far from the urbanization rate from 65% to 70%, the critical point of labor shortage caused the sharp rise of labor costs. Thus, it is reasonable for China's proportion of residents' income to be stabilized at about 50% between the middle and the end of industrialization.

It took Japan, South Korea, and China Taiwan about ten years to go through the process from the moment when the industrialization index was at 80 to the completion of industrialization. When the industrialization index reached 95, close to the completion of industrialization, the proportion of residents' income of the three countries and regions increased by around five percentage points, with Japan up to 55.1%, South Korea up to 45.9%, and China Taiwan back to 54.7% upon rapid growth. Later, their changes in the proportion of residents' income differed. In accordance with the rule of change, China will likely approach the completion of industrialization in 2030, with the possibility for China's proportion of residents' income to go on a rise by five percentage points than that in 2020, up to 55%.

C Policy Suggestions on Improving China's Proportion of Residents' Income

According to the space-time standard on changes of China's future proportion of residents' income, although the proportion of residents' income went on a rise in the late stages of the middle stage of industrialization and the stage of post-industrialization, the range of rise was limited, due to taking into consideration that residents enjoy the benefits of economic growth and guaranteeing the smooth advancement of industrialization. To achieve such balance, it required actions in the following aspects.

First is to improve the salary formation mechanism to promote reasonable rise of salary. For a long time, China's migrant workers salary was determined in accordance with the basic rule for survival, which made the salary of migrant workers remained almost unchanged from 1990s to early 2000s. If considering the price factor, it even declined, which affected the enthusiasm of the employment of migrant workers. With the economic growth and the change of labor structure, the formation mechanism of the salary of migrant workers was gradually priced upon market bargaining, which led to certain rise of their salary. However, the current salary formation mechanism is still not perfect. It is critical to establish the salary formation mechanism that reflects change of supply and demand in labor market and includes guarantee of migrant workers, so as to ensure the reasonable rise of salary.

Second is to speed up the transformation of governmental functions and taxation system reform to reduce the burden on enterprises. In industrialization, the proportion of government's income of Japan, South Korea, and China Taiwan was relatively stable with slight reduction. The income of residents and enterprises in these countries and regions grew or declined, while China's turned out to be slightly more. If all administrative fees are included, the proportion of government's income rose more obviously. In this context, to raise the proportion of residents' income will further reduce the margin of enterprises' profits and hinder capital accumulation and industrialization. It requires the speed-up of transformation of governmental functions so as to reduce the burden on enterprises and benefit enterprises by further expanding the scope of replacing the business tax with the value-added tax and other tax reform.

Third is to improve quality of urbanization and increase aspiration of labor supply. In 2013, China's urbanization rate based on registration population was only 36%, far below the urbanization rate calculated based on residential population, with low quality of urbanization. Migrant workers could not enjoy the same public services as urban residents. Low city integration brought about problems of the left-behind elderly people and children, which greatly affected the willingness of supply of rural labor. Concerning the change of the current labor age structure, the "Lewis turning point" prematurely occurred, which resulted in the pressure on the rise of salary and increased the difficulty of industrialization. It required a targeted solution to the problem that labor supply aspiration was suppressed, so as to improve the quality of urbanization.

Fourth is to raise human capital and increase labor productivity. Through the rapid development of education, China's human capital was greatly improved. However, in the era of knowledge economy, China was unable to replicate technical progress and innovation path of the later-developed countries in the era of industrial economy but had to promote industrialization in competition with developed countries. It puts forward higher requirements on human capital. At present, there is still a big gap between China and developed countries in the situation of human capital. In 2010, the average education of people aged over 25 in the United States last 12.4 years, and that in Japan was 11.6 years. Both were longer than China by

3.8 and 3 years, respectively. Therefore, it is necessary to speed up the development of education, improve the quality and level of human capital, and raise the labor productivity of enterprises, so as to set aside the room for salary increase for enterprises.

Fifth is to promote upgrade of industrial structure and accelerate economic transition. With the advance of industrialization, serious overcapacity and ecological and environmental pressure occurred in China. The original model of development was not sustainable, which requires China to attach great importance to innovation-driven development and to actively promote the upgrade of industrial structure and added value of manufacturing industry, so as to synchronize the rise of salary and sustainable advancement of industrialization.

Notes

1 This achievement was sponsored by the project of Study on the Reform of Primary Distribution System with Coordination of Efficiency and Fairness, a key project on the subject of philosophy and social science research launched by the Ministry of Education (project number: 08JZD0013) and by the project of Youth Funds of Institute of China's Economic Reform & Development of Renmin University of China.
2 However, owing to the influence of urbanization rate, the industrialization index in China Taiwan was in fluctuation, failing to reach 100 by 2004.
3 As China's previous industrialization remained low, it began to investigate the changes in the proportion of its residents' income after the reform of the urban economic system in 1984.
4 According to the scholars' investigation, the proportion of China's residents' income has declined greatly since 2004, mainly due to the adjustment of statistical caliber. See relevant studies for details of Chongen et al. (2009b), Luo Changyuan et al. (2009), and Xiao Hongye et al. (2009).

Bibliography

Alwyn Young. "The Tyranny of Numbers: Confronting the Statistical Realities of the East Asian Growth Experience." *The Quarterly Journal of Economics*, vol. 110, no. 3, 1995, pp. 641–680.

Bai Chongen, Qian Zhenjie. "Analysis of Influence Factors on China's Capital Proportion of Residents' Income and Reasons for Its Changes – A Study Based on Provincial Panel Data", *Journal of Tsinghua University (Edition of Philosophical Social Science)*, no. 4, 2009a, pp. 137–147,160.

Bai Chongen, Qian Zhenjie. "Factor Distribution of National Income: A Story Behind Statistical Data", *Economic Research*, no. 3, 2009b, pp. 27–41.

Cai Fang. "Exploration on Fair Distribution Mechanism Adapted to Economic Development", *People's Forum*, no. 10, 2005, pp. 31–32.

Cai Fang. "To Realize Maximized Economic Employment: Economic Foundation of Harmonious Society", *Wen Hui Daily,* 24-10-2006(005).

Chen Jiagui et al. *Blue Book of Industrialization: Report on Industrialization in China from 1995 to 2005*, Beijing: Social Sciences Academic Press, 2007.

D. Acemoglu. "Labor and Capital Augmenting Technical Change", *NBER Working Paper*, 2000 (7544).

D. Gollin. "Getting Income Shares Right", *Journal of Political Economy*, no. 2, 2002.

Li Daokui. *China's GDP Share of Labor Gradually Declining*, (www.caijing.com.cn).02-07-2007, <http://www.caijing.com.cn/2007-07-02/100023720.html.>

Li Daokui, Liu Linlin, Wang Hongling. "U-shaped Rule in Evolution of Labor Share in GDP", *Economic Research*, no. 1, 2009, pp. 0–82.

Louis Kuijis. "How Will China's Saving-investment Balance Evolve?", *World Bank China Office Research Working Paper*, no. 5, 2006.

Luo Changyuan, Zhang Jun. "Proportion of Labor Income in Economic Development: An Empirical Study Based on China's Industrial Data", *China's Social Science*, no. 4, 2009, pp. 65–79, 206.

N. Kaldor. *Capital Accumulation and Economic Growth*, London: Palgrave MacMillan, 1961.

S. Bentolina, G. Saint-Paul. "Explaining Movements in the Labor Share", *Contributions to Macroeconomics*, vol. 3, no. 1, 2003.

Victor J. Elias. *Sources of Growth: A Study of Seven Latin American Economies*, San Francisco: ICS Press, 1992.

Wang Tongsan. "Reform Income Distribution System to Solve Imbalance of Investment & Consumption",*Financial Perspectives Journal*, no. 22, 2007, p. 23.

Xiao Hongye, Hao Feng. "China's Initial Income Distribution Structure & International Comparisons", *Finance and Trade Economy*, no. 2, 2009, pp. 13–21, 45, 136.

Index

Note: **Bold** page numbers refer to tables; *Italic* page numbers refer to figures and page numbers followed by "n" denote endnotes.

Printed in the United States
By Bookmasters